Scottish Border

D1493315

SWEPT CHANNELS

UNIFORM WITH THIS WORK,
AND BY THE SAME AUTHOR

ENDLESS STORY

Being an account of the work of the flotilla-leaders, destroyers, torpedo-boats and patrol boats in the Great War.

A MINE EXPLOSION.
From a photograph kindly supplied by Commander G. Cunningham Glen,
D.S.O., O.B.E., R.N.

SWEPT CHANNELS

BEING AN ACCOUNT OF THE WORK OF THE MINESWEEPERS IN THE GREAT WAR

BY

TAFFRAIL

CAPTAIN TAPRELL DORLING, D.S.O., F.R.HIST.S.,
ROYAL NAVY

HODDER AND STOUGHTON LIMITED
LONDON

First published, 1935

BORDERS REGIONAL LIBRARY

ACCESSION No.	CLASS No.
~~A Dortle~~	Bennclé

0072173432

Made and Printed in Great Britain for Hodder and Stoughton Limited,
by Butler & Tanner Ltd., Frome and London

TO THOSE,
WHO IN HOURLY PERIL OF THEIR LIVES,
KEPT THE CHANNELS
SWEPT
OF
MINES,
SO THAT SHIPS MIGHT PASS
IN SAFETY,
THE INHABITANTS OF BRITAIN
MIGHT BE FED,
AND
THE ALLIED CAUSE MAINTAINED.

INTRODUCTION

IN the first chapter of this book I have explained how it came to be written. My work has largely been that of an editor and compiler, for where those engaged in minesweeping during the war have been good enough to write of their personal experiences, I have incorporated their accounts practically without alteration, comment, or embellishment.

The names of those to whom I am indebted appear on another page. Here, however, I would say that it would have been impossible for this book to have been written without material generously placed in my hands by Admiral Sir Lionel Preston, K.C.B. He was in command of the Grand Fleet Sweepers during the earlier part of the war, and in 1917 became Director of Minesweeping at the Admiralty, a post he retained until the end of the Mine Clearance in 1919. His experience of Minesweepers and of the Minesweeping Service is unrivalled.

I think the salient points of the Minesweepers' war may be epitomised as follows :

(i) Our comparative unpreparedness in 1914 for minesweeping on any considerable scale, mainly through our trust in a Hague Convention which forbade the promiscuous laying of mines outside territorial waters.

(ii) The tremendous strain imposed on our minesweeping resources by the advent of minelaying submarines in 1915, and the subsequent intensive U-boat campaign against shipping.

(iii) The truly surprising growth and development of a Minesweeping Service which started the war as a handful of old gunboats and trawlers, and ended in November, 1918, with a fleet of 726 Minesweepers stationed at 26 ports at home and 35 abroad.

That we possessed a Trawler Section of the Royal

Naval Reserve which in 1912 consisted of 142 trawlers and 1,279 ranks and ratings ; and allowed numbers of trawlers to be taken up and equipped and manned with the greatest rapidity on the outbreak of war, was due to a suggestion made by Admiral Lord Charles Beresford when Commander-in-Chief of the Home Fleet in 1907. In view of the cataclysm that was to burst upon us seven years later, we owe a debt to the prevision of Lord Charles, and to those others who inaugurated the nucleus of a Minesweeping Service.

Like other seamen who served afloat during hostilities and saw something of their work, I have always treasured the greatest respect and admiration for the work of the Minesweepers and those who had the gigantic task of their organisation and operation. My many months of work entailed by the writing of this book have enhanced that respect and admiration a hundredfold.

During the war the Germans laid 43,636 mines in all parts of the world, though principally in the North Sea and round about the British Isles. The bulk of the minesweeping fell upon Britain. At one period one Minesweeper was lost for every two mines swept up, while each time a sweeper was sunk half her crew were killed or drowned. In all, we lost 214 Minesweepers during the four years and three months that the war lasted.

I need not emphasise the part played in the work by the Royal Navy, for, after all, its officers and men were trained as fighting seamen. What I hope I have made clear is the truly magnificent and devoted service given to the country by the officers and men of its Merchant Navy and Fishing Fleets, not to mention civilians from every profession and walk of life, who flocked into the Minesweeping Service through the R.N.R. and R.N.V.R. when the call came. To these fine men the country owes a debt that can never be over-estimated.

TAFFRAIL.

New Year's Day.
    1935.

CONTENTS

LIST OF ILLUSTRATIONS

LIST OF MAPS AND DIAGRAMS

SHORT BIBLIOGRAPHY

Naval Operations, Vols. I., II. and III. Sir Julian Corbett.

Naval Operations, Vols. IV. and V. Sir Henry Newbolt.

The Times History of the War.

The German Submarine War. R. H. Gibson and Maurice Prender-gast.

The Dover Patrol, 2 vols. Admiral Sir Reginald Bacon.

Encyclopædia Britannica, 14th edition.

The Merchant Navy, Vol. II. Sir Archibald Hurd.

Naval Memoirs. The Narrow Seas to the Dardanelles, 1910–1915.
   Admiral of the Fleet Sir Roger Keyes.

Publications of the United States Navy Department, Historical Section :
   No. 2. 'The Northern Barrage and other Mining Activities.'
   No. 4. 'The Northern Barrage' (Taking up the Mines).

Our Navy at War. Josephus Daniels.

Cross-Channel and Coastal Paddle Steamers. F. Burtt.

Endless Story. 'Taffrail.'

70° North. 'Taffrail.'

A Naval Lieutenant, 1914–1918. 'Etienne.'

ACKNOWLEDGMENTS

(Directly or Indirectly)

Captain H. T. Baillie-Grohman, D.S.O., O.B.E., R.N.
Captain C. C. Bell, D.S.O., R.N.
Lieutenant-Commander G. E. Blackmore, O.B.E., D.S.C., R.N.
Captain M. W. S. Boucher, D.S.O., R.N.
A. Merton Brown, Esq.
Captain Wilfrid M. Bruce, C.B.E., R.D., R.N.R.
Commander A. E. Buckland, D.S.O., D.S.C., R.N.
Captain A. C. Dewar, O.B.E., R.N.
Chief Skipper Martin Fielding, R.N.R.
Commander G. Cunningham Glen, D.S.O., O.B.E., R.N.
Commander C. E. Hamond, R.N.
Skipper John E. Harwood, R.N.R.
Captain the Hon. Claude P. Hermon-Hodge, D.S.C., R.N.
Captain Vansittart Howard, D.S.O., R.N.
Captain Colin S. Inglis, D.S.O., R.N.
Rear-Admiral Sir Thomas J. S. Lyne, K.C.V.O., C.B., D.S.O.
Francis E. McMurtrie, Esq., A.I.N.A.
Commander R. D. Oliver, D.S.C., R.N.
Captain H. W. Noakes.
Admiral Sir Lionel Preston, K.C.B.
Commander H. M. J. Rundle, O.B.E., R.N.
Commander A. E. Thomson, D.S.C., R.N.
Commander Alexander D. Thomson, D.S.C., R.N.R.
Rear-Admiral Aubrey T. Tillard, D.S.O.
The Librarian and Staff of the Admiralty Library, London, and others whose request for anonymity I must observe.

CHAPTER I

THE MINESWEEPERS' WAR

I

BRITAIN is not a self-supporting country, and the British Empire is an Oceanic Commonwealth of free nations linked together by the sea. Throughout the war of 1914–18 the vital lines of communication were the sea-lines – the main arteries for the carriage of men, munitions and raw materials, and the daily food of every man, woman and child in these islands.

By keeping the enemy's Fleet locked in its harbours, the Royal Navy kept the seas open for ourselves and our Allies, thereby making ultimate victory possible. It is not too much to say that it was the British Fleet that stood between the Central Powers and victory, and that Sea Power was the hub upon which the whole Allied cause revolved. Without it British troops could neither have been landed in France, nor reinforcements from Britain, the great Dominions, or the United States have been guaranteed a safe passage to any oversea theatre of war. Without Sea Power our people would have starved, and every Dominion and Colony would have been open to invasion. The end would have been an ignominious peace and the disruption of the Empire.

The Royal Navy held the seas. Nearer at home the minesweepers, by their daily sweeping of the coastal traffic lanes to clear them of enemy mines, contributed in no small measure to the free movement of fighting ships, transports and cargo-carriers upon which all else depended. Once this free movement became seriously interrupted, disaster stared us in the face.

Ask any man who served at sea between 1914 and

1918 which was the most perilous, monotonous, and bitterly uncomfortable work of the war afloat – that which demanded the greatest hardihood, courage, individual resource, and unfailing good seamanship. The reply, nine times out of ten, and justly, I think, will be : ' The work of the minesweepers.'

Day in and day out, month after month, fair weather or foul, in gales, fog, snow or sleet, we, in the regular fighting ships, saw the little minesweepers going about their vital business of keeping the channels swept clear of mines, so that we and the merchantmen might pass in safety.

When the war started, our regular minesweeping force consisted of six old torpedo-gunboats fitted as fleet sweepers. By August 8, 1914, under a scheme suggested by Admiral Lord Charles Beresford in 1907, 94 ordinary fishing trawlers had been mobilised and were at sea sweeping for mines with their usual crews of fishermen. Within a fortnight another 100 trawlers had been requisitioned and were fitting out.

The needs of minesweeping, however, had only partly been foreseen. It soon became evident that intensive minelaying was part of the German naval strategy, and our minesweeping force grew and grew.

At the time of the Armistice it comprised 726 vessels – 110 regular naval vessels, mostly built during the war, and divided into twenty fast sweeping flotillas ; 52 hired paddle steamers of the type patronised by excursionists in peace time ; 412 fishing trawlers ; 142 drifters ; and 10 shallow-draught ' tunnel ' mine-sweepers of the ' Dance ' class.[1]

We lost a total of 214 minesweepers during the 4 years 3 months and 7 days that the war lasted – on a rough average, one a week.

In these days of disarmament conferences, treaties for the limitation of navies, and the clamouring of a noisy but largely uninstructed minority for further unilateral naval disarmament on the part of the British Empire, it is perhaps well to recall that during the war 1,360 minefields, containing in all some 25,000

[1] See p. 360.

H.M.S. *ETTRICK* (RIVER CLASS DESTROYER).
MINED JULY, 1917.

mines, were laid by the Germans in British waters, 90 per cent. of them by submarines.

For the first two months of the war one minesweeping trawler was sunk for every five mines swept up, while one vessel of some sort or another was blown up for every two mines destroyed.

During 1917, 28 mines were swept up for every ship sunk, and in 1918, 85.

Throughout the four years of hostilities an average of half the crew of a trawler was lost every time a vessel was mined.

The work of the German submarines in the war is of course remembered by some. It should be known to and remembered by every man, woman and child among us. The situation was bad enough before February 1, 1917; but on that date the enemy started his unrestricted submarine campaign in which any ships – British, Allied or Neutral – round about the British Isles, France and in the Mediterranean, were liable to be sunk on sight, entirely without regard to the lives of their non-combatant crews and passengers.

In 1914–15, 568 British, Allied or Neutral merchantmen were sent to the bottom by submarines. In 1917, the total was 1,098. But in February, 1917, the first month of the unrestricted submarine war, 260 merchant ships were sunk; in March 338, and in April 430.

On April 19, the worst day of the worst month of the war, eleven British merchantmen and eight fishing craft were destroyed. One out of every four ships that left the British Isles in that awful month never returned.

From this great increase in the rate of sinkings it appeared probable that the submarines would win the war for Germany. They were being built and sent to sea faster than they could be destroyed. The submarine menace, though relatively few civilians realised it at the time, and far fewer realise it now, was the gravest peril that has ever threatened the British Empire. By cutting off our food supplies from oversea, the U-boats brought us to the verge of starvation. The situation was only saved by the introduction of the Convoy System, where merchantmen were grouped into fleets and escorted through the danger zones by cruisers and small craft.

But gunfire and torpedoes were not the only methods used. In April, 1917, during the height of the unrestricted submarine campaign, an average of one German mine was laid off the British coast every hour of the day, and each day we lost one minesweeper. Throughout the year 1917, moreover, an average of one submarine's cargo of mines was deposited off the British coast *every 30 hours*.[1]

According to an official return issued in 1919,[2] 44 of His Majesty's ships were lost by mines during the war. Since that return was compiled, however, later information would make it appear that two torpedo-boats, listed as having been sunk by submarines, were, in fact, destroyed by mines.

Of the auxiliaries employed on Admiralty service, 225 were destroyed by mines, of which 140 were hired, and four were Admiralty trawlers.

Our losses in minesweepers from the same cause, as already mentioned, totalled 214. Mines, not all laid by submarines, were responsible for the destruction of 259 British merchant ships and 63 fishing vessels with the loss of 1,825 lives, and the damage of another 84 merchant vessels with the loss of 64 lives.[3]

There was hardly an important harbour, headland or channel in the whole of the British Isles which was not mined at least once during hostilities in the hope of destroying Allied shipping. The denser traffic

---

[1] Minelaying submarines were a product of the war. In 1917 ten of the larger German submarines designed for distant oversea work (U.71–U.80) each carried 36 mines, while seventy-nine smaller U.C. boats, not all of which were operating from Germany or Flanders, carried 12 or 18. As showing the intensity of the German minelaying effort against Allied shipping in the later stages of the war, it may be said that nineteen large and over one hundred small submarine minelayers were built during the period of hostilities. Some eighty-eight more were cancelled at the Armistice, a few being completed for surrender to the Allies.

[2] Navy Losses. August, 1919. H.M.S.O. 4*d*.

[3] For details of these and other losses through enemy mines, see Appendix 1.

areas were mined more or less continuously. For instance, in the Dover area alone – this including portions of the French coast – 695 mines were swept up between January and September, 1917. In the same period 500 mines were disposed of round about Harwich.

Portsmouth, Dartmouth, Plymouth, the entrance to the Thames, every port and anchorage throughout the whole length of the east coasts of England and Scotland, received their quotas of mines. They appeared also off Liverpool, in the approaches to the Clyde, and the Irish Sea ; off Belfast, Lough Swilly, Waterford and in the waters round Mull, Coll, Skye, Harris and Stornoway, on the west coast of Scotland.

The west coast of Ireland was not immune. The mines laid there, however, did no damage, except in one case where the villagers mistook a specimen which had drifted ashore for a new sort of liquor cask. Forgathering cheerfully on the beach with tools and receptacles, they tried to open the novel barrel. The results were disastrous. There was a funeral – for nine.

Not all the mines that broke adrift from their moorings became harmless, as they were supposed to be by the terms of the Hague Convention for the ' humanising ' of war, if such a thing were ever possible.

Later, I shall tell the tale of a Boer farmer in South Africa, who also suffered a somewhat shattering experience through tampering with a mine washed up on the beach. But he, though badly startled, was luckier than the nine poor Irishmen.

Though the intensive minelaying on the part of the Germans was confined to the waters round about Great Britain, both sides of the English Channel, and the Mediterranean, mines also appeared in the White Sea, the Bay of Biscay, and so far afield as off the eastern seaboard of North America, in the South China Sea, and off South Africa, Aden, India, Ceylon, Australia and New Zealand. And wherever mines appeared, the minesweepers had to follow.

2

Our minesweepers were at it eternally. When the organisation was in full swing, a channel between the Firth of Forth and Portland Bill, a distance of some 540 miles, was swept daily, as well as the approaches to all ports. Other channels were periodically swept between Duncansby Head at the north-east corner of Scotland, to the Orkneys and Shetlands, the Skaw, the Firth of Forth, the Flannan Islands off the Outer Hebrides, Rathlin Island, the Skelligs off the south-west corner of Ireland, the Smalls off Milford Haven, and Ushant. At a rough computation the total distance covered by these periodical sweeps cannot have been much less than 5,000 miles.

Between 1915 and 1917, says Admiral Sir Reginald Bacon in his book, *The Dover Patrol*, the minesweepers in his area alone swept a distance equal to twelve times round the earth. The trawlers were used as patrol craft as well, and had practically no rest. Even during their brief spells in Dover harbour, they rolled twenty to twenty-five degrees each way during the ordinary southerly and south-westerly gales. And while nominally ' resting ', one trawler unit was ready to go to sea at five minutes' notice, and no leave was allowed to anyone on board. Another was coaling ; a third had to draw stores and provisions ; and a fourth, the ' stand off ' unit, sent most of its men ashore for instruction in gunnery and signals.

During the whole of the time that the trawlers were employed on the Dover patrol, they never once took shelter or left their beats in heavy weather.

To quote Sir Reginald Bacon again : ' It is doubtful if we could have defeated the Germans, at any rate as quickly as we did defeat them, if it had not been for the assistance which the Royal Navy received from the fishing community . . . the officers and fishermen of the trawler patrol, and of the paddle minesweepers, showed great fortitude and a fine spirit by implicit obedience to orders, zeal, and devotion to duty. No call was made to them without obtaining their most

willing and ready response, and it is with pride that
I recall the memory of having had such a splendid
body of officers and men under my orders.' [1]

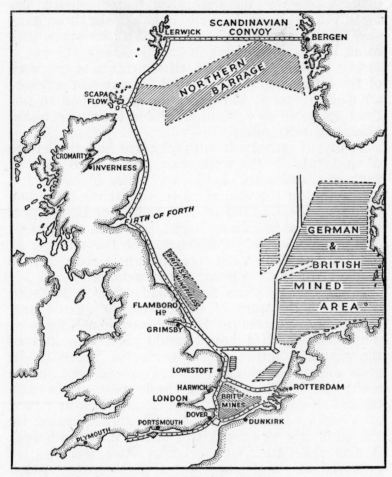

THE EAST COAST SWEPT CHANNEL

That eulogy must not be confined to Dover. It
applied everywhere.

The minesweepers had none of the excitement of
going into action against a visible foe with a fair
chance of success. Like the merchantmen, who braved

[1] *The Dover Patrol* (Hutchinson), vol. i, pp. 112, 143.

the truly hideous danger of the submarine campaign, they were combating an enemy hidden beneath the sea – the mine, or rather groups of mines, which did not make themselves manifest until they exploded and destroyed a ship, or else were caught by the thrumming sweep-wires and brought to the surface, where they could be destroyed by gun or rifle fire.

This book is designed to tell something of the work of the minesweepers in the war. I say ' something ' advisedly, since it is beyond the wit of man to put down on paper more than a tithe of their hair-raising work and adventures.

Really, if competent authority had had the leisure to undertake it, the work should have been done in 1922 or thereabouts – before the minor incidents and happenings of the war, vivid enough at the time they occurred, became blurred and indistinct in the dim background of human memory ; and when the various different phases and components of the struggle at sea had had time to fit into the whole great picture in their true and appropriate perspective.

Not so many years ago I had occasion to write a book on the work of the destroyers [1] in the war. It did not purport to be a *history*, but merely a miscellany which I hoped would give some idea of the manifold duties of destroyers in wartime. In some measure it succeeded. It received appreciative notices in the Press all over the Empire. It has run through several editions ; first at a guinea and then at a more popular price. Copies were procured by the Admiralty for official issue to His Majesty's Ships ; it was translated into French, while portions re-appeared in the United States of America. Added to a huge correspondence from Great Britain, it has brought me letters from all over the British Empire and the world, from the most unexpected places.

' I have just finished reading your book *Endless Story*,' writes a correspondent in St. Louis de Gonzaque, Province of Quebec, Canada. ' I have been prompted to send you these few lines . . . merely as a warm

[1] *Endless Story*. Hodder and Stoughton. 7s. 6d.

appreciation of a . . . work which I enjoyed immensely. It will, I'm sure stand out . . . particularly so to the many who considered it their good fortune to serve in a little ship during those . . . days of war.'

' Even with such a lapse of time,' he continues, ' it is not difficult, while perusing each page, to live again through the squalls and storms, long night patrols, etc. One hears old familiar sounds – grating steering-gear, clanging engine-room telegraph bells, the lush of great bow-waves, and the hiss of the seething bank of foam astern. With subsequent years of a monotonous bush existence and a total absence of everything associated with destroyer life, one is, after emerging from *Endless Story* rather overwhelmed with a longing for the glamorous far-off days and the old crowd. But now I fear I'm waxing sentimental.'

Well – perhaps !

Here is another letter, this time from Warsaw, Poland, and written by a woman :

' I have just read with infinite pride and great pleasure your book *Endless Story*. War must always be a dreadful thing, but when it is accompanied by such wonderful heroism and self-sacrifice as is portrayed in your book time and time again, its horror seems to fade a little into the background, leaving only an unbounded admiration for such men and a feeling of great pride that one can claim kinship with them. The reading of the " Have we won, sir ? " of men in their last agony leaves behind an impression difficult to express in words.

' Having married a Pole I am theoretically no longer a British subject, although I am afraid it would be difficult to find a more loyal one, and so I hope you will accept this very small tribute to your . . . book which is offered by a woman proud of the land of her birth.'

I do not quote these letters with any idea of self-praise or advertisement ; but merely to show that there *are* people who still cherish enough care for their country's destiny to read about a war which is fast fading into oblivion.

And the story of the minesweepers, or that part of it that one man may write, has never been told. Part of their gallant record lies scattered piecemeal in some scores of volumes of personal reminiscences or in books dealing with other aspects of the war; hidden in hundreds of official returns and semi-official documents, and in diaries, letters, notes and personal records. There is no lack of material if one knows where to look and has the time and industry to search, besides engaging in a lengthy, and sometimes unprofitable, correspondence with those who swept for mines during the war. Though I have persuaded one or two fishermen to come to the point of putting their experiences on paper, my chief regret has been that the majority have proved stubbornly inarticulate. It is their nature so to be, being men of deeds and not words.

Nevertheless, for many months, in the intervals of other work, I have been immersed in a sea of books, documents and papers – collecting, sorting, collating rejecting here and there; trying to evolve order out of chaos in order that I might write in some sort of logical sequence. It has not been, and could not be, an easy task.

I did not volunteer to write this book. It was suggested to me by others. But it has none the less been a labour of love.

I never served in minesweepers, though, having commanded destroyers throughout the war, I came to know a good deal about the work of those who maintained the swept channels. Having commanded a minelaying destroyer during the last two years of hostilities, I also know a little about mines. Like other seamen who were afloat between 1914 and 1918, I conceived an immense admiration and respect for the sweepers.

Their work meant hard, monotonous drudgery in all weathers, punctuated by days and hours of deadly peril, mingled with moments of excitement so tense that it seems wonderful how human brain and flesh and blood could bear the strain.

H.M.S. *AZALEA* (SLOOP).
MINED JULY, 1917.
View showing the damage to Fore-part of Ship.

And when, so often and often, this work was accompanied by magnificent heroism and self-sacrifice, the horror of war, to use the words of my correspondent from Poland, ' seems to fade a little into the background, leaving only an unbounded admiration for such men, and a feeling of great pride that one can claim kinship with them '.

Let this, then, be my justification for attempting to tell something of their story.

CHAPTER II

MINES, MINELAYERS AND SWEEPERS

I

W HEN the war started, comparatively few people in the Navy, and fewer still outside it, had any idea of how potent a weapon the mine might be if used intensively. Certainly they had no notion that during the next four years or so the Germans would lay 43,636 mines in all parts of the world, and that, in the North Sea and English Channel alone, British minelayers would deposit something like 116,000 mines, and the Americans 56,033.[1]

These latter, with 15,093 British mines, were laid in the well-known 'Northern Barrage', stretching for 230 miles between the Orkneys and the coast of Norway, and designed to prevent the egress of U-boats on to the trade routes through the northern part of the North Sea.[2]

I, personally, had not the vaguest conception that in 1917 and 1918 I should be in command of a mine-

---

[1] See Appendix 1A.

[2] The Northern Barrage was laid in depths varying between 45 and 150 fathoms. As originally designed, it required the colossal total of 120,000 mines laid in nine rows—three at an upper level of 80 feet; three at 160 feet; and three at 240 feet. A huge organisation for transporting, filling, loading and laying the mines grew up round the scene of the work. The British minelaying base was at Grangemouth, in the upper reaches of the Firth of Forth. The American base was at Inverness, their mines being landed in the Kyle of Lochalsh near Skye, and sent across by the Caledonian Canal and by rail. Ten large American minelayers, with a total capacity of 5,530 mines, took part in the work, laying about 56,033 mines between the end of May, 1918, and the time of the Armistice. (Laying in the British section of the Northern Barrage had begun on March 3.) The barrage was not complete by the time hostilities ceased, though six German submarines are supposed to have been blown up in it. This approximated to an expenditure of 11,686 mines for each submarine destroyed!

laying destroyer involved in 37 minelaying operations in the Heligoland Bight and off the Flanders coast to lay some 1,480 mines.

Primitive sea-mines, however, designed to be attached to the bottom of a wooden ship by a species of one-man submarine running awash, were used by the Americans during the War of Independence, when, in 1777, David Bushnell tried unsuccessfully to blow up H.M.S. *Cerberus*. For a similar purpose, between 1801 and 1805, the American inventor Robert Fulton built a submarine called the *Nautilus*; but failed to evoke the interest of the British, French or United States Governments.

Canisters charged with gunpowder, moored under water, and designed to explode on contact with an enemy vessel, were used by the Russians at Kronstadt in 1854, by the Austrians in Venice in 1859, and five years later by the Danes in Alsen Sound. These contrivances were first known as ' torpedoes ' – from the torpedo, or electric ray, a fish provided with electrical antennæ for numbing and killing its prey.

Torpedoes, or moored ' mines ', as we should now call them, assumed considerable importance during the American Civil War of 1861–5, when they are stated to have destroyed seven iron and eleven wooden vessels. It was Admiral David Farragut, at the battle of Mobile Bay on August 4, 1864, who, just after the monitor *Tecumseh* had been blown up in the Confederates' minefield, made his name famous and saved the situation by shouting ' Damn the torpedoes !' and taking his flagship, the *Hartford,* in over the danger area at a moment when his squadron was in some confusion. The mine-cases could be heard rumbling along the flagship's bottom. By sheer good luck none exploded.

Mines, of an infinitely more potent kind, were used by both sides in the Russo-Japanese War of 1904–5, the Japanese losing two battleships and the Russians one, besides smaller units.

But though the successful use of mines by the Russians and Japanese had evoked great interest in England, their offensive power and real place in naval strategy had not been properly appreciated in 1914. In the years before the war, every available penny of the Navy Estimates was needed for the expansion of the Fleet.

Mines were regarded as rather expensive luxuries, and our minelaying squadron in August, 1914, consisted of seven old 14-knot, 3,400-ton cruisers.[1] The details and design of the efficacious Russian ' Carbonit ' mines, which were possessed by the Germans, were also fully known, and we could have had them if we had cared to pay the price – £200 apiece. Instead of that we evolved badly designed mines of our own which cost £40 each, and possessed no more than 4,000 of them when war broke out. Our policy in this respect was penny wise and pound foolish.[2]

The mines we had soon came to be recognised as inefficient. Not only did they break adrift with appalling frequency; but they failed to explode when struck. ' German submarines could carry these ineffective engines on their bows, shake them off, or bump against them with impunity. Many German warships had as a souvenir a British mine mounted on a stand.' [3]

Even in 1917, British mines laid in the Dover Straits failed to stop the enemy submarines. The strong currents depressed them below their proper depth, and if they were laid shallow they were swung to and fro in the heavy sea. Moorings chafed through and parted, allowing the mines to drift away. They bumped harmlessly against the U-boats, or betrayed their positions by floating on the surface. ' So through this defile poured one long stream of submarines, to spread themselves over the western approaches, where they could extirpate all seaborne trade as it flowed in from the outer world.' [4]

[1] *Andromache, Apollo, Intrepid, Iphigenia, Latona, Naiad,* and *Thetis.* Built under the Naval Defence Act of 1889 and launched in 1890 and 1891.

[2] During the early months of the war a cargo of Russian 'Carbonit' mines was delivered at Devonport, having been brought from Vladivostok by the Russian Volunteer Fleet s.s. *Penza* at the average speed of 16 knots.

[3] *The German Submarine War.* By R. H. Gibson and Maurice Prendergast (Constable), pp. 38, 39.

[4] *Ibid,* p. 145.

In the course of experiments carried out during the war, only one-third of the old pattern British mines exploded on being struck by a target submarine. Of our stock of 20,000 mines in April, 1917, only 1,500 were fit for laying![1]

It was not until September, 1917, that a new type of mine, mooring gear and sinker, known as the ' H.2 ', became available in any quantity. It was modelled upon the weapon which had been used by the Germans since the very outbreak of war.

Imagine a spherical or pear-shaped buoy roughly three feet in diameter and containing between 250 and 350 lb. of guncotton, trinitrotoluene (T.N.T.), or amatol. This explosive, together with the firing batteries, occupies about half the space available, the rest being used as an air chamber to give the contrivance its necessary buoyancy.

On the top of the mine, on the outside, are five or more leaden ' horns ' each about five inches long and an inch and a quarter in diameter. Each of these horns has inside it a glass tube containing a chemical mixture. A blow of about 50 lb. will fracture a horn, which smashes the glass tube which releases the liquid, which energises the battery, which fires a detonator, which detonates the explosive, which destroys or seriously damages the object – generally a ship, though on one occasion, at least, a whale – which has struck the mine and crumpled the horn in the first instance.

During the war mines were not sown broadcast all over the ocean to drift about at the mercy of wind and tide. They were laid in fields or groups in certain prearranged positions, each mine being anchored to the bottom by means of a wire mooring rope attached to a heavy sinker.

The German sinker varied somewhat from the British. It is unnecessary to go into abstruse details, but in German minelaying, the mine and sinker, weighing roughly half a ton went straight to the bottom on being dropped from the laying vessel. After a short interval, sufficient to allow the laying vessel to

[1] *The German Submarine War*, p. 179.

get clear of the spot, the mine was automatically
released and started to rise under its own buoyancy,
unreeling the mooring wire as it rose.

Underneath the mine was a device known as a
'hydrostat', which could be set beforehand for the
depth below water which it was desired the mine should
take up soon after laying. When the mine had risen
to this height above the sea bottom, the hydrostat
came into action, gripped the mooring wire, and
anchored the mine to its sinker.

In British minelaying the final result was the same,
though the mine became detached from its sinker the

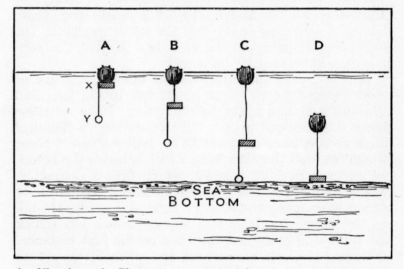

A. Mine dropped. Plummet runs out to end.
B. Mine still on surface. Sinker descending.
C. Mine still on surface. Plummet hits bottom and prevents more cable
unreeling.
D. Sinker descends and pulls mine with it. Depth of mine below the sur-
face equals the distance XY on plummet chain in Fig. A.

moment it was laid. The mine case floated for a few
seconds while the heavy sinker descended towards the
sea bottom, the mooring wire unreeling from its drum
as it travelled downwards. Beneath the sinker proper
was a small auxiliary weight known as a 'plummet',
attached by a chain to the main sinker. This chain

was adjustable in length according to the distance it was required the mine should be below the surface when laid. The plummet hit the bottom first, and the slackening of its chain automatically locked the drum on the main sinker and prevented any more wire from running out. The main sinker then came into play and pulled the mine itself down to the pre-arranged depth beneath the surface.

The diagram on the opposite page may help to simplify this explanation.

In other respects, the principle and firing arrangements of the British H.2 mines evolved during the war, and laid in huge quantities from the autumn of 1917 onwards, were practically the same as the German.

2

A mine being anchored to its sinker by means of a wire mooring rope varying between $1\frac{1}{4}$ and $2\frac{1}{2}$ inches in circumference – single in the case of the British mine, and double rope passing over a species of pulley at the bottom of the mine in the case of the German – it follows that minesweeping in its simplest form consists of towing a sunken sweep-wire between a pair of vessels, two or more pairs working together so as to cover as wide a front as possible.

The sweep-wire is much the same size as the mine mooring. However, in order that the mine should quickly be cut free from its moorings and float up to the surface for destruction, instead of being dragged with the sinker still pounding along the bottom, thereby causing delay and difficulty, what was known as a ' serrated ' sweep-wire was brought into use during the war. Instead of the rope being laid up in the ordinary way, it has one irregular strand which, when under strain, exercises a sawing effect on the mine mooring, and, cutting it, allows the mine to float up. Serrated wire is certainly efficacious. It has been known to cut clean through a heavy steel mooring bollard.

Various forms of minesweeps were evolved and

successfully used during the war ; but a minute description would involve the reader in technicalities
rather beyond the scope of this book. In essence,
they are all the same.

Each minesweeper drags a ' kite ', a heavy, prismatic wooden appliance which dives under water when
towed, in precisely the same way as an ordinary kite
rises in the air due to wind pressure. It also acts on
much the same principle as the ' otter boards ' used
by an ordinary fishing trawler which swim out laterally
under water and keep the mouth of the trawl net open
when it is towed along the sea bottom.

The kite, towed from an ordinary steam winch, goes
down to the depth permitted by the amount of wire
paid out. The actual sweep-wire passes through rings
on the kites towed by a pair of vessels, thus forming
a span of wire roughly parallel to the sea bottom but
well beneath the surface. The actual distance apart
at which sweepers can work – generally three to five
hundred yards – naturally depends upon their power,
towing capacity and the state of the weather. It can
also be understood that the centre of the sweep-wire
will sag a little with its own weight, and will thus be
somewhat deeper than the kites.

The sweep-wire used to be passed from ship to ship
by hand, so to speak, both vessels steaming ahead
and so close as to be nearly touching. Then, while
one of the pair secured the end of the sweep and
moved off at an angle to open out to sweeping distance,
her consort eased out the wire. The kites having been
streamed and lowered to the right depth, the sweepers
were ready for work. Later on in the war, to avoid
the risk of collision between the larger vessels that
came to be used, the practice was introduced of one
sweeper steaming about 100 yards ahead of her consort, and passing the sweep-wire across by means of
a grass line and barricoe towed astern.

It is unnecessary here to deal with other varieties
of sweeps, including one that can be used from a single
vessel, and another that can be towed along the bottom
to sweep up mines which have never left their sinkers,

H.M.S. *AZALEA.*

IN DOCK. PORT BOW OF VESSEL, LOOKING FORWARD.

or have been moored very deep. That already described was the means of destroying 30,000 mines during and after the war, and is still in use in the small minesweeping flotilla we now maintain. A few simple diagrams, however, may serve to make the general scheme of minesweeping somewhat clearer.

The sweep which did most of the work in the war and stood the most exacting tests of efficiency in all weathers, certainly had the merit of simplicity. It was easily handled by trawlermen who, after years of

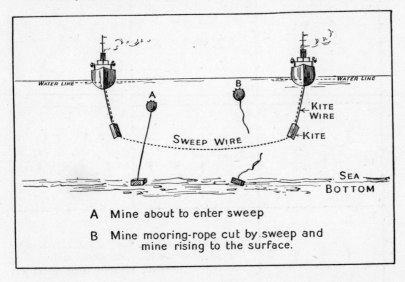

WATER LINE — — — — — — — — — — — WATER LINE
B
A — — KITE WIRE
SWEEP WIRE — KITE
SEA BOTTOM

A Mine about to enter sweep
B Mine mooring-rope cut by sweep and
   mine rising to the surface.

experience on the fishing grounds, were well accustomed to handling their ships and dealing with taut wires and steam winches in the bitter cold, and the gales and heavy seas, of our northern winter. Most of these men were inured to the sea from boyhood. Other men also became accustomed to its use – officers of all types, seamen of the Royal and Merchant Navies, and those thousands of landsmen from every walk of life, who found themselves serving in minesweepers during the war.

But a good deal more was required besides good seamanship. Like other military operations, minesweeping rapidly became a science.

3

Imagination was required by those responsible for its direction, not merely in their dealings with the men who flocked into the Service, but by anticipating when and where the enemy was likely to lay mines.

And by those commanding groups of minesweepers, accuracy in navigation was of the first importance, since a minefield wrongly plotted upon a chart might spell disaster to shipping. The same might be said for accurate station-keeping while minesweeping was

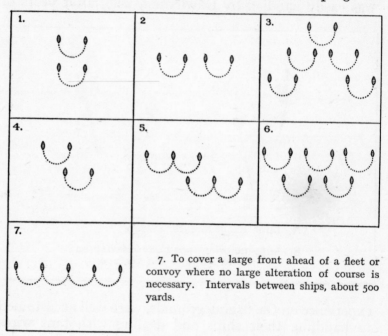

7. To cover a large front ahead of a fleet or convoy where no large alteration of course is necessary. Intervals between ships, about 500 yards.

VARIOUS SWEEPING FORMATIONS

in progress. If sweepers were out of position and gaps were left, an area which had been swept and was therefore supposedly safe might really have mines left in it and still be dangerous.

A knowledge of tides, and their rise and fall, was also essential. Mines being laid at a certain distance from the sea bottom, it can be understood, for instance, that they were closer to the surface at low water, and therefore more dangerous to sweepers. Moreover, when the tide was flowing, the current acting on the mine and its mooring rope caused it to be deflected below its set depth and therefore less dangerous.

All these things, and a great many others, had to be taken into consideration. So while the Royal Navy had something to learn from the fishermen, the fishermen had also a lot to learn from the more scientific methods of the officers of the Royal Navy and the Royal Naval Reserve.

To take one's courage in one's hand and to rush bald-headed at a minefield, as so often occurred in the early days of the war, might be brave. But it was certainly not prudent.

Magnificent, perhaps; but not war.

3

It was Admiral Lord Charles Beresford,[1] when Commander-in-Chief of the Home Fleet in 1907, and after a visit to ports on the east coast of England, who first recommended the use of Grimsby trawlers for minesweeping.

' Our fishing fleets, in war, will be rendered inactive', he wrote, ' and will in consequence be available for war service. Fishermen, by virtue of their calling, are adept in the handling and towing of wires and trawls, more so than are naval ratings. Small naval vessels, if used in minesweeping, will be used at the expense of other urgent war requirements.'

This was the germ of the idea which eventually brought about the formation of the Royal Naval Reserve (Trawler Section) – the R.N.R.(T.) – a force consisting of 39,000 officers and men when the Armistice was signed, of whom 10,000 were employed in minesweepers and the rest in the auxiliary patrol.

In December, 1907, two Grimsby trawlers were hired by the Admiralty with their fishing crews and sent down to Portland for experiments. The first trials, carried out against a field of dummy moored

---

[1] Afterwards Admiral Lord Beresford of Metemmeh and Curraghmore, G.C.B., G.C.V.O., D.C.L., LL.D.

mines with a sweep not unlike an ordinary fishing
trawl, were not successful. However, on a wooden,
prismatic water-kite being introduced, and a sweep of
the sort already described being towed between the
two trawlers, its efficacy and simplicity was at once
apparent.

The sweep was adopted for use, the first of the six
ex-torpedo-gunboat minesweepers was commissioned
in 1908, and a senior officer was appointed to the
Admiralty to conduct further experiments and to
develop the system more fully.

Soon afterwards the Trawler Reserve was instituted
with approval for 100 trawlers to be mobilised during
any future period of strained relations, and for the
immediate enrolment of 1,000 officers and ratings to
man these vessels. This brought a new rank, that of
' Skipper ', R.N.R., into the Navy List, and the first
officer enrolled at Aberdeen on February 3, 1911.
His name deserves to be remembered. It was Peter
Yorston.[1]

Fifty-three skippers had joined by the end of 1911 ;
twenty-five more enrolled themselves in 1912, and
thirty-one more before the war period – a total of 109.

In 1912 the Trawler Reserve was augmented to 142
trawlers and 1,278 ranks and ratings, and in this same
year and the next, minesweeping trials were carried
out with the old torpedo-gunboats.[2] Certain of the
' River ' class destroyers were also fitted out for minesweeping with a view to their relieving the 20-year-old
gunboats. The shortage of patrol destroyers, however,
led to this decision being revoked.

In the year before the war, however, and in spite
of the lessons of the Russo-Japanese War, minesweeping, like minelaying, did not receive the attention

---

[1] Now Skipper Lieutenant Peter Yorston, M.B.E., D.S.C. (Retd.).

[2] I find the names of nine of these ships in the Navy List for October,
1914. Attached to the Grand Fleet for minesweeping purposes, they
were under the command of Commander Lionel G. Preston (now
Admiral Sir Lionel Preston, K.C.B.) in the *Skipjack*. The others were
the *Circe, Gossamer, Hebe, Jason, Leda, Seagull, Spanker* and *Speedwell*.
The *Speedy* had already been sunk by a mine off the Humber on
September 3, 1914.

it deserved. Money was short, for one thing. For another, minelaying from submarines was utterly unknown. The rulings of International Law also laid down that mines must only be laid in the territorial waters of an opponent, and it was thought that any surface minelayers attempting to do this could effectually be dealt with by our coastwise patrols.

We had rather been lulled into a sense of security by the Hague Conference of 1907, when Baron Adolf Von Marschall Von Bieberstein, the chief German delegate, declared: 'That a belligerent who lays mines assumes a very heavy responsibility towards neutrals and towards peaceful shipping we are all agreed. – No one will resort to this instrument of warfare unless for Military reasons of an absolutely urgent character. But Military acts are not solely governed by the stipulations of International Law. There are other factors. Conscience, good sense, and the sense of duty imposed by principles of humanity will be the surest guides for the conduct of sailors, and will contribute the most effective guarantee against abuses. – The Officers of the German Navy, *I loudly proclaim it*, will always fulfil in the strictest fashion the duties which emanate from the unwritten law of humanity.'

The man who spoke these words died at Baden-weiler on September 24, 1912.

On the early morning of August 5, 1914, six or seven hours after the outbreak of war, the *Königin Luise*, a small fast mail-steamer of the North German Lloyd which had been taken over by the German Admiralty and converted into a minelayer, was seen by a British trawler 'throwing things overboard' twenty miles north-east of the Outer Gabbard Lightship. This spot lay to the west of Longitude 3° east, or roughly thirty miles off Southwold. The 'things', which were 180 mines, had therefore been planted regardless of the Hague Convention or the time-honoured customs of sea warfare, which permitted them to be laid only in an enemy's territorial waters. In international waters, the *Königin Luise's* field was just as likely to destroy neutral ships as British.

The minelayer was caught and sunk by British destroyers; but at 6.35 next morning, on the return towards Harwich, the cruiser *Amphion* struck a mine and sank with a loss of 151 lives.

There is some evidence that the *Königin Luise* laid her cargo further to seaward than was the intention of the German Admiralty, and that her actual orders were to mine the approaches to Harwich, a perfectly legitimate operation provided the mines were planted within three miles of the coast.

Be that as it may, the fact remained that the Germans continued the practice of laying mines in the open sea. And when Britain formally protested Germany excused herself on the plea that any International agreement for the restriction of mine-laying to territorial waters was binding only if all belligerents had ratified it. Russia, said Germany, was a belligerent. Russia had not ratified the Hague Convention. Therefore mines could be used where Germany liked, irrespective of the law and principles of humanity so loudly proclaimed by the German spokesman seven years before at the Hague.

So much for the value of peace-time enactments for the ' humanising ' of warfare.

At the beginning of the war, I happened to be serving in a small cruiser attached to the 9th Destroyer Flotilla, which had the duty of patrolling the north-east coast of England.

On the morning of Thursday, August 27, 1914, we were lying in the Tyne in touch, as usual, with our outlying patrols, when, at about 4.30 a.m., we received a signal from one of our torpedo-boats. This is what I wrote in my diary the same day:

' She told us that an Icelandic trawler, the *Skuli Forgeti*, had been blown up by a mine at 10.0 p.m. last night. It happened about 30 miles to the eastward of the Tyne, right in the track of shipping, and in the midst of a favourite fishing ground. The men had been picked up by a South Shields drifter, which communicated with the torpedo-boat on her way in.

'I made all the necessary arrangements with the doctor for sending the wounded to hospital, and one great strapping Dane or Icelandman came on board to give information. We had to send for an interpreter before we could understand him. Our four minesweeping trawlers, under the orders of Commander R. W. Dalgety, R.N. (Retd.), were sent out to sweep the area, and left harbour at about 5.30 a.m.

'During the forenoon we heard that a Norwegian steamer the *Gottfried*, of 600 tons, had been blown up on another mine in much the same place at 2.15 a.m. The crew had no time to get out the boats, for the ship went down in a minute and a half, to leave the survivors in the water for over five hours before they were picked up by a British drifter.

'Torpedo Boat No. 13, who was out by the mine-field with the sweepers, told us during the afternoon that a Danish sailing ship had been blown up and sunk. T.B. 13 also said she was anchored right on top of the minefield, and that some of the mines were 15 feet down, some at 4 feet and some on the surface. For some time she could not find a way out, and told us she had felt mines scraping across her bottom when she went ahead.

'Next, at 5.30 p.m., we heard that Hired Trawler No. 61, the *Thomas W. Irvin*, one of those that had gone to sea that morning, had been blown up and sunk. Three-quarters of an hour later we got similar information about No. 106, the *Crathie*. The Germans, therefore, by laying mines 30 miles out at sea, have bagged two British ships and three neutrals. So far as I can gather, the following are the casualties : *Skuli Forgeti*, Icelandic trawler, 4 killed ; *Gottfried*, Norwegian steamer, 8 killed or drowned ; *Ena*, Danish sailing ship, 3 killed ; *Thomas W. Irvin*, 3 killed ; *Crathie*, 2 killed. Apart from wounded and injured, of which there were a good many, 20 men lost their lives, of whom 15 are neutrals. We heard later that the British steam drifter, *Barley Rig* had also been lost. Popular opinion says that the mines were laid to catch the *Agincourt*,[1] or to blow up ships from Scandinavia voyaging to the Tyne.

' The Skipper of No. 61 came on board when he arrived in harbour at about 8 p.m., and had some food in the wardroom. He is a splendid fellow; but is naturally rather shaken by his experience. When asked what he intended to do, he said casually, in broad North Country lingo – " Oh, I suppose they'll find me another ship ! "

' He was in the wheelhouse with Commander Dalgety when the mine went off underneath him. He doesn't remember how he got out of the wheelhouse; but imagines he was blown out through the roof, for the next thing he remembers was that he was drenched in water and running aft to launch the one boat they carried in the stern. He says it was a horrible experience. He didn't have time to think of much. The ship went down in less than five minutes, her boiler exploding as she did so. It is exasperating to know that this minelaying has been going on only 30 miles out at sea – almost under our noses.'

That particular minefield, containing 194 mines, had been laid by the German minelayer *Albatros* escorted by the cruiser *Stuttgart* soon after dark on August 26. On the same date a field of 200 mines was laid by the *Nautilus* off the Humber.

Like the field which sank the *Amphion*, both were well outside territorial waters.

---

[1] ' *Tuesday, August* 18*th*. The *Agincourt*, the battleship built for the Turks by Armstrongs and taken over by us on the outbreak of war, went down the river early this morning. She has fourteen 12-inch guns, and is a peculiar looking ship, very un-English.' (My diary.)

CHAPTER III

FLEET SWEEPERS, 1914

I

WHAT afterwards came to be known as the 'Grand Fleet' sailed from Portsmouth for Scapa Flow on Wednesday, July 29, 1914.

'We may now picture this great Fleet,' writes Mr. Winston Churchill,[1] then the First Lord of the Admiralty, 'with its flotillas and cruisers, steaming slowly out of Portland Harbour, squadron by squadron, scores of gigantic castles of steel wending their way across the misty, shining sea, like giants bowed in anxious thought. We may picture them again as darkness fell, eighteen miles of warships running at high speed and in absolute blackness through the narrow Straits, bearing with them into the broad waters of the North the safeguard of considerable affairs.'

Passing outside the shoals off the east coast, the Fleet reached its war station at Scapa Flow on August 2.

The flotilla of gunboats attached to the Grand Fleet for minesweeping purposes – the only sweepers manned by regular naval crews we then possessed apart from a few trawlers which had been bought by the Admiralty for experimental purposes a few years before – preceded the squadrons of heavy ships. Sailing from Dover under the orders of Commander L. G. Preston in the *Skipjack*, these little ships, with their minesweeps out, actually swept the water presently to be used by the battleships on their way up the North Sea.

For the first six months of the war the gunboats

[1] *The World Crisis, 1911–1914*, vol. i (Thornton Butterworth), p. 212.

were never idle. Whenever practicable, they explored
the water through which the big ships moved on their
frequent excursions to sea. They hunted possible submarines, and searched areas where mines were expected.

Fortunately, they found nothing. Mines were not
laid near the Fleet's bases in the windswept, misty
north until later, by which time the overworked gunboats had been considerably augmented.

They had an arduous time. Strenuous days, sleepless nights and frequent bad weather were their
common lot. And round about Scapa Flow and the
Pentland Firth, as anyone who has been there will
tell you, the tides and currents are fierce and wildly
erratic. A heavy, confused, tumbling sea is kicked
up by the five- or seven-knot stream running against
even a moderate gale of wind. Thick or misty weather
is frequent even in summer ; and it is dark for three-
quarters of the day during winter. With an iron-
bound shore which in most places is ' steep-to ', and
thus gives no warning of its proximity by the use of
the lead, with a multitude of outlying rocks and
skerries, the locality is the bane of navigators.

The gunboats were old craft – little ships more
than twenty years old which had been retained or
snatched from the scrap-heap for service as minesweepers. They were about 800 tons, roughly two-
thirds of the size of our modern destroyers, and by
no means so habitable. Their antiquated engines and
boilers, like the ships themselves, had to be nursed.
They burnt coal instead of oil, which meant that during
their brief spells of rest in harbour, the grimy fuel had
laboriously to be shovelled into bags in the hold of a
collier and hoisted on board to replenish the hungry
bunkers.

' We had a comparatively small steaming radius,'
writes one officer. ' On some of our longer trips we
had to carry 50 or 60 tons of extra coal on the upper
deck, making our passages through the Pentland Firth
or the North Sea in winter very dangerous. Even
so we sometimes had to be towed home, or reach our
base with empty bunkers.'

It must have been a dog's life; though few dogs ever know so little ease.

But ancient though they were, those little ships did the job that was expected of them, and a good deal else besides. It was said that Commander Preston,[1] who was the 'Senior Officer, Minesweepers' – 'S.O.M.S.' for short – practically never slept. Having known him for more than twenty years, and being fully aware of his tireless energy, I can quite well believe it.

Lionel George Preston was well known in the Navy even before the war. As the junior promotion of his batch, he had been specially advanced to commander in June, 1907, for the skilful and seamanlike handling of his destroyer H.M.S. *Bruizer* in the Mediterranean.

During a gale of wind on a pitch-dark night with a very heavy sea, the destroyer *Ariel* went ashore on the rocks off Malta and was rapidly sinking. Well knowing the risk to himself, his men, and his ship, Preston ran his little vessel alongside the wreck and succeeded in saving most of her officers and men.

A destroyer is no easy craft to handle in bad weather, and the *Bruizer*, one of the earliest destroyers built, was a '27 knotter' of something under 300 tons. Her steel sides, stretched tight over an interior framing, were no thicker than stout cardboard. The least mishandling, the smallest error in judgment, might have sunk her alongside her consort. Cool bravery is not the prerogative of war.

Sailors have many hobbies, and in his spare time, Sir Lionel Preston, as he now is, has constituted himself a real authority, a highly knowledgeable amateur, in the matter of antique furniture, pictures, china and glass. He started to acquire his knowledge, he once told me, in his destroyer in the Mediterranean by setting himself to read one chapter of a book on one or other of the subjects in which he was particularly interested, each night before going to sleep. Be that as it may, he is now an expert whose opinion is valued by professional salesmen and buyers.

[1] Now, July, 1934, Admiral Sir Lionel G. Preston, K.C.B.

Perhaps one day he may be tempted to write a book on the romance of collecting. The tale of how he saw a valuable bow-fronted chest-of-drawers in a cobbler's cottage on Dartmoor, and tracked it down years later when he happened to be possessed of the return half of a ticket from London to Plymouth which it seemed a pity not to use, is worth hearing. And it must be a thrilling experience to buy a picture for £2 2s. at an auction, under the noses of many experts who failed to recognise its value, and afterwards to dispose of it for £650 !

Anyhow, the S.O.M.S. in the *Skipjack* in the early days of the war was very much of a character, and much beloved by the officers and men of his command. Many are the stories told of him.

As one officer writes : ' We felt so confident of his efficiency and leadership, that we were prepared to follow him anywhere. He certainly demanded full measure, and looking back I sometimes wonder how we were able to stick it, specially during the first year of the war. . . . It was a real privilege and pleasure to have served under him, and I know further how he has looked after our welfare, then and ever since. Often to the point of being severe, he never forgot those who served with him. . . .'

Many are the stories told of ' L. G. P. ', as he was affectionately known.

Quite early in the war another gunboat was sweeping with the *Skipjack*, Commander Preston's ship, when the S.O.M.S. noticed that the other vessel's mine-sweeping kite was behaving most erratically, jumping out of the water at one moment, and diving deeply the next. The depth of the kite, in relation to the amount of kite wire out, had previously been determined by experiments, and was always signalled by numeral flags when passing the sweep.

So the S.O.M.S. signalled to the commanding officer of the gunboat with the offending kite asking what was the matter. The C.O., very unwisely, replied, ' I find from experience the kite keeps more accurate depth if kite wire is less than signalled.' Commander

Preston replied, ' Your experience of minesweeping is very limited and not yet very convincing. Do things according to the book.'

The majority of minesweepers carried no medical officer, and on another occasion a vessel at sea reported by wireless that a man on board was in great pain and ought to see a doctor. Kidney trouble was suspected. The senior officer's reply was laconic : ' Turn him in. Put hot fomentations on his back. Pass your sweep-wire with all despatch.'

Another time, when news of an advance in France was being expected hourly, the same minesweeper signalled to the S.O.M.S. asking if there was anything exciting in the press news, and was told to listen on P. wave at 1800 (6 p.m.). At five minutes past the hour the petty officer telegraphist of the sweeper duly handed his captain a signal. It was very short and had nothing whatever to do with the news from France : ' *Foxglove* take wireless guard till 2200.'

Yet again, when a flotilla of minesweepers happened to be lying in harbour on a Sunday, they were ordered to land parties for Divine Service. ' Two men pleasantly but firmly declined to go,' writes the commanding officer of the ship concerned. ' They asserted they had decided to have *no* religion, probably to save themselves the trouble of a walk. I told them that their souls were their own ; but that what *I* cared about was their earthly discipline. I went over to see S.O.M.S. and asked him what I should do. He very soon made up his mind. " Tell them ", he said, " that as they have *no religion*, they can't be buried in any ordinary cemetery if they get killed. It is an unpleasant idea that corpses should be left lying about ; therefore they must deposit with you a sum of money to enable you to buy a plot of land to bury them in if they should die. Choose an expensive plot, say in the middle of a football field, so that the deposit may be generous." These men were finally sent to a ship with a chaplain, labelled " For conversion ". I don't know what happened.'

In order to ensure clear water for the fleet if the

necessity arose, the gunboats were occasionally put on to sweeping an area some 50 miles square well over the other side of the North Sea and close to the enemy coast. Their full speed was 17 to 18 knots,[1] but so small was their coal capacity, that they were unable to remain long enough on the spot to do really good work. Hence one boiler was kept in reserve with banked fires, and was only brought forward when the German wireless signals became particularly loud and prolific. Escorted by heavier vessels they once continued this sweep for nearly three weeks, working three days out and two days back at Aberdeen for rest and coaling. No mines were apparently encountered; but neither the escort nor the Germans dared to enter the supposed minefield. If the enemy had maintained wireless silence, and had ventured to pounce on the gunboats at dawn, they would have been easy meat.

But risks had to be taken. Useful as the minesweeping trawlers were, their speed of 6 to 7 knots when sweeping was insufficient to allow them to work far enough afield and to give the Commander-in-Chief elbow room for his heavy ships. The gunboats, which could sweep at 12 knots, had to do the job.

Until such time as new, specially designed vessels could be built,[2] however, it was decided to supplement these already overworked craft of the Fleet Minesweeping Flotilla by eight fast railway packets commandeered from the Mercantile Marine. They were the *Reindeer, Roebuck* (renamed *Roedean*) *Lynx* (renamed *Lynn*) and *Gazelle* of the Great Western Railway; the *Folkestone* and *Hythe* of the South Eastern and Chatham Railway; and the *Clacton* and *Newmarket* of the Great Eastern Railway.

Fitted out and commissioned in a great hurry, they were manned by officers with temporary commissions in the Royal Naval Reserve without any knowledge

---

[1] I am informed that on one occasion when chasing a submarine on the surface both the *Circe* and the *Leda* exceeded 19 knots.

[2] For an account of the minesweepers constructed during the war under Admiralty building programmes, see Appendix 6.

of minesweeping, and, with a few exceptions, no previous experience of naval work or discipline.   Their crews were also a hybrid collection enrolled under four different scales of pay, some being inexperienced landsmen, and others merchant seamen who had never served in small craft.[1] Their hearts were very much in the right place, but their inexperience led to difficulties.   Reorganisation brought gradual efficiency, though just as they were becoming capable of helping the gunboats in their arduous exploratory sweeps, the railway packets were sent off to the Mediterranean for service at Gallipoli.

One incident that occurred in 1914 shows the peculiar state of discipline that sometimes prevailed among these auxiliaries.

A large force of minesweepers, including the railway steamers referred to, was collected at Invergordon. Protected by a division of destroyers they were required to steam across the North Sea to a position about 100 miles from Heligoland, and to sweep towards Germany along the track which would probably be taken by the British battle-cruisers in chase of any enemy raiding force.   At the far end of their journey they were to be met by a cruiser squadron which would act as an escort.

All the arrangements had been cut and dried, when, as so often happened, a heavy gale intervened.   The whole force of minesweepers had therefore to take shelter at Aberdeen, where they were crammed into the docks.

The arrival of the Navy in some strength excited the generosity of certain Aberdonians, who had never seen such a spectacle before.   Sentries had been placed round the ships in the quaysides.   Nevertheless, bottles of whisky in quantity found their way on board some of the vessels.

During the night the weather moderated sufficiently

[1] As a matter of interest, the men were drawn from the Royal Navy, Royal Fleet Reserve, Royal Naval Reserve, Royal Naval Reserve (Trawler Section), Royal Naval Volunteer Reserve, while a considerable number of Mercantile Marine ratings were specially enrolled under a form of contract known as T. 1242.

to allow the expedition to sail. By steaming at the anticipated speed it was just possible to rendezvous with the cruiser squadron on the other side of the North Sea at the time ordered.

However, for the first two hours, the speed of the large flotilla fell a good three knots below that ordered. Frequent doses of whisky had gone to the heads of some of the stokers. Fire-hoses had to be turned on to them to bring them to their senses. Speed gradually increased as the fumes wore off, and the rendezvous was made more or less at the proper time.

But one man, over-attracted by the delights of Aberdeen, had broken out of his ship, and this is a considerable crime in the naval calendar. It might even amount to desertion in the face of the enemy.

The commanding officer of the ship in question thought it his duty to report the absentee by signal. During the night he had had plenty to occupy his mind; but shortly after the flotilla had reached its rendezvous and had passed its sweep-wires, he had time to think of other things. So when his bows were pointed for Germany, with the whole of the High Sea Fleet, and its attendant cruisers, destroyers and submarines not a hundred miles distant, he broke forth into wireless. He did not even trouble to put his message into code. In plain, unvarnished English, he reported to anyone who happened to be listening that William Smith, or whatever his name might be, was absent without leave in Aberdeen.

Now this is a true tale, and the German wireless operators must have heard that signal nearly as clearly as the senior officer to whom it was addressed.

Whether or not William Smith's delinquency was reported to the German Commander-in-Chief one cannot say. If it was, he probably took it as a very palpable ruse to entice him into battle with the Grand Fleet, or into the arms of some waiting British submarine. At any rate, no German forces appeared to interrupt the sweepers.

Their work continued.

ADMIRAL SIR LIONEL G. PRESTON, K.C.B.

[p. 43.

2

The U-boats were soon busy in the northern part of the North Sea. U.15 had been rammed and sunk by the *Birmingham* off Fair Island four days after the outbreak of war. Late at night on September 2, a German Kapitän-Leutnant named Hersing had taken U.21 up the Firth of Forth and as far as the Forth Bridge. Finding nothing to attack, he made his way out to sea again, and on September 5, in bad weather, torpedoed and sank the small cruiser *Pathfinder* off St. Abbs' Head with heavy loss of life.

On September 22, U.9, commanded by Otto Weddigen, sank the cruisers *Aboukir*, *Cressy* and *Hogue* in the ' Broad Fourteens ', off the coast of Holland, with the loss of 1,459 officers and men. ' This cruel loss of life ', as says Mr. Winston Churchill, ' although small compared to what the Army was suffering, constituted the first serious forfeit extracted from the Navy in the war. It greatly stimulated and encouraged the enterprise of the German submarines.' [1]

On October 15, Weddigen, still in U.9, sank the old cruiser *Hawke* – patrolling on a line well to the eastward of Aberdeen – with a loss of another 500 officers and men.

This disaster, coupled with what had gone before, drove home the terrible menace of the U-boats. They were working further and further afield, and the great sheet of water which is Scapa Flow, in which the Grand Fleet lay, was unprotected against submarine attack. People had thought it impossible that any submerged vessel could penetrate into the anchorage through the swirling currents of its intricate, rock-studded channels. But now they were not so sure. There began to be reports of submarines actually inside the Flow. The sense of security which every fleet demands in its war anchorages was destroyed. ' The climax came on October 17. Guns were fired, destroyers thrashed

[1] *The World Crisis, 1911–1914,* vol. i, p. 326.

4

the waters, and the whole gigantic Armada put to
sea in haste and dudgeon.' [1]

'The first day after the departure of the Fleet was
very exciting,' an eye-witness writes. 'About forty
vessels were barging round independently at high
speed, and periscopes were seen in all directions.
Guns opened fire, and it was a miracle none of us got
hit. About 11.30 one of the destroyers taking part
enlivened the proceedings by accidentally firing a
torpedo. Several people tried to ram it, and still
more opened fire. One of the gunboats claimed to
have sunk a submarine; but when the divers went
down they found nothing . . . the hunt went on,
with searchlights being used at night.'

In point of fact no enemy submarine ever penetrated
Scapa Flow during the war, and at the time, the
Commander-in-Chief of the Grand Fleet, then Sir
John Jellicoe, could not state with 'absolute certainty'
that submarines were inside the anchorage. Nevertheless, consummate seaman as he was, he was of the
opinion that it was 'not difficult for a submarine to
get inside at slack water'.

It is easy to be wise after the event, and to pooh-
pooh the idea as ridiculous. The fact remains that
Scapa Flow *was* undefended, and that the risk of
submarine attack was a very real one.

Pending the completion of its anti-submarine
defences, the Commander-in-Chief was therefore
empowered to use anchorages on the west coast of
Scotland, or to go so far afield as Berehaven, in the
south of Ireland.

'The menace of mines and submarines is proving
larger every day,' Sir David Beatty, then commanding
the Battle Cruiser Squadron, wrote from the *Lion*
to the First Lord of the Admiralty on October 17.
'Adequate means to meet or combat them are not
forthcoming, and we are gradually being pushed out
of the North Sea, and off our own particular perch
. . . we have no Base where we can with *any* degree
of safety lie for coaling, replenishing, and refitting and

[1] *The World Crisis, 1911–1914*, p. 381.

repairing, after two and a half months of war . . . we have no place to lay our heads. We are at Loch Na Keal, Isle of Mull. My picket boats are at the entrance, the nets are out and the men are at the guns, waiting for coal which has run low, but ready to move at a moment's notice. . . . We have been running now hard since 28th July; small defects are creeping up which we haven't time to take in hand. . . . The men can stand it, but the machine can't, and we must have a place where we can stop for from four to five days every now and then to give the engineers a chance. Such a place does not exist. . . .' [1]

The battle-cruisers, like other ships, were very hard worked in those early days of the war. Forty-eight hours in harbour with steam ready to move at short notice was their usual spell of rest, and during this period they had to coal on an average 1,400 tons a time, every ton being laboriously dug out of the holds of colliers and filled into bags by hand.

To the seamen who were fighting the war afloat it seemed hard and inexplicable that they should have no place where they could safely lay their heads. ' We are not enjoying ourselves,' Sir David Beatty wrote. ' But the morale is high and confidence higher.'

It was as well that the spirit of the men remained unimpaired.

3

I have wandered a little from the story of the mine-sweepers to explain the situation of the Grand Fleet as it appeared in October, 1914 – driven for the time out of the North Sea by the ever-present and increasing threat of the submarines.

In point of actual fact, Otto Weddigen, after sinking the *Hawke, did* make an attempt to enter Scapa Flow, and after nearly torpedoing a destroyer, was all but rammed by another.

The defences of Scapa Flow were hurried on with all speed; but on October 27, while the Grand Fleet

[1] *The World Crisis, 1911–1914,* vol. i, pp. 389, 390.

was using Lough Swilly – in the north of Ireland – as a base for gunnery exercises, it suffered its first serious loss in the sinking of the battleship *Audacious*.

Two hundred mines had been laid the night before off Tory Island by the North German Lloyd liner *Berlin*, a ship of 17,000 tons with a speed of about 17 knots. It was sheer bad luck that one of her mines sank the *Audacious*, since her objective had been the merchant traffic bound to and from Liverpool round the north of Ireland.

The submarine scare in Scapa Flow had thrown a lot of extra work on the minesweeping gunboats, so that their routine sweeping was considerably behindhand. On the evening of October 26, the flotilla had returned to Scapa Flow to coal, after which officers and men were looking forward to a night in bed, the first for a considerable period.

But the unexpected always happens. The *Leda* and *Circe* suddenly received orders to raise steam for full speed, and to report when ready. A ship called the *Manchester Commerce* had struck a mine off the north of Ireland, and the two gunboats were required to see that the approaches to Lough Swilly – then being used by the Grand Fleet – were clear of mines. They sailed soon after midnight, and shortly afterwards were somewhat surprised to receive a wireless signal – 'Keep a good lookout for floating mines.' This seemed strange, as the night was pitch dark. But the matter was soon cleared up. The word 'mines' in the signal should have been 'dock', for soon after leaving harbour they sighted a new floating dock which was being towed to Scapa for repair work for the Fleet. 'With numerous tugs and attendant craft all lit up, it looked like a town coming along,' runs one account.

However, steaming at their best speed, the two gunboats continued their journey to the south, passing through the Minches – between the Hebrides and the west coast of Scotland. On the morning of the 27th they received an urgent signal to go to the assistance of the *Audacious*. I have the follow-

ing account from an officer who was present in the
Circe : [1]

' Just as we were reaching the area and were passing
sweeps, we received orders to go to the help of the
Audacious. We slipped sweeps and proceeded at
full speed towards her position, steaming head on
to a heavy Atlantic swell. The lookout reported a
submarine on our starboard bow, and we altered course
towards it. After shipping a good Atlantic comber
which flattened out the bridge and washed a signalman
on to the fore-and-aft bridge, it was discovered that
the supposed submarine was really the discarded battle-
practice target at which the *Audacious* was to have
carried out her firing.

' On closing the *Audacious* I was lowered in the
cutter – a very unpleasant experience as she was not
fitted with dropping-gear – and taken in tow by the
Circe. After being nearly swamped a couple of times,
I cut the tow and proceeded under oars to the
Audacious' starboard quarter where I was instructed
to lie off and await orders. She was lying stern to
swell on an even keel but well down by the stern.
The seas were breaking well over her after 6-inch
gun ports ; otherwise one could see nothing the matter
with her.

' We lay there for about three hours, watching the
Olympic take her in tow. When the tow had been
passed, it was very interesting to note that although
we could not see any movement of the *Olympic* through
the water, the towing hawsers slowly rose out of the
sea, grew bar taut, and parted. On being recalled to
the *Circe* we were hoisted after a great deal of trouble,
and then proceeded to take in tow the *Audacious'*
launch and pinnace, and also any of the *Olympic's*
lifeboats we could collect.'

Owing to the following sea the tow was continually
parting, so that the lifeboats had to be abandoned.
Meanwhile, the *Circe* was crowded with men from
the *Audacious*, who were all wet through and hungry.

[1] Lieutenant-Commander A. E. Thomson, D.S.C., R.N., then a sub-
lieutenant.

It was a difficult matter to provide dry clothing for the multitude, and everything edible soon disappeared.

' Placing a petty officer in each boat,' Lieutenant-Commander Thomson's account continues, ' we made the launch fast to the sweep-wire, and the pinnace on the kite wire, and proceeded to Lough Swilly. As we were closing the entrance the *Olympic* asked us to lead her in, as she had no charts of the place. It was a very proud moment for our Navigating Gunner.' [1]

No wonder. The *Circe's* Navy List displacement was 810 tons, while she drew 12½ feet of water. The *Olympic's* gross tonnage is 46,439, and at the time of the incident described she was drawing 33 feet !

' As we reached the narrowest part of the entrance the pinnace sheered across the bows of the launch, and as the latter fell astern in the trough of the swell the sweep-wire tautened out and capsized the pinnace – P. O. Kean being given a very unexpected swim. It was dark by now. We lowered a lifeboat and picked him up after the use of searchlights, all very upsetting to the *Olympic*. Then we proceeded up harbour, with the pinnace floating upside down, and every few minutes either diving nearly to the bottom or trying to ram the launch. Just before our excitement with the boats, we had seen an enormous column of flame out to sea – looking just like a large red Prince of Wales's Feathers. Although we were a good many miles away from the *Audacious*, the illumination was bright enough to recognise most people on our upper deck. That, I suppose, must have been the last of her. We anchored the *Olympic* in a safe billet, and went to our own anchorage with the flotilla.'

I persuaded Mr. Blackmore to give his version of the pilotage incident. ' It was certainly a great moment for me,' he writes, ' but a great responsibility increased by the attendant circumstances – bad weather, a long tow of boats continually breaking adrift, little time and practically no facilities for working up the chart, and sending all messages by light.

[1] Mr. George E. Blackmore. Now Lieutenant-Commander, O.B.E., D.S.C. His name will appear later in this book.

On top of that we had the man overboard incident, causing us to stop in the narrow entrance. It was a great risk which could only be justified by the circumstances of war, which might have caused the *Olympic*, and all her passengers, to have shared the fate of the *Audacious*. . . . I was relieved when she was safely anchored, and glad when, after sounding all round her, I could get a little rest.'

The gunboats certainly had a strenuous time, and in November were again hunting submarines near Scapa Flow.

On November 24, U.18, commanded by Kapitän-Leutnant Von Hennig, made an attempt to enter the anchorage. Following in the wake of a steamer in the early hours of the morning, he got as far as the boom in the Hoxa entrance, only to discover that the Grand Fleet was absent. Sir John Jellicoe, in fact, was carrying out one of his periodical sweeps towards the Heligoland Bight.

Turning to make out to sea again, U.18 was sighted by the armed trawler *Tokio*, and soon afterwards by another armed trawler, the *Dorothy Gray*, Skipper Alexander Youngson, R.N.R. After a chase, Youngson succeeded in ramming the submarine, which, with her periscope and hydroplanes damaged, dived, hit the bottom and then again broke surface. It was on this occasion, the story goes, that when the first ramming occurred the engineer of the *Dorothy Gray*, leaving his engines, appeared on deck with a sledge hammer ready to deal with the enemy at close quarters.

Rammed once more by the destroyer *Garry*, U.18 disappeared for a time, then again struggled up to the surface. Completely disabled, she drifted past the Pentland Skerries, with her crew firing distress signals. All but one of her men were rescued by the *Garry*, when, having been scuttled by her crew, she vanished for the last time off Muckle Skerry.

The *Dorothy Gray* had the supreme honour of being the first auxiliary vessel in naval history to be the means of destroying a submarine. ' Hearty congratulations to Trawler No. 96 for brilliant service which Their Lordships will mark by a substantial reward,' the First Lord of the Admiralty telegraphed. In due course Skipper Youngson and his men received £500, while £100 went to the *Tokio*.

Quite apart from the pecuniary prize, the knowledge that a fishing trawler manned by fishermen had performed excellent service in ridding the sea of a dangerous enemy created a most encouraging precedent and incentive.

Within a day or two Commander Preston in the *Skipjack* was in touch with U.16 off Lerwick, in the Shetlands. The submarine managed to make her escape ; but again the ubiquitous armed trawler had given chase. ' I consider most praiseworthy ', Commander Preston reported, ' the way these two trawlers 79 and 80 carried out the chase and promptly gave information.'

The British auxiliary patrol, manned from outside the Royal Navy, was coming into its own as a most effective fighting force. A retired German admiral wrote letters to the German Press suggesting that no fishing vessels should be spared.

4

All this early war experience in minesweeping, and in dealing with all manner of ships and men, must have been of incalculable value to the S.O.M.S. in the *Skipjack*. In 1917, having been promoted on December 31, 1914, Captain Preston became Director of Minesweeping at the Admiralty.

One particularly hair-raising series of incidents that befell him in the *Skipjack* in a minefield off Scarborough will be told later. Here, however, I may fittingly mention a few more incidents connected with the Fleet Sweepers in the earlier days of the war.

One of them, the *Circe*, spent the Christmas period of 1914 in dock at Devonport, being fitted with a heavy type of bow defence gear against mines, and having her masts lengthened to 120 feet to increase the range of her wireless. Early in January she sailed

for Scapa Flow via the West Coast. The weather was
not particularly bad, but off the Lizard the seas
bumping the new bow defence gear caused the rivets
to leak and flooded the forepart of the ship. Then
both masts broke and went overboard. 'With one
thing and another we had a hectic night, and returning
to Devonport gave everyone the impression of having
been in action. They reduced the height of our masts
and repaired the bow gear, but the latter gave us
no end of trouble on the way north and was eventually
removed at Scapa.'

In a later chapter I have mentioned the large minefield laid in the Moray Firth by the *Meteor* in August,
1915. I have a few more details of its clearing from
an officer who was present.

Because of the depth at which the mines were laid,
and the draught of water, between 11 and 12 feet, of
the gunboats and the new ' Flower ' class sloops engaged in clearing the field, actual sweeping was restricted to about 3½ hours either side of high water.
During the periods when sweeping was impossible
the flotilla used to anchor at various places along the
coast of Elgin and Banffshire – Buckie, Banff and
Lossiemouth – which provided a chance of landing
officers and men for recreation. But on its first visit
to Banff the flotilla incurred some unpopularity. ' We
came in at dusk,' writes my informant, ' and anchored
among various small buoys and floats. They were
soon investigated, and were found to be crab and
lobster traps. Word was quickly passed round . . .
you can imagine the result. Anyhow, we were discovered, and the next morning a deputation from
Banff waited on Captain Preston, with the result that
anyone having had crab or lobster was invited to
plead guilty and to subscribe to a fund to making
good the loss to the fishermen. Bar oysters, I think
they were the most expensive shellfish I've ever
eaten.'

The new sloop *Lilac* was one of the ships blown up
in this Moray Firth minefield. She struck the mine
with her stem, and blew off her bows nearly as far

as the bridge. The wreckage dropped down and hung from the keel, and for various reasons, such as obstructing the channel, it was decided not to tow her into Cromarty, but into Peterhead. Two ships, one of which was Captain Preston's, towed her round, and on berthing the *Lilac* alongside the breakwater it was found that the wreckage was drawing nearly 40 feet of water. It was lucky that the weather remained fine, otherwise the *Lilac* might have sunk. As it was, a new bow was built on to her and she rejoined the flotilla in a few months.

The sweepers were very hard worked at this period, and to provide some sort of rest for the personnel, Sir John Jellicoe, the Commander-in-Chief, arranged that whenever they visited Rosyth for refuelling or any other purpose each little ship should be looked after and mothered by a battleship. It was greatly appreciated.

' Immediately we arrived we went alongside, were relieved of all duty, and entertained on board. Officers and men from the battleship coaled and cleaned the sweepers, corrected all our charts, completed any defects, and had us spick and span ready to leave harbour next day. They left nothing undone that could possibly increase our comfort, and always gave us a warm welcome. You can realise how grateful we were, for we got practically no rest at sea.'

At one period of the war delay action mines laid by enemy submarines greatly complicated the work of the sweepers. On several occasions the Fleet Sweepers were sent south from Scapa Flow to assist in clearing minefields laid well to seaward of May Island, off the Firth of Forth. They would carry out the sweep, and report the area clear, when the next day, or two or three days later, mines would reappear in the same positions. Grave suspicion rested on the sweepers until a mine was salved, and was discovered to be fitted with a delay action mechanism which was capable of releasing the mine from its sinker at any time up to a period of thirty days.

In March, 1917, two of the gunboats, the *Circe* and

Jason, were sent down the west coast of Scotland to sweep a channel and to locate mines that had been reported there. On April 7 the *Jason* – Lieutenant-Commander C. P. Franklin [1] – struck a mine well forward, and sank almost at once. The *Circe's* boats succeeded in rescuing about 50 of the crew ; but there were about 40 casualties.

Some of the men saved died on board the *Circe*, and others were in a very bad way, as she proceeded full speed to Oban. Here the inhabitants showed their sympathy by attending the funeral, and starting a fund for the dependents of those who had lost their lives. The subscriptions were most generous, and the *Circe's* prize bulldog ' Turk ', wearing a coat made of the Union Flag and carrying a box on his back, collected over £60 in one day !

[1] Now Commander C. P. Franklin, D.S.O., R.N. (Retd.).

CHAPTER IV

IMPROVISATION

I

IT takes on average five or six years to make a fully qualified deep-sea fisherman.

So far as trawlers are concerned, a man may join as a ' deckie learner ' at the age of sixteen. If he can endure the life and proves himself, he can become a deck-hand after a year or so at sea. If ambitious, he may rise to 'third hand', then to 'second hand' or mate, and finally to skipper. Four years have to be spent on deck and one year as mate before sitting for the examination for command.

A trawler skipper, let it be remembered, is generally a man of substance. Nowadays, the earnings of the skippers of Murman Coast and Icelandic trawlers are never less than £700 a year, though it is common knowledge that they must make at least £1,200 if their ships are to pay their owners in proportion to their capital outlay of about £18,000 a ship.

Skippers of ' single boaters ' in the North Sea earn less, about £400 in a bad year and £1,000 in a good one. Between £500 and £600 is the maximum for North Sea Trawlers which work in a fleet and send their fish daily by ' carriers ' to Billingsgate Market.

I once wrote a book [1] which purported to be a novel round the fishing industry from Hull. Long before I ever thought of writing it I knew that trawlermen were tough and hearty. After meeting them, I realised they are as hard and as rugged as granite – not hard in any inhuman sense ; but tough in body and spirit. They are absolutely fearless, inured to discomfort, con-

[1] *70° North.* Hodder and Stoughton.

temptuous of danger, and fiercely independent. No
man is their master. Taking it all in all, I should
imagine that their lives are the most arduous of any
seamen afloat.

Even before the war fishing grounds extended from
the coast of Morocco, in the south ; round the whole
of the British Isles, including, of course, the Atlantic
slope and the North Sea ; to Iceland, and, in the far
north, to well beyond the Arctic Circle.

Trawlers must not be confounded with ' drifters ', of
which I shall say something presently.

The former are stout, weatherly little steam vessels,
built of steel, with high, upstanding bows and a length
of anything between 115 and 138 feet. Their tonnage
is between 215 and 325, their speed anything up to 11
knots, while they draw about 13½ feet of water, sometimes a little more. The largest, manned by about
twelve men, make voyages lasting as long as three
weeks. They fish on the bottom with trawls. A
trawl can be described as a heavy, elongated purse-
shaped net dragged along the sea bottom by means of
a warp, or thin towing wire. Its mouth is kept open
by means of ' otter boards ', and the fish are scooped
up, so to speak, from the sea bottom and find themselves trapped in the cylindrical end of the net known
as the ' cod end '.

' Ye'll mind what it's like handlin' wires up in the
Arctic in the winter when its dark most of the day
round,' a trawler skipper once said to me. ' Ye can
p'r'aps imagine it, though ye'll never *really* know unless
ye comes with us for a trip.'

I shuddered at the prospect.

' The temperature'll be way down near zero,' he
continued. ' Your hands are freezin', an' the ship's
rollin' and pitchin' her guts out wi' the sea breakin'
aboard in solid masses. Maybe there's snow an' sleet,
wi' the iron deck all slippery wi' ice an' fish slime –
like a blinkin' skatin' rink all on the wobble.'

He went on to describe other horrors and accidents,
casualties and shipwrecks – told me how he had known
men to be on deck hauling and clearing the trawl, and

gutting and cleaning fish, for thirty hours at a stretch. When they had finished the job in hand, they just threw off their sea-boots and oilskins and turned in 'all standing', to be up again in an hour or two to repeat the process.

A tough life, I thought it – essentially a hardening process which cannot fail to weed out the ' softies '.

Drifters are quite different from trawlers, being small steam or motor-vessels of less than 100 tons manned by no more than nine or ten men and often built of wood. They make quite long voyages, those from the English ports, for instance, going north during the Scottish herring season, and west to Donegal, while the Scotsmen come south to Yarmouth and Lowestoft later in the year. They fish for the herring with drift-nets – lines of nets sometimes $2\frac{1}{2}$ miles long, supported from the surface by floats or ' buffs ', and hanging like a curtain in the water from a depth of about 12 to 50 feet. The herring, in dense shoals, try to force their way through the nets, to find themselves entrapped in the pliable meshes by the broad part of their bodies.

It is impossible to say how many vessels of each type, manned by their fishermen crews, served under the White Ensign during the war for minesweeping and patrol purposes. What I know is that from 1914 to 1918 we lost in action, or through submarine, mine, fire, collision, shipwreck, or ' various ' or unknown causes, 18 Admiralty and 246 hired trawlers, together with 130 hired drifters – a total of 394 fishing vessels.

Thank heaven that they, and the sturdy men who manned them, were available when the crisis came in August, 1914. Without them, we could not have pulled through.

2

As has already been mentioned, the R.N.R., Trawler Section, formed in 1911, allowed for 100 trawlers, fully manned by fishermen who had had some training in minesweeping, to be commissioned on the outbreak of war. On August 4, 1914, many of the trained men were absent at sea on the fishing grounds. Nevertheless, 94 trawlers were soon ready, and within a week of the Declaration most of them were in harness at their allotted stations.

In those early days, in spite of the minefield laid by the *Königin Luise* well out from Southwold on August 5, it was not realised that the Germans would soon be sowing mines more or less indiscriminately outside territorial waters. So the first batches of trawlers were sent to the ports of chief ' military importance ' – Cromarty, the Firth of Forth, the Tyne, the Humber, Harwich, Sheerness, Dover, Portsmouth, Portland and Plymouth.

The groups were commanded by naval officers, some of them from the retired list, who had received a brief training in minesweeping. It must be confessed that at the outset they had but the vaguest idea of what their duties would entail.

The laying of the Southwold minefield, however, and the loss of many merchant vessels, neutral as well as British, showed that a much larger minesweeping force was needed. Another 100 trawlers were requisitioned on August 10, and so rapidly did the fishermen respond to the call for men that in eleven days the whole force was manned and fitted out at Lowestoft. It is impossible to state the number of fishermen who came forward; but 113 skippers had joined the Trawler Reserve before the outbreak of war. Three hundred and fifteen more had been enrolled by the end of the first week in October.

Apart from the skippers, officers were also required to supplement the handful of naval officers, of the existing minesweeping service. Most of the trained pre-war R.N.R. and R.N.V.R. officers had already been called up for service with the Fleet. For the new minesweeping and auxiliary patrol flotillas officers were obtained from the Mercantile Marine through the instrumentality of the Imperial Merchant Service Guild, an organisation which rendered yeoman service throughout the war. These Mercantile Marine officers, and the civilians who were given temporary commissions in the R.N.R. and R.N.V.R., played no small part in making the Minesweeping Service the splendid force it eventually became.

Under Captain A. A. Ellison, R.N.,[1] originally the captain of H.M.S. *Halycon*, the senior officer's ship of the North Sea Fisheries, Lowestoft became the very large base for minesweeping operations which it remained during the war.

On August 21 yet another 50 trawlers were taken over by the Admiralty. There was never a moment's delay for lack of men or the supply of stores, for which latter Captain T. P. Bonham,[2] the Inspecting Captain of Minesweeping Vessels at the Admiralty, and his assistant, Commander Hubert H. Holland,[3] were mainly responsible.

Eight days later a clear channel had been swept and buoyed inshore of the Southwold minefield laid by the *Königin Luise*. This was the start of the fairway, known as the 'War Channel', a buoyed traffic lane which eventually extended from Dover to the Firth of Forth and was swept daily for mines. The minesweeping forces employed on this service were based on the Nore, Harwich, Lowestoft, the Humber, the Tyne and Granton in the Firth of Forth. 'These six ports', Sir Lionel Preston writes, 'gained us a great deal of our early experience, while the friendly rivalry between them did much to bring about efficiency and to initiate the fine spirit that pervaded the whole minesweeping force.'

Improvisation won, though at first the fishermen were inclined to boggle at the restrictions of naval discipline. Various Royal Fleet Reserve and pensioner petty officers were distributed among the vessels for the purpose of inculcating naval ideas and habits. As a whole they did their work well, if here and there their dealings were marked by a lack of appreciation of the characteristics and outlook of the

---

[1] Now Rear-Admiral A. A. Ellison, C.B. (Retd.).
[2] Afterwards killed at Jutland in H.M.S. *Black Prince*.
[3] Now Rear-Admiral H. H. Holland, C.B. (Retd.).

H.M.S. *CIRCE.*
One of the Gunboat Sweepers, 1916.

[*p.* 53.

entirely new type of personnel with which they had
to deal.

It was only to be expected. The fishermen were
intensely conservative and independent, accustomed
to thinking and acting for themselves. Skippers might
be related by birth and marriage with cooks and deck-
hands, and might live in the same streets. So there
was a certain amount of free and easy familiarity
which, while all very well in a fishing vessel, hardly
fitted in with the tradition of the Navy. If trouble
arose in a trawler during peace, settlement was generally reached via the strong right arm of the skipper
or second hand, helped by the toe of a heavy sea-
boot.

The institution of ' leave forms ' and free railway
passes in August, 1914, was at first imperfectly understood by some of the skippers to whom they were
issued. The intention was that the skipper should
sign a form saying that a man could be spared during
his time in harbour. The man then took it to the
Base – I am referring to the custom at Lowestoft –
with his request for leave.

On his return from his first minesweeping trip, one
gallant Aberdonian signed a leave form and a railway
pass for himself and every member of his crew. There-
upon, apparently disliking Lowestoft, they left their
ship entirely unattended and went off to Scotland *en
bloc* by the first available train.

The skipper, who knew no better, being entirely
ignorant of naval discipline, had to be severely dealt
with when he returned, with an escort. Later, he
became a first-class man, and was commodore of his
group of trawlers.

The spirit was naturally individual and undisciplined. The men from Hull looked sideways at
those from Grimsby, or North or South Shields, while
the Grimsbyites might despise the gentlemen from
Lowestoft or Fleetwood, and regard the Aberdonians
as being no more than foreigners. There were frequent fights ashore – riotous scenes when the leave
parties returned to their ships.

Each of these different clans and factions, all steeped in their own peculiar traditions, had to be reconciled and brought together to work in unison. This was the work of the officers – retired naval officers fresh from civil life ashore ; officers from liners, large cargo vessels and tramps ; enthusiastic yachtsmen, and many whose experience of the sea was confined to a summer holiday at Broadstairs, Southsea or West-ward Ho !

Even some of the officers couldn't quite grasp the new regime, so utterly different from anything they had experienced before.

Seniority is something of a fetish in the Navy. It has to be. Though two officers may be promoted to commander or lieutenant on the same day, the one whose name appears lowest in the Navy List has to obey the orders of the other if the pair are drawn into official contact. They may call each other ' Shorty ' or ' Mike ' off duty ; but not so on the bridges of their ships engaged on some operation.

Hence the point of the true story of two temporary officers of the R.N.R., both in command of mine-sweepers. The senior, by virtue of an earlier dated commission, was leading into harbour, and hoisted a signal to his mate – " Take station two cables astern."

Resenting the interference, the junior officer took station as the spirit moved him, and expostulated by semaphore.

The senior man replied – ' Obey orders. Kindly don't argue.'

Hardly had the semaphore arms ceased to wave, when a reply came back from the junior – ' Don't you argue with me. Do you think the Cunard takes orders from a Burns Line tramp ? '

I never heard what happened.

3

Nothing could have been more wonderful than the spirit of officers and men alike. I have before me a letter written by Captain Wilfred M. Bruce, C.B.E.,

R.D., R.N.R., who was working with minesweepers at Lowestoft throughout the whole of the war.

' As a general rule there was little to disturb the monotony of the grim routine of the sweepers – twelve days at sea, and four in harbour, in all weathers. The prospect of death and mutilation must always have been in the minds of the crews, but was accepted with the fatalistic composure which is such a marked characteristic of the class of men by whom these vessels were manned. Occasionally a man's nerves gave way completely, and, curiously enough, it was often the biggest, burliest and roughest who had to be " passed out " by medical inspection.

' For over four years these little ships, in many cases keeping their small crews intact throughout, swept continuously the different sections of the War Channel. The men knew full well, and often witnessed the fact, that four or five seconds after striking a mine, no trace of a trawler would be left, and that those of the crew still surviving would be struggling in water poisoned by high explosive. Their steadfastness under these conditions cannot be spoken of too highly, and it is doubtful if anyone – save those who were working with them, and, perhaps, the crews of the merchant ships which passed safely through the swept channels round our coasts – will ever fully understand the debt that England owes to the men of the minesweepers.' [1]

Those words are corroborated by Rear-Admiral Edward F. B. Charlton, C.B.,[2] who, on September 1, 1914, became Admiral in command of minesweepers on the East Coast of England.

' Although something can be learned from peace training, the real excitement of minesweeping was not there. The knowledge that your unseen enemy was capable of completely destroying without warning, and at the most unexpected moment, was not present. Nor

[1] Over 2,300 mines were accounted for by Lowestoft during the war. Of the 76,000 odd vessels that passed through the swept channel during the four years that a record was kept, 248 were lost from all causes, a percentage of 0·32 in the Lowestoft area.

[2] Now Admiral Sir Edward F. B. Charlton, K.C.B., K.C.M.G. (Retd.).

was the practical certainty that, from the methods employed, the odds were precisely twenty to one whether you got the mine, or the mine got you.

' "And how were the sweepers being manned?" the Admiral went on to ask." Principally with North Sea fishermen – men certainly inured to every sea hardship, and accustomed to every ordinary danger of the deep ; but untrained (as were other naval forces) to face the destructive efforts of an unscrupulous enemy. The question was in what manner would these fishermen acquit themselves? They were men of the sea – rough, sturdy, undisciplined, accustomed mostly to pleasing themselves as to the manner of doing their work, or whether they went to sea or not. Would they be amenable to naval discipline, all important in minesweeping, as in every other branch of the Service, or would they prove an element of discord, and fight shy of the fresh dangers they were now called upon to confront ?

' The manner in which they replied to these questions and justified the trust of the country which was placed in them is now a matter of world-wide knowledge.'

In short, the ratings were admirable, and so were the officers, who rapidly attained the initiative, the quick perception and decision, the resource, and the power of command that enabled their arduous and dangerous work to be carried out without intermission.

These men were honoured in the days when they were carrying on a life-and-death struggle for us, and for a few years afterwards.

They should not be forgotten now.

' I have worked with all classes and many nationalities of men in all corners of the world,' Captain Bruce writes. ' I never want, or hope, to work with a finer lot than the crews of the Lowestoft minesweepers.'

And as showing the comradeship that obtained, here is a letter written by the officer of a group of minesweepers to the man about to relieve him :

H.M. Trawler *Sargon*
Nothin' Doin' Section,
Ellaferlongway
Sunday.

DEAR ALEC,

Please let me know by Thursday's mail-boat which
tide you are coming out on on Sunday next, as I don't
want to toddle down to Corton Roads and have Old
Brucie jumping on me for nix.

Luv,
DUGGIE.   x x x x x

I must leave the reader to imagine who ' Old Brucie '
might be.

4

Innumerable are the strange yarns of minor difficulties with the minesweepers during the early days
of the war.

'Getting the fishermen into uniform, and bringing
them under naval discipline, were necessary preliminaries to make them into a Minesweeping Service,'
writes Captain M. W. S. Boucher, D.S.O., R.N., who
in 1914 was the Lieutenant (N) of the *Halycon* at
Lowestoft. ' Enough officers' uniforms could not be
produced at short notice for so many skippers. Each,
therefore, was given an officer's cap and badge, and a
set of uniform buttons which he was told to sew on to
his best suit ! The results were sometimes amusing,
but were thought sufficient to comply with the terms
of the Hague Convention whereby all combatants had
to be in uniform.

' At Lowestoft the skippers were haled on board
the *Halycon*, where they were given simple instruction in naval discipline. They then went back to
their ships, and instructed their mates and crews on
similar lines. But their ideas of discipline were often
peculiar. One quiet Saturday forenoon an unusually
violent commotion began in a trawler lying alongside
the wharf not far from the *Halycon*. An officer and
a couple of armed men went to investigate, and look-

ing down from the wharf on to the deck of the trawler were amazed to see the entire crew, engineers and all, rushing wildly about the deck. The clatter and shouting was echoing up and down the harbour. They would huddle together on one side, then scatter and rush to the other, pursued by a tousled, unshaven man waving a chopper.'

The mate had run amok.

Lieutenant C. E. Hamond,[1] then first-lieutenant of the *Halycon*, went on board, and, in his own words, ' took up a point of vantage by the winch, tripped up the mate as he passed and managed to disarm him. Explanations followed. The mate was after cookie, and cookie said the mate had come on board at 11 a.m. and had started ' cursing and blinding him ' for his breakfast. No breakfast was forthcoming. When I asked him what he meant, the mate could only say – " Am I mate of this blinkin' ship or am I not ? – I asks cookie for my breakfast, and he's 'nowt to do but start swearin' and cursin' like one possessed and don't get me none. What'll I do, I asks ye, but 'ave a go at 'im with chopper ? I just wanted to frighten 'im like ; but I'd dearly love to see the ruddy cook in 'Ull, Grimsby, Aberdeen or sanguinary Lowestoft as'll stop *me* 'aving me grub ! Discipline must be maintained at all costs. That's what we're told ! " – The statement about frightening cookie was somewhat discounted by the condition of the galley door, which had a panel knocked out and the lock shattered.'

' Eventually,' Captain Boucher writes, ' the trawlers' crews settled down to a sort of compromise between naval discipline and fishing discipline. But no sort of discipline ever seemed to regularise the relationship between the skipper and the cook. Even when order prevailed everywhere else, the *Halycon's* doctor was frequently repairing skippers and/or cooks. It was unfortunate that so many fights took place in or near the galley. The galleys of trawlers are small and not easy to move about in, so the cook, being on his own ground, usually won. . . . Dealing with such

[1] Now Commander C. E. Hamond, R.N. (Retd.).

cases, and finding scraps of relevant evidence among
the tangled statements of the witnesses was most
difficult. But they all yielded the same lesson. –
Never assault a cook in his own kitchen. Have it out
with him on deck.'

Cooks seemed often to be in trouble. ' Once in the
trawler *Dreadnought II* when firing at a Zeppelin off
the Swarte Bank,' writes an officer, ' I shamed the
cook by double-shotting the gun with some of his
suet dumplings which we had been unable to eat
for dinner.'

Law and order, however, soon came to prevail. The
trawlers worked in groups of six, each group being commanded by a Lieutenant R.N.R. with a skipper in each
ship. The group officers, mostly young fellows with experience of large merchant ships only, were at first regarded with the deepest suspicion by the older men.
It was not long, however, before the groups became
' family concerns ' headed very ably by their C.O.'s.
A healthy rivalry sprang up, and clean ships with holy-
stoned decks and shining brightwork were the rule
rather than the exception.

Early in the war, before the trawlers' crews reached
their later stage of efficiency, they frequently smashed
their large, prism-shaped minesweeping kites against
their propellers, or elsewhere. So many kites were
expended, that the stock ran out. Lowestoft sent
S.O.S. telegrams to other bases ; but no kites could
be supplied. Appeals were broadcast to the Admiralty, the Royal Dockyards, and to any other likely
establishment, beseeching, demanding kites. Meanwhile, minesweeping had ceased from Yarmouth and
Lowestoft, a very serious matter.

For two days nothing happened. Then arrived a
few railway trucks laden with kites. Joy prevailed,
and a party from the *Halycon* began to unload them.
The kites were large and heavy, each weighing about
a ton. Two of them completely filled a five-ton truck,
where they lay wedged and difficult to get out.

Working with the party was a man with red hair
– very zealous, but very stupid. His efforts were re-

sponsible for smashing more than one of the precious kites, when a straight right and left from the petty officer of the party put a stop to his misdirected energy. But he meant well. Moreover, he was only a volunteer, and had nothing really to do with the business in hand. His one complaint when he picked himself up was : ' I only coom 'ere to oblige.'

Captain Boucher, who vouches for this incident, goes on to say that the dearth of kites in Lowestoft had now been broken. ' Every authority to whom appeals had been sent responded actively. Kites poured in. Every day and all day, trainload after trainload arrived. It seemed as though the entire manufacturing resources of the country had set to work on kites. Each day, from sunrise till late at night, everyone in the port was unloading kites. Even the man with the red head became perfect at it. The wharves were stocked high with kites. The Town Hall square in North Lowestoft became filled with them, and still more arrived hourly.

' The telegraph wires were kept busy with messages about kites arriving. The post office staff nearly went off its head. So busy were they, that they could hardly pass out the stack of urgent messages which they had orders to send every two hours to all kite exuding authorities : " Stop sending kites ! "

' Before the supply was quenched, all naval and railway personnel were completely exhausted. Even the by-streets were filled, and the sidings and permanent way were all so choked with trucks of kites that railway communication with the rest of England practically ceased. Then, extraordinary as it may seem, telegrams began to arrive from other ports asking for kites. Lowestoft had every kite in the country ! The station-master's face relaxed into surprised joy when he heard it. Then he, too, began to wire. He wired for engines and guard's vans ! '

' We were always in a rush in those days,' another officer [1] wrote, ' and working parties from trawlers in

_____
[1] Commander C. E. Hamond, R.N.

from sea for their short spells in harbour had sometimes to be requisitioned. I must say they worked
with a will, and so did the civilian workers from the
Great Eastern Railway. " Billy ", the crane-man, and
the shunters with their horses knew nothing of eight-
hour days, and toiled without a murmur seven days
in the week. " Billy ", incidentally, was always a
sick man and has since died, but never held off
through the war except after a very occasional ' bust
night ' when he would appear late and rather ashamed
of himself.

' A great character on the quay was " Ginger ", one
of the shunters. He was a wonder with horses, and
loved them. One night when the Germans bombed
the place they killed one of his horses. This so in-
furiated " Ginger " that he walked straight round to
the Base and joined up in the R.N.R., Trawler Section. He was no youngster, and had never been to
sea before. He had, I believe, two sons serving, and
one was killed later on. Anyhow, " Ginger " was
taken on and went to sea in a trawler for awhile,
though later he was shifted to a shore working
party which he adorned till the end. Some years
later I saw him back at his old civilian job on the
quayside.'

Mines, or supposed mines, were treated with a
curious mixture of deference and disrespect in those
early days.

A fishing vessel made a harbour flying a signal,
' Have important news to communicate ', and reported
a drifting mine in the channel outside. A motor-boat,
with her crew fully armed, was sent out to deal with
the danger, and presently returned with the ' mine '.
It was an Association football !

On another rather similar occasion it was a dead
cow !

Mines, as already explained, cannot be guaranteed
to be safe when they have broken adrift from their
moorings, while the horns are their most dangerous
feature. On one foggy morning, in the Humber this
time, a small fishing vessel just in from sea appeared

close alongside a slightly larger one flying the White
Ensign.

' Oi ! ' shouted a raucous voice from the fishing
craft. ' Wake up, mister ! Here's a present for the
Navy ! '

There was a bustle on the upper-deck of the little
man-o'-war. An officer appeared.

' What is it ? ' he hailed.

' No need to 'urry, guv'nor,' the fisherman yelled
back. ' We got a mine aboard, found it floatin'
around-like. – But it's quite safe now, mister. I've
knocked off it's 'orns with me lil' chopper ! '

Scandalised astonishment on the part of the man-
o'-war.

Didn't these innocent fishermen realise that floating
mines were not altogether harmless ?

There was another incident when, in the dusk of the
evening, a bargee in the Thames estuary mistook a
mine which had broken from its moorings for a convenient mooring buoy, and made fast to it for the
night. His disgust in the morning when he discovered
he had drifted many miles in the wrong direction,
should have been surpassed by his feeling of thank-
fulness that he was alive to tell the story.

Yarns ? One could go on interminably with yarns
– and all true.

There was a skipper in a Lowestoft minesweeper who
was the proud father of nineteen children, and had
nine sons serving in the army and Navy, and another
– I believe his name was Frederick Henry Hodgson
who, I trust, will not sue me for libel if I am correct
and he happens to read these words – who applied for
a commission. After giving a long and amusing account of his qualifications in writing, he concluded as
follows : ' If, after perusing the above-mentioned sum-
mary, you have a vacancy for an indomitable little
Commodore who does not care a button for Kaiser
Bill, nor his servant, nor his maid, nor his ox, nor his
ass, nor nuffink what is his – 'nuff said – I'm *it.*'

Captain Bruce is responsible for that story. ' Some
of the letters received were extremely amusing,' he adds.

The Naval Base was apparently on or near the pier at Lowestoft. 'One of the funniest addresses was:

THE HEAD ONE OF THE SAILORS,
ID. PIER,
LOWESTOFT.'

All sorts and conditions of men came into the Minesweeping Service, including a longshore fisherman hailing from somewhere near St. Abb's Head, who was rather addicted to the bottle. He was a man of nearly 50 when he was drafted to one of the paddle minesweepers working from Granton. His commanding officer complained that he always looked dirty. 'Yes, sir,' a petty officer agreed. 'He's one of those men who washes clean and dries dirty.'

But even the grimy one was useful. One day, in a thick fog, he was on the bridge as a look-out. The paddler, after several days at sea, was rather uncertain about her position, when a lobster fishing boat was sighted. The look-out man borrowed a pair of glasses and gazed at her attentively.

'You're fifteen miles nor'-east of St. Abb's Head, sir,' he said to his commanding officer.

'I don't believe it,' the officer replied. 'That's nowhere near where I think we are.'

The dirty one sniffed and shrugged his shoulders. 'I can't help where you *think* you are, sir,' he answered. 'That's Andy MacPherson in that boat. He's run that line o' lobster pots for forty years, an' he's now handlin' his fourth pot!'

The position given was perfectly correct.

Here is another Lowestoft story which can best be told by signal:

From Paddle Minesweeper X to Naval Base, Lowestoft. *Smack 'Revenge' dragging her anchors near South Holm Buoy. Am going to her assistance.*

Half an hour elapsed, and then:

From Paddle Minesweeper X to Naval Base, Lowestoft. *Submit while assisting smack 'Revenge' have sunk her. Message ends.*

5

The spirit of the men was indomitable.

A trawler dragged her anchor and went ashore in a heavy gale. The lights were put out by the seas breaking over her; but the second engineman remained at his starting gear for two hours, feeling the telegraph pointer with his fingers, and working the engines until he was called on deck. The ship was bumping heavily and water washing about the engine-room all the time.

Another trawler, the *Charmouth*, commanded by the same Skipper Hodgson who has previously been mentioned, dragged her anchor one vile night and went ashore on the North Scorby Sand, where she bumped heavily and lost her propeller. Rockets were sent up, the Caister lifeboat was launched, and managed to get alongside, rescuing the crew.

But Hodgson refused to leave. It was then low water, and he thought there was just a chance of the ship driving over the shoal into the deep water when the tide rose. As soon as the crew had gone he set about making his preparations. Single-handed, he lit the fire in the donkey boiler, passed out a wire, and managed to shackle it on to a spare anchor, which he got out over the bows by his own unaided efforts. All this time the ship was lying broadside on to the seas in a turmoil of broken water. Pounding heavily on the sand, she was being swept for and aft.

Hodgson waited.

As the flood-tide gradually made, the *Charmouth* bumped right over the sand and into deep water. When finally clear, the gallant skipper let go his anchor and brought her up. Then, unable to do more, he turned in, being found in his bunk when the lifeboat came off again at daylight.

If ever a ship was saved by the grit and good seamanship of one man it was the *Charmouth*. It was a magnificent piece of work, and Hodgson was officially commended by the Court of Enquiry which sat to investigate the grounding.

On another occasion two trawlers were blown up within two hours of each other quite close to the town of Lowestoft. The four remaining vessels of the group, though shaken from stem to stern by the explosions, picked up the survivors and sent them into harbour in a drifter sent out for the purpose. Then, without asking for or awaiting further orders, they calmly passed their sweeps, swept up the remainder of the mines and cleared the channel for a crowd of waiting merchantmen.

One of the earliest problems was to provide the minesweepers with signalmen. Comparatively few of the ships had wireless, and without signalmen they were deaf and dumb outside hailing distance. A number of Sea Scouts, and youngsters from the training-ship *Exmouth*, volunteered for the duty, and were given a short training in morse and semaphore.

Once, in the very early days of the war, two drifters were blown up by mines while sweeping with drift-nets. Few of the men could swim, but the two young signal boys swam about among them passing them bits of flotsam, laughing and singing to them all until the rescuing boats arrived.

It is difficult to read of the cool heroism and matter-of-course gallantry displayed on every occasion by the men, even the very youngest, without feeling emotional.

They were truly magnificent.

CHAPTER V

ORGANISATION

I

BEFORE the last day of August, 1914, the German surface minelayers, as already mentioned, had laid three large minefields off the East Coast of England – off Southwold, the Humber and the Tyne.

Lowestoft, too, had become one of the principal minesweeping bases in the North Sea, and here it was that many of the trawlers were collected, fitted out as minesweepers, and sent off to their various stations.

The mine danger was increasingly obvious and real. Various merchantmen, several of which were neutrals, had been lost, and though the trawler minesweepers had worked their hardest and with unremitting bravery, they had achieved little.

By September 1 no more than twelve mines out of the several hundreds laid [1] and not yet properly located, had been swept up and destroyed. For this meagre result six trawlers had been blown into smithereens with more than half their crews.

The men were entirely new to the work, and the whole matter of minesweeping was still at the experimental stage. The scientific approach to the problem which came afterwards was lacking. The average of losses was a cruelly severe test of the finest morale, and Germany might go on laying mines week after week, month after month.

A real antidote had obviously not yet been found for the new weapon of destruction, and it was natural,

[1] Off Southwold.   180 mines laid August 5.
Off the Humber. 200 ,,   ,,   ,, 26.
Off the Tyne. 194 ,,   ,,   ,, 26.

perhaps, that the method of sweeping fell under grave suspicion. It was evident, too, that trawlers, though excellent minesweepers in other respects, drew too much water with their draught of $13\frac{1}{2}$ and $14\frac{1}{2}$ feet.

It was as well, then, that the enemy gave us a respite[1] from minelaying in the North Sea between August 26 and November 3, when the *Kolberg* laid 130 mines off Smith's Knoll, a shoal about 30 miles north-east of Lowestoft.

Meanwhile, on September 1, Rear-Admiral Edward F. B. Charlton had been appointed as Admiral of Minesweepers (A.M.S.). Broadly, his functions were to supervise and to co-ordinate the work of the minesweepers on the East Coast of England. By force of circumstance, he also became involved in the enrolment of the personnel.

The difficulties and perplexities confronting the A.M.S. were enormous. But he was well known throughout the Service as a good practical organiser full of initiative and resource. Moreover, though minesweepers were new to him, he had long experience of small ships through his contact with destroyers.

One of his first actions was to visit Grimsby, and to fly in a seaplane over the spot where ships had been sunk in the Humber minefield to see if mines could be spotted from the air. He soon discovered, however, that the sandy water of the North Sea was insufficiently clear to permit mines to be sighted, though later on this method of location was to prove most valuable in the blue transparence of the Mediterranean.

Another attempt was made to locate minefields by the use of the long drift-nets used by herring fishermen. It was feasible enough to allow the nets to drift down on a minefield with the tide, but the result was a serious loss of life and material. When caught in the nets mines became entangled without exploding. The nets, with the mines still in them, had then to be slipped and buoyed. Left for time alone to eradicate, the mines became an added danger to shipping.

[1] It is now known that the Germans employed the interval in using their limited number of minelayers against the Russians in the Baltic.

Further experience with the wire minesweep, however, brought it back into favour, though there still remained the unsuitability of trawlers for general minesweeping purposes. They drew too much water, and were too slow for work with the Fleet. As against this, however, they had certain outstanding advantages – they were available in large numbers, were very seaworthy, and, having a small coal consumption, were able to keep the sea for long periods.

Trawlers were therefore of the greatest utility for the daily routine minesweeping in the coastwise traffic lanes. When mines were once located, however, it was better and more economical to sweep them up with vessels of shallower draught.

What ships were immediately available for this work ?

Whose idea it may have been in the first instance one cannot pretend to know ; but somebody suggested using ordinary paddle-steamers of the type patronised by excursionists. They were moderately fast, and whilst perhaps not suitable for really bad weather, drew comparatively little water. The *Devonia* and *Brighton Queen* were the first pair to be commissioned towards the end of September, 1914. They proved so successful, that some dozens more were requisitioned and put into service during the war. Over fifty were at work at the time of the Armistice.[1]

The names *Westward Ho, Lorna Doone, Balmoral, Erin's Isle, Yarmouth Belle, Clacton Belle, Walton Belle, London Belle,*[2] *Southend Belle, Marmion, Queen of the North, Lady Ismay, Duchess of Hamilton, Duchess of Montrose, Duchess of Fife, Duchess of Rothesay, Ravenswood, Cambridge (ex Cambria), Snowdon, Glen*

---

[1] See Appendix 6. Hired paddlers at Grimsby, Portsmouth, Dover and elsewhere.

[2] After four strenuous years of minesweeping, the *Walton Belle* and *London Belle* were returned to their owners in 1919, only to be requisitioned again within a week for service as hospital tenders in the Dvina River during the post-war operations in North Russia. They did four months' service round about Archangel, and were under fire on several occasions, being returned to their owners with many bullet marks on funnels, ventilators and hulls.

A MINE EXPLODES IN THE SWEEP OF THE HIRED PADDLE SWEEPER
DEVONIA.

Avon, Glen Usk, Kylemore, Albyn (ex Albion), and others crop up from time to time in the records of the war. They all did excellent service, and several were lost during hostilities. Many are still running during the balmy days of summer with their wide decks crammed with holiday trippers.

One rather amusing little incident befell the *Brighton Queen, Westward Ho, Glen Avon* and *Cambridge* in August, 1915. Working from Grimsby, they were sweeping for mines near Smith's Knoll. The U-boats had been devoting some of their attention to the fishing smacks, and it happened that some Lowestoft smacks were near the sweepers.

At 2.15 p.m. the paddlers sighted a submarine of the U.B. type near the fishermen. Slipping their sweeps immediately, they made for the raider at full speed, opening a brisk fire with their small guns. The *Brighton Queen* claimed to have hit the enemy's conning tower with her third shot ; though whether or not this was true cannot be verified. All the same, their prompt action put the U-boat to flight, and saved the fishing smacks from molestation. There is a spice of humour in a bunch of excursion steamers chasing a man-o'-war, albeit a submarine.

Here I am constrained to digress for a page or two to mention the fate of that particular submarine, U.B.4, which was sunk the same evening.

Some weeks before, a fishing smack called the *Young Jack*, with three hands, put out from Lowestoft to fish by Smith's Knoll. In the words of an officer who was at Lowestoft at the time – ' A German submarine came along. When the smacksmen saw the submarine, they put on their lifebelts. The Germans sank the smack, removed the lifebelts from the crew, left them on deck, closed up the hatches of the submarine and submerged : One of the three was a powerful swimmer and managed to reach one of the buoys of the swept channel, whence he was rescued by a minesweeper and brought in. The incident, as you may imagine, caused a lot of hate : We fitted out one or two smacks with a concealed gun, and put a gun's crew from one of our gunboats in each. I suppose they were almost the first of the " Q " ships. The enclosed piece of cardboard tells the rest of the tale, or at least, part of it. It sounds pretty nasty.'

Three of these decoy-smacks were the ' G. and E.', the *Pet* and the *Inverlyon*. And on the evening of the incident when the four ex-excursion steamers chased the submarine, U.B.4. came into contact with the *Inverlyon*. This vessel was a sailing ketch, an ordinary Lowestoft smack, a type now practically obsolete. Her crew consisted of her fishing skipper and three men, all temporarily enrolled in the R.N.R. (Trawler Section), four seamen of the Royal Navy from the gunboat *Dryad*, and Mr. Ernest Martin Jehan, the Gunner of the same ship. She carried a concealed 3-pounder gun.

The ' piece of cardboard ' to which I referred, evidently torn out of a notebook, lies before me as I write. It is Mr. Jehan's report hastily scribbled in pencil.

' *Sunday*, 16*th*. *Smack* " *Inverlyon* ". Submitted – I have the honour to report – 8.10 p.m., position N. by E. 3 miles spar buoy Smith's Knoll, 8.20. Submarine sighted steering N.N.E. Smack's crew at once manned ship side with rifles and lying under cover, 2 men at gun, one below to pass up ammunition. When within 30 yds I ob(served) G(erman) ensign and heard off. of sub. shouting. All I could understand was " boat ". Sub. stopped, I at once gave the order up ensign and stand by to fire. I then fired my revolver at officer steering, which was signal for to open fire. First and third shots pierced centre of conning tower and exploded inside. Second shot cleared aft. part of conning tower and ensign, the officer steering falling over Starbd. side. Sub. coming round our stern with tide 10 yds. from smack the wounded shouting " Stop stop " : Sub. sinking with two men lying with part of body down hatch and head hanging over side. Then she was brought to bear on starb. quarter, 1st, 2nd, 3rd and 4th shots striking conning tower, 5 and 7 over, 6, 8 and 9 hitting hull.

'Sub, sinking at angle of 80° head down. 3 bodies appearing, one shouting. Skipper Philips undressed and swam with lifebuoy but could not reach man before he sank. A large volume of water and oil was thrown up. Smack having trawl down drifted over Sub. and brought up. We are lying by trawl which is foul of submarine. There were no casualties on board as they only fired about 6 rds. I emptied 4 revolvers and one repeater. All rifles were emptied. No. of casualties on board Sub. before sinking were 6. The Smack crew behaved splendidly, also the *Dryad's* men, especially the Gun Layer. The greatest distance between ships was 30 yards, nearest 10 yards. Pigeons were sent (out) at 5 a.m. Also Smack *Arthur Williams* left soon after sinking of Sub. with verbal message to nearest Drifter. Respectfully

E. M. JEHAN, Gr.'

This bloodthirsty but gallant little action brought Mr. Jehan the Distinguished Service Cross, and rewards to the other members of his crew. Promoted to Lieutenant on January 4, 1916, Mr. Jehan retired in this rank after the war, and in due course became a Lieutenant-Commander. He died some years ago.

2

Meanwhile, as summer gave way to autumn, and autumn to winter with its cold and gales and heavy seas, the minesweeping force grew apace and the organisation gradually became perfected under the energetic direction of Admiral Charlton.

Apart from commandeering the pleasure steamers, he realised the undesirability of attempting to clear the existing minefields during the approaching bad weather.[1] Instead, he organised a method of imparting accurate information of minefields to all merchantmen, and took the sound course of concentrating

[1] The uncleared minefields, having been defined, became a partial protection to coastwise traffic, since enemy submarines were unwilling to enter them.

all his available sweepers on the approaches to important harbours, and on the regular sweeping of a coastwise channel marked by buoys at regular intervals.

This fairway, known as ' The War Channel ', extended at first from the Thames to the Humber. From time to time it was lengthened, and at the Armistice stretched from the Firth of Forth to Dover and Portland Bill, a distance, as already mentioned, of about 540 miles. Every yard of this was swept daily except in the very worst weather. In 1917, when the submarine campaign was at its height, it became one of the principal arteries of supply to the whole country.

The Germans were bound eventually to become aware that such a traffic-lane existed ; but at first it could not be broadcast to the world that a safe but secret route existed. Neutrals used it, and it was a problem how to ensure their safety without divulging information which would inevitably reach the ears of a watchful enemy.

It was difficult, too, to induce some neutral shipmasters to understand that the direct route from port to port in wartime was not necessarily the shortest. At all periods of the war, avoidable and considerable losses of merchantmen occurred in minefields through their inattention to orders, if not to flagrant disobedience.

A yacht, the *Zarefah*, was allotted to Admiral Charlton as flagship, and in this vessel he visited the various ports on the East Coast to see matters for himself. One result was a readjustment of forces and the establishment of closer co-operation.

Officers, known as Port Minesweeping Officers (P.M.S.O.), were appointed at the principal ports for the purpose of organising and controlling the minesweeping forces in their own definite areas. This was a most satisfactory innovation, though it was a pity that the co-ordination did not embrace the whole of the British Isles under one central controlling authority. It was not until October 26, 1914, that the *Berlin* laid the first minefield *outside* the North Sea, though considerably before that time it must have been obvious that the enemy's minelaying activities would eventually be extended.

The operational side of the whole of the minesweeping round the British Isles did not come under one single head until Captain Preston was appointed to the Admiralty in October, 1917, as Superintendent, afterwards Director, of Minesweeping.

The first dozen of the regular war-built minesweepers were ordered by the Admiralty on January 1, 1915, and thereafter their construction proceeded apace.[1] The first of these ships, the *Foxglove*, joined the Grand Fleet in April, 1915. Before the advent of these vessels, however, minesweeping was gradually falling into the divisions which ensured the best type of vessels being used for each particular sort of work.

The new grouping did not come at once, for the ships were not immediately available. Moreover, when they were, the extraneous work entailed by the submarine campaign necessitated many vessels built primarily for minesweeping being relegated to other functions. But sweepers fell into three main categories :

(1) *The Fast Sweepers*, comprising the original gunboats and minesweepers built during the war, which swept ahead of Fleets and Convoys and searched the approaches to Fleet bases and Convoy ports.

(2) *The Routine Sweepers*, consisting of the trawlers and drifters, assisted by motor launches (M.L.'s), which carried out the daily search of the War Channels and the approaches to harbours.

(3) *The Clearance Sweepers*, consisting of shallow-draught, paddle excursion steamers, which cleared minefields when located. When weather permitted, motor launches were also most useful for clearance work.

The grouping was more or less elastic. More than once it was a case of ' all hands to the job ', though the Fleet Sweepers were always left with the Grand Fleet.

[1] See Appendix 6.

It is unnecessary here to weary the reader with a mass of figures, together with the names of officers and places. Appendices 1A and 2, however, give the number of mines laid and swept up or destroyed in the different years of the war; Appendix 3 shows more clearly than words can express how the mine-sweeping organisation grew; while Appendix 6 shows how the mine menace was countered by a succession of large building programmes.

3

A word should be said about the *Zarefah*, the yacht which became Admiral Charlton's first flagship as Admiral of Minesweepers before the *Sagitta*.

Commanded by Lieutenant W. H. S. Garnett, R.N.R., a Cambridge wrangler and an enthusiastic yachtsman, who volunteered and received a commission at the beginning of the war, the crew of the *Zarefah* was probably unique. It was composed almost entirely of University graduates and under-graduates and other kindred spirits who had joined up in the Royal Naval Volunteer Reserve. Among them was a J.P., a Commissioner for Oaths, two sons of millionaires, and a gentleman of means of whom it was recorded that he was found smoking his special brand of cigars when on duty as a sentry.

Many of these, who had started as A.B.'s, after-wards obtained commissions, and rendered excellent service in minesweepers. They were the pioneers of the R.N.V.R. officers, who, after the temporary R.N.R. officers from the Merchant Service, formed the largest class from which the Minesweeping Service was eventually officered.

At the outset, the gentlemen of the *Zarefah* do not appear to have taken the war too seriously. The yacht was ordered from Grimsby to Harwich, and off the latter port, while waiting to go into harbour, one of the amateur signalmen is said to have amused himself by sending messages in German to the station ashore. (The Admiral, I think, can hardly have been on board.)

People were suspicious in those days. The air was full of stories of spies, and strange ships seen off the coast for the purpose of supplying petrol to submarines (*sic*). So the *Zarefah* was arrested, brought into harbour, and the Admiralty asked if they knew anything about her. The answer came back in the negative, and for a time things looked serious.

Then a senior naval officer boarded the yacht and discovered a young relative among the crew. Matters were explained, and the over-jocular signalman . . . well, the story does not relate what happened to him.

On another occasion a minesweeping trawler which had become parted from her mates sent off a wireless signal saying – 'Enemy aeroplanes 300 feet overhead dropping bombs ', which was the literal truth.

The message was received by the Admiral in his yacht, which proceeded at once into the minefield to assist, meeting the aircraft on the way. There was considerable difficulty in locating the trawler, as all signals by wireless remained unanswered. Finally she was found, with her boats away. The following conversation took place by semaphore.

Admiral. ' What are you doing ? '

Reply. ' Picking up fish killed by bomb explosions.'

Admiral. ' Why don't you answer my wireless signals ? '

Reply. ' Wireless operator is collecting fish in one of the boats.'

Considerable consternation on the flagship's bridge. What could be done with such people ?

Some months later, while in command of the yacht *Sagitta*, Lieutenant Garnett performed a very noteworthy action.

A specimen of a German mine was needed for expert examination The *Sagitta* was sweeping with the *Westward Ho*, when a mine exploded in their sweep. A little later the moorings of another were cut, and it came bobbing to the surface.

A mine, as already explained, could not be guaranteed to be harmless when drifting. Garnett, however, stopped his ship, jumped overboard, swam to the mine,

and cut the electric wires about it.   Then it was hoisted
on board without any further ado and brought into harbour in triumph.   It is all the more to be regretted that
the hero of this incident, having transferred to the
Royal Naval Air Service, met his death some months
later in a flying accident.

Besides fishermen, the minesweeping force contained
men from every walk of life, and from every Dominion
and nearly every Colony before the war was ended.
There was a clergyman serving as an A.B., and the
schoolmaster, who, after three years' active sweeping
work afloat, during which he was awarded the D.S.C.,
became the senior instructor in a school of minesweeping. Australia, New Zealand, Canada, South
Africa, India, Ceylon, Malta – all contributed men to
the Minesweeping Service. There was a Chinaman
from Hong-Kong and several coloured gentlemen from
the West Indies.

CHAPTER VI

THE SCARBOROUGH MINEFIELD

I

AS already mentioned, the German auxiliary vessel *Berlin* laid a large minefield off Tory Island on October 26, 1914, which was responsible for the loss of the battleship *Audacious* the next day. This further emphasised the necessity for a large and efficient minesweeping service, more particularly because the White Star liner *Olympic*, crowded with passengers, had gone to the assistance of the *Audacious* and had run a grave risk of being blown up.

So far every minefield had been discovered by the loss of ships. It was realised that in future there would have to be a daily systematic search of all the coastal waters round about the British Isles, and that the actual minesweeping must be linked up with the control of traffic. On November 2, 1914, largely because of the mine menace, the British Government declared the whole of the North Sea a prohibited area. All neutrals were warned that unless their ships confined themselves to the regular routes laid down by the British authorities, the area was used at their own risk.

The Minesweeping Division of the Naval Staff at the Admiralty became primarily responsible for the framing of all instructions regarding the avoidance of mined areas in the North Sea, round about the British Isles, and off the north and west coasts of France. The information and instructions were sent out in the form of ' Q messages ', so called from their index letter. They were priority messages sent by land telegrams to all shore stations; and by wireless from Cleethorpes W/T Station to all ships at sea.

The moment a mine was discovered or swept up, the position was buoyed, and the local traffic diverted. If the mine was in the regular War Channel, shipping was held up. As soon as tidal conditions permitted, the dangerous area was swept. The text of a 'Q message' was sent to the Admiralty by the senior officer on the spot, checked by the Minesweeping Division, and then broadcast to all ships and stations. The average time from the discovery of a mine to the issue of information to vessels at sea was about $1\frac{1}{4}$ hours.

The system worked extraordinarily well. Over 4,000 'Q messages' had been issued by the time of the Armistice, and after the scheme became generally known, hardly a vessel that obeyed instructions was sunk by a mine. What losses did occur were due either to disregard of the instructions issued; to encountering a freshly laid minefield or group of mines; or to causes beyond human control like fog or bad weather.

2

For some time prior to the end of October, 1914, the enemy's heavy ships were inactive in the North Sea.

Then, early on the morning of November 3, the Admiralty received the disturbing message that several German battle-cruisers had been sighted in the mist off Gorleston by the gunboat *Halcyon*, and that the latter was in action.

Soon afterwards, heavy shells were reported to be bursting in the water and on the beach at Yarmouth. Then the old 30-knot destroyers *Leopard* and *Lively*, patrolling off that town, reported that they also were under fire and were proceeding to attack with torpedoes.

For the first time since the outbreak of war Sir John Jellicoe, the Commander-in-Chief of the Grand Fleet, had been summoned to London to confer with Lord Fisher, who had recently been appointed First

Sea Lord. Because of the submarine menace, and the unprepared state of Scapa Flow, the Grand Fleet was temporarily based upon Lough Swilly, in the north of Ireland. Its only detachment in the North Sea was the Battle Cruiser Squadron, under the command of Sir David Beatty, which lay in the Cromarty Firth, far away to the northward.

What was portended by the sudden appearance of German heavy ships off the coast of Norfolk ?

It was unbelievable that they would have been sent merely to bombard an open town like Yarmouth. It must be a demonstration to divert the attention of the British Fleet from a German coup elsewhere – perhaps an attempt to land troops on the coast of Northumberland ; a raid in force on the English Channel ; or an attempt to interfere on the Belgian Coast, where a large number of ships were co-operating in the desperate fighting that was going on ashore.

The situation was alarming – pregnant with possibilities.

The Grand Fleet could not appear in the vital portion of the North Sea until late next day. Meanwhile, our slender forces at Harwich, in the Dover Straits, and in the Channel must do the best they could.

'Several hours of tension passed,' Mr. Winston Churchill writes. 'And then gradually it became clear that the German battle-cruisers were returning home at full speed, and that nothing else was apparently happening ; and the incredible conclusion forced itself upon us that the German Admiralty had no other purpose in hand than this silly demonstration off Yarmouth beach.' [1]

What had happened was that the small cruiser *Kolberg*, either during the approach or the retirement, laid a field of 130 mines in scattered groups off Smith's Knoll. The existence of this minefield became known almost immediately through the British submarine D.5 being blown up while trying to attack the retreating enemy.

This same field, close to Yarmouth and Lowestoft,

[1] *The World Crisis, 1911–1914,* pp. 441–2.

took a melancholy toll of fishing craft. On the very night after it had been laid it accounted for four drifters, which were destroyed with heavy loss of life. More mines were exploded in the drift-nets, and for a time fishing in the area was prohibited. The hard-bitten herring fishermen volunteered to continue their work at sea if the Government would indemnify them for the possible loss of their nets. The Government declined, so the men took the law into their own hands and continued to fish.

But the demonstration off Yarmouth was not altogether one-sided. On her way home the German cruiser *Yorck* struck a mine off the Jade River and was sunk with considerable loss of life.

3

Shortly after daylight on December 16, 1914, German battle-cruisers bombarded the Hartlepools, Whitby and Scarborough, killing 120 men, women and children, wounding over 400 more, and inflicting severe damage on these coast towns.

Hartlepool had a battery of guns, and might, by a stretch of imagination, be considered ' fortified '. Whitby and Scarborough were entirely unprotected, and what justification there may have been for their senseless and inhuman bombardment nobody can say. It was only another example of that war-mindedness, or ' frightfulness ', as it afterwards came to be called, which regards the massacre of innocents as something of ' military importance '. As Mr. Winston Churchill wrote – ' The bombardment of open towns was still new to us.' [1]

How the Admiralty had previous knowledge that some offensive action was to be taken by portions of the German High Seas Fleet against part of the British coast, is hardly germane to this story. Briefly, however, German wireless signals were being deciphered with the help of certain codes, signal books and secret charts found on the body of a drowned German under-

[1] *The World Crisis, 1911–1914,* vol. i, p. 467.

officer by the Russians after the cruiser *Magdeburg* went ashore and was blown up off the island of Odensholm – at the southern entrance to the Gulf of Finland – on August 26. These codes and signal books were sent to the Admiralty, and together with tit-bits of information picked up by the British directional wireless stations, caused the authorities in Whitehall to realise that some important movement was afoot.

The whole story is told by Mr. Winston Churchill in *The World Crisis*. Squadrons and flotillas were moved to deal with the expected raid, and our scouting forces actually made contact with the enemy during their retreat, and opened fire. At one period the British and German battle-cruiser forces were only twenty-five miles apart, and were still closing in on each other. Further to seaward there was a powerful battle-squadron under the command of Sir George Warrender. Action was imminent, and it could only have one result.

Then, as so often happened, the weather supervened.

The wind sprang up and the sea started to run high. The North Sea mist came down until the horizon became blotted out in a curtain of thin vapour. The weather gradually thickened, the visibility dropping from 7,000 to 5,000 yards, then to 3,000. In the driving rain-squalls the area of vision was bounded by a circle whose radius was sometimes less than a mile.

Between fifteen and twenty heavy ships, and a number of light cruisers and destroyers, all steaming at high speed, were groping for each other within a space of about sixty square miles. Their wireless signals could be overheard in Whitehall, where their positions were constantly plotted on the large chart in the War Room at the Admiralty. It was like a nerve-racking game of Blind Man's Buff played in the dark, with huge ships instead of children – and the enemy escaped.

There was much indignation and outcry at the failure of the Navy to prevent the bombardment of coastal towns, or to punish the raiders. Civilians were wantonly massacred, and the Admiralty did nothing to prevent it !

What was the Navy doing ? What was the Navy for ?

No word of explanation could be given at the time for fear of compromising our secret sources of information as to the German movements. Nothing could be told the public of how narrowly the enemy had been missed, and how the weather alone had prevented an engagement which, with such an overwhelming superiority in our favour, must have resulted in their destruction or severe chastisement. As the Germans had *not* sighted the whole of our ships, it would never have done to have broadcast through the Press what vessels we had on the spot, or how they happened to be there.

To those who had suffered in the bombardment, and to the British public generally, there was little consolation in the Admiralty *communiqué* which appeared in the newspapers on the morning of December 17. The two final paragraphs alone need be quoted !

' The Admiralty take the opportunity of pointing out that demonstrations of this character against unfortified towns or commercial ports, though not difficult to accomplish provided that a certain amount of risk is accepted, are devoid of military significance.

' They may cause some loss of life among the civil population and some damage to private property, which is much to be regretted ; but they must not in any circumstances be allowed to modify the general naval policy which is being pursued.'

In short, the east coasts of England and Scotland, from the Straits of Dover to the Pentland Firth, covered a distance of some 500 miles. It was thus possible for the enemy, emerging from the Heligoland Bight at their own selected moment, to make what may be called a ' tip and run ' raid on any one or more of the numerous towns or commercial ports on this long seaboard. It was manifestly impossible for detachments of the Grand Fleet *always* to be in the chosen area to give battle to the raiders.

What the public did not realise, and what comparatively few people realise to-day, is that in war it is the task of the British Fleet to obtain effective Control of the Sea by destroying or immobilising the naval forces of the enemy. In so doing our Fleet ensures the protection of our own essential seaborne trade and the destruction of that of the enemy, and can ensure the free movement by sea to any part of the world of our military forces, while denying this advantage to the enemy.

At the same time, a dispersion of the main fleet in detachments weaker than the main fleet of an opponent is contrary to sound strategy, since it leaves such detachments open to defeat in detail before concentration with the main body. The whole aim of naval strategy is the concentration of the maximum possible strength at the decisive point.

In the war of 1914–1918 it was the Grand Fleet, operating from Scapa Flow and the Firth of Forth in the grey, inhospitable welter of the North Sea, that stood between the Central Powers and victory. Without this Fleet, British troops could neither safely have been landed in France, nor reinforcements from any one of the great Dominions or the United States have been guaranteed a safe passage to any oversea theatre of war. Indeed, every Dominion would at once have been open to invasion.

The war was won on the Western Front ; but the British Fleet, by maintaining the integrity of the sea communications, was the hub upon which not only the British, but the entire Allied cause revolved. Without its silent menace and constant watchfulness, the German Fleet, and a swarm of commerce raiders, would have been free to pass out into the ocean to wreak their will upon our essential seaborne trade. The results would have been the starvation of Great Britain ; the stoppage of all Allied troop movements by sea ; the despatch of German expeditionary forces oversea for the subjugation of the Dominions and Colonies ; followed by an ignominious peace and the disruption of the British Empire.

The Great War was won on the Western Front ; but it provides a most cogent example of the immense importance of the effective Control of the Sea. In 1917 we were nearly beaten by the intensive German submarine campaign against our commerce. This was only defeated by the Convoy System.

It was Sea Power, and Sea Power alone, which made it possible for the Allied Armies ashore to bring hostilities to a triumphant conclusion. The Armies might be likened to the sharp point of a sword – the Fleet to the strength behind its thrust.

In these days of disarmament and a sadly attenuated British Navy, it is well that these facts should be remembered.

4

It was very soon discovered that the German bombardments of December 16, 1914, were intended to cover an operation by the *Kolberg*, in which that ship laid 100 mines close inshore between Scarborough and Filey, right in the track ordinarily used by the coastwise shipping.

It was not long before this minefield took the usual toll of shipping. The first loss was that of the Norwegian S.S. *Vaaren*, which struck a mine about $3\frac{1}{2}$ miles N.E. by N. of Filey and foundered. Twelve hours later the British steamship *Elterwater* suffered the same fate 3 miles east of Scarborough, while the same evening the *Princess Olga* went down 5 miles E.N.E. of Scarborough. It was reported that the sea off Scarborough was strewn with mines.

The area was within the usual beat of the minesweeping trawlers from Grimsby, and they were directed to clear it. But on this occasion there were to be no ' bull at a gate ' tactics. The exact limits of the danger area had to be defined, and the mines swept up. Time was an important factor, for the War Channel to the north was blocked. Until such time as a fairway was found the stream of traffic must be held up or diverted.

Mines, let it be repeated, remain at a fixed distance

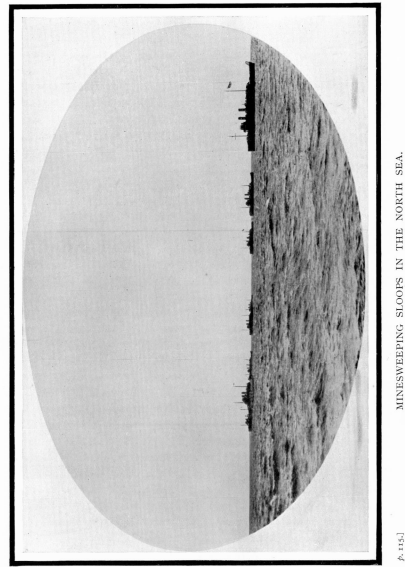

MINESWEEPING SLOOPS IN THE NORTH SEA.

from the sea bottom. The tide rises and falls above them, so to speak, and hence it will be realised that they are nearest the surface at low water, and therefore most dangerous. Given a sufficient rise and fall of the tide, then, it follows that in calm weather vessels of shallow draught can sweep a minefield round about high water in comparative safety provided no mines have been seen on the surface at low tide.

Neglect of this simple rule had already cost many valuable lives and minesweepers. It was no good rushing at a minefield with thoughtless gallantry, and this was recognised by Admiral Charlton, who, as already mentioned, was in charge of all the mine-sweeping operations on the east coast of England. So before sending off the trawlers from Grimsby, the Admiral had given orders that sweeping should not take place for two hours either side of low water. This should provide a margin of safety.

On December 19, shortly after dawn, a group of trawler minesweepers from Grimsby steamed past Filey Brig on their way towards Scarborough, some seven miles up the coast to the north-westward.

' They were busy-looking, eager little vessels,' wrote one who saw them from seaward at daylight. ' Their high bows and bridges, and their sturdy grey hulls, each with its distinguishing number, showed clear against the dull green background of coast. They were in a hurry, too. Volumes of black smoke poured from their funnels. They were now in training as a unit of the Fleet, and their station-keeping would not have disgraced a battle-squadron. They were steaming in divisions in line ahead, with flags fluttering at the mastheads of the leaders, and somebody at a semaphore passing the orders of the day. The little squadron was under the command of a retired naval officer – Lieutenant Godfrey Parsons – whose " flag-ship " was the trawler *Passing*.'

Away in the distance, some six miles to seaward, three of the minesweeping gunboats of the Grand Fleet were also steering to the north-westward with their sweeps out. They were the *Skipjack*, *Gossamer*

7

and *Jason*, under the orders of Commander Preston in the *Skipjack*, which had been sent south on some expedition which never actually materialised. On their way north again to rejoin the Fleet a wireless message from the Admiralty had diverted them to help with the new minefield off Scarborough.

Something has already been said of the work of the gunboats since the outbreak of war. Many times they had searched for mines ; but hitherto in vain. More than once they had swept all the way across the North Sea to the Horns Reef, and down towards Heligoland, with the whole of the Grand Fleet behind them. But to-day, with the certain knowledge of a minefield, they were full of expectancy, hoping at last to be blooded.

They were not disappointed.

It was a brilliantly fine morning, calm and peaceful, and somewhere about 8 a.m. the gunboats were off Cayton Bay, not far from Scarborough. The smell of bacon frying for the officers' breakfast was being wafted up to the bridge from the galley below, when a round, black object suddenly appeared in a swirl of water astern of, and between, the *Skipjack* and *Gossamer*. It was followed immediately by another.

There could be no doubt what they were. Each had four long, black horns – German mines !

The deadly things were destroyed by gunfire, and as it was now within two hours of low water the gunboats ceased their sweep and steered in towards Scarborough with the intention of anchoring during the restricted hours.

Further inshore the Grimsby trawlers were also steaming in the same direction with their mine-sweeps out. Commander Preston approached them to communicate.

The *Skipjack* was quite close to the trawlers when the stillness of the morning was rudely shattered by the thudding boom of a heavy explosion. A column of white water mingled with greyish smoke leapt out of the calm sea. It was as high as a church spire, and seemed to hang for a moment in mid-air before curling over to fall sizzling and hissing back to the surface in the midst of a blackened area dotted with the silver bodies of dead fish.

The detonations continued, one after the other. Within five minutes eighteen mines were swept up, or had exploded in the trawlers' sweeps. The *Kolberg's* cargo had been very thickly sown. Never afterwards throughout the whole period of the war were mines discovered in such profusion, or so close together.

But the situation was alarming. The 'safety period' had passed. The tide was falling fast, and every minute brought the mines nearer the ships' bottoms.

The scene was extraordinary. Trawlers, most of them with their sweeps parted, were intermingled with mines torn from their moorings and floating ominously on the surface. The mines were being fired upon.

Two trawlers had been blown up. One, the *Orianda*, unable to stop her engines, steamed on, sinking as she went, until nothing remained but the tip of her mast-head travelling along the surface like the periscope of a submarine. Then this last trace of her disappeared.

A second trawler, Lieutenant Parsons' *Passing*, was down by the bows, badly on fire, and blowing off dense clouds of steam from a severed steam-pipe. Her sweeping consort promptly went alongside to render what help was possible.

A third little ship, commanded by Lieutenant Crossley, R.N.R., was in immediate danger of sinking owing to leaks caused by the heavy explosions close alongside her. Crossley himself was below in the cramped space near the screw shaft trying to stop the inflow of water by divesting himself of his clothing and stuffing it into the stern gland. He plugged it sufficiently to allow the pumps to keep down the inrush of water, and so saved the ship.

It was a hideous mêlée of trawlers and unexploded mines drifting with the tide. The rattle of rifles and heavier guns rent the air. Now and then a mine hit by gunfire detonated with a mighty roar, or was punctured and sank bubbling to the bottom. Low water was rapidly approaching. The extent of the minefield was unknown.

Commander Preston was the senior officer on the spot at the moment. In the midst of this hideous danger he did not hesitate, but gave the order to anchor as the only possible method of avoiding further heavy loss.

Many men, confronted with the same problem, would have trusted to luck and beat a hasty retreat. But Preston argued to himself that the ships would be comparatively safe at anchor until the tide turned. And when it did turn, the risk of striking mines as the ships swung was infinitesimal compared with the danger of trying to extricate the whole flotilla then and there. At high water all vessels could be withdrawn in safety.

So the anchors rattled down to the bottom, and for a time there was peace.

This sudden and dramatic emergency in the Scarborough minefield, more than anything else, cemented the friendship and mutual respect between the fishermen-minesweepers on the one hand, and the Royal Navy on the other. They had fought the hidden danger together. And while the trawler reservemen had obeyed orders and behaved with splendid courage, the naval men in their heavier ships had not hesitated to enter the minefield.

The Navy conceived an immense admiration for its new auxiliaries. The trawlermen had displayed the same calm, cool bravery in the face of hidden death as was their habit when facing the ordinary perils of the sea. Also, they had learnt the true spirit of discipline – quick, unquestioning obedience to orders in the face of horrible danger.

'I shall never forget that day,' Sir Lionel Preston was to write later. 'The paddle steamer *Brighton Queen* came in from seaward and joined us. Commander R. H. Walters,[1] in charge of the general operations, was on board her. One obstinate mine which had refused to be sunk or exploded by gunfire drifted

[1] Now Captain R. H. Walters, D.S.O., R.N. (Retd.).

quietly down on the *Skipjack* just as he arrived. It was finally hit and exploded within a few feet of our bows. There were no dry clothes on our bridge or forecastle after it went up.

' The immediate sequel sticks in my mind as showing the types of officers in the trawlers,' Sir Lionel continues. ' Having been to seaward during the mine battle, Walters was thirsting for news, so I went over to lunch in the *Brighton Queen*. There were four of us – Walters, myself, Lieutenant Parsons, whose trawler, the *Passing*, had been mined and was afterwards beached, and Lieutenant W. Boothby, R.N.R.,[1] the C.O. of the *Orianda*, which had been sunk. He had only managed to escape from the wheelhouse window with many bruises just before she finally went under.

' Parsons, whose ankles were both badly damaged, was still wearing his blown-out swimming collar. The meal consisted mostly of salt pork, and both Parsons and Boothby leisurely cleared their plates and seemed quite unperturbed by their experience. Boothby, who was nearing the forties, took command of another trawler at once and was mined again within the week. Parsons also continued minesweeping at once and was mined again later. Both ended the war in minesweepers, though their experiences left their inevitable marks. Parsons, sad to say, has since died.'

Here is Lieutenant Parsons' own report on the mining of the *Passing* :

' The ship was rapidly going down. Little of the bows was left, and nothing at all of the poor fellow who was there when we struck the mine. I gave the order to abandon ship, and then found what wonderful fellows I commanded. The situation was of course utterly novel to them. Our consort, also mined, appeared a little distance away in a similar predicament. Our ship was likely to sink in a matter of minutes, if not seconds. Yet not a voice was raised, nor was there any sign of fear.

[1] Lieutenant Boothby eventually received the D.S.O. for his services in minesweepers.

' The engineer reported quite calmly that he had stopped the engines, and regretted that he had done so without orders. I apologised for the oversight, which I explained was due to the telegraph and voice-pipe from the wheelhouse both being blown away. Most of the crew by this time were in the boat. They were baling her out with their caps, as she was leaking badly. But cookie was anxious not to waste his precious tea. I noticed him drawing jorums from an enormous enamel teapot and passing them over the side into the boat.'

Parsons was the hero of another story. It was desired to obtain a German mine for purposes of vivi-section, and he was ordered to salve a specimen which had been washed up on the beach. A floating or stranded mine, let it be added, can by no means be considered safe.

The sequel is best described in his own words :

' One morning I received a signal worded as follows : *" You are to proceed and locate a German mine which has been washed ashore 20 miles to the Northward. Having located it, you are to render the mine safe, place it on board your ship, and then return to your base."*

' Now what the blazes was I to do ? The place where the mine was washed ashore was on some very dangerous rocks, beneath a two hundred feet cliff. There was generally a nasty swell running, so how on earth was I going to get the mine off to the ship *even* after it was rendered safe ?

' Having duly located the mine, I went ashore and made arrangements to begin operations the next day. Accompanied by the whole of the local population, and a company of Territorials which I had borrowed in case of need, I proceeded to the top of the cliff. From there I was lowered down right on top of the mine. I made it harmless, much to the disappointment of the gallery on top of the cliff. I really think they felt that the Navy was not doing its job by not providing a melodrama, if not a tragedy.

' At any rate, as soon as they saw I was safe, they all went home with the exception of a few enthusiasts, who waited to see me pulled up the cliff. They were not disappointed. Carried away with zeal, the Territorials pulled enthusiastically. They brought me up feet first and unconscious, and managed to break the rope. Fortunately, I had taken the precaution of tying a second rope round myself in case of accidents. Otherwise, the melodrama would have indeed concluded with tragedy.

' After considerable trouble, and a call on the local Rocket Brigade for the use of their apparatus and lines, it was possible to get a wire rope ashore from the ship and secure it to the mine. It was then pulled off to the ship.

' My ship's company first shook the horns to see if I had done my job thoroughly. Then the mine was hoisted at the derrick head, and we proceeded proudly back to the base with the first mine salved during the war.'

5

The minefield laid by the *Kolberg* off Scarborough continued to give trouble until April, 1915.

The sweeping was carried on throughout the gales and bitter cold of the winter, the work being carried on under the orders of Commander R. H. Walters, who had under his command the gunboat *Halcyon*, fourteen trawlers, and twelve drifters. The whole area was thickly mined. Fathom by fathom the water had to be swept over at high water, and swept again. Traffic was safely resumed ; but this side-show of the spectacular bombardment of Scarborough accounted for nearly 100 lives, fourteen steamers, and six minesweepers and patrol vessels before it was finally cleared.

The hazardous work was varied by the still more risky duty of rescue.

On December 20, for instance, the armed yacht *Valiant*, on her way to Cromarty, had her bows and propellers blown off in this same minefield. Two trawlers went to her rescue, and though it was low water steamed fearlessly in to the yacht's assistance and brought her safely into Scarborough.

Incidentally, the *Valiant* was commanded by Admiral Charles J. Barlow, D.S.O., who had retired some years before. He was a veteran officer over sixty years of age who had served in the Egyptian war of 1882 and the Burmah campaign of 1887. His D.S.O., awarded in 1887, was the second ever given to the Navy after its establishment the year before. Like other retired Flag Officers, he volunteered his services on the outbreak of the Great War, and was given the command of an armed yacht with the rank of Commander, R.N.R.

On the same day as the *Valiant* incident, the patrol trawler *Garmo* was mined off Scarborough with a loss of one officer and five men. Sub-Lieutenant W. L. Scott, R.N.R., of the drifter *Principal*, was responsible for saving the remainder. But by Christmas Eve the swept channel was clear as far as Scarborough, though on Christmas morning the minesweeping trawler *Night Hawk* was blown up off Whitby with the loss of six men.

Further south, two merchantmen had also struck mines. One of these was the Norwegian steamship *Gallier*. In going to her rescue the trawler and drifter skippers gave a wonderful display of cold-blooded bravery and devotion to duty.

It was blowing a gale at the time, but the little drifters *Hilda and Ernest* (Skipper Ernest V. Snowline), and the *Eager* (Skipper William Allerton) stood by the *Gallier* until she sank. Though it was pitch dark, dead low water, and the *Gallier* was showing no lights, the trawler *Solon* (Skipper T. W. Trendall) also steamed into the minefield in search of her.

As Sir Julian Corbett was afterwards to write in the second volume of *Naval Operations* – the official Naval History of the war – ' It is difficult to gain a full impression of all the toil and danger, the skill and devotion, which went to make up what the Minesweeping Flotillas were giving to the common cause. Their part was but the sober background against which the more conspicuous exploits of the Navy are thrown up into relief . . . we must never forget how that background was being worked in patiently, incessantly, stroke by stroke, in fair weather and in foul, with the old tasks never complete and new ones constantly being set.'

Writing again of the minesweepers, and the vast anti-submarine organisation which brought about the commissioning of innumerable trawlers and drifters as fast as guns and gear could be provided, Sir Julian wrote :

' We have been taught to be proud of how in days gone by the sea spirit of the nation answered the call at the hour of danger. But never in all our long story had there been such an answer as this.'

Speaking in the House of Commons on March 7, 1916, on the motion for going into Committee on the Naval Estimates, Mr. Balfour, the First Lord of the Admiralty, paid a warm tribute to the minesweepers, armed trawlers, and other fishermen engaged in the war. ' I am afraid ', he said, ' I cannot do justice to all I feel about the work of these men. Necessarily, it is little known to the public. They do not work in the presence of great bodies of men, to applaud and admire them for their gallantry. Small crews in stormy seas suddenly face to face with unexpected peril, they never seem to me to fail. No danger, no difficulty is too great for them. The debt of this country to them is almost incalculable.'

Indeed, by the end of the year 1914 there were in all 750 yachts, patrol and minesweeping trawlers, drifters, paddle sweepers, motor-drifters and motor-boats serving under the White Ensign as an integral part of the Royal Navy. It is impossible to state the full number of the personnel employed at this particular period, but the force included 190 officers of the R.N. and R.N.R., together with 250 of the R.N.V.R.

CHAPTER VII

THE GERMAN MINELAYING OFFENSIVE

I

THE actual method of minesweeping has already been described, while something has been said of the many trawlers which were taken up in the first few months of the war, and the fishermen who flocked to enrol themselves under the White Ensign. Then came the hired paddle excursion steamers, useful for minesweeping because they drew less water and were faster than the trawlers; the development of an efficient minesweeping organisation combined with an intelligence system for the guidance of shipping; the gradual extension of regularly swept War Channels; and the placing of orders for the building of the first of the new sloops to replace the old gunboats as Fleet sweepers. Here, even at the risk of occasional repetition, it is advisable to give a rapid survey of the German minelaying offensive throughout the war.

Before the end of 1914, 840 German mines had been laid off the coasts of Britain, all by surface minelayers. In that same five months upwards of fifty merchant vessels or fishing craft had been mined, and 300 mines had been swept up or rendered harmless by other means. Certain of the enemy minefields were purposely left in position as a protection, and channels were swept through them for traffic.

By April, 1915, about 238 vessels were employed solely in minesweeping in British waters. They were distributed as follows, the figures all representing trawlers except where otherwise mentioned : Grand Fleet, 6 gunboats, 1 new sloop, 10 ; Peterhead, 8 ; Cromarty, 18 ; Granton, 21 ; North Shields, 12 ;

Grimsby, 30 and 6 hired paddlers[1]; Lowestoft, 47; Harwich, 8; the Nore (for Thames Estuary), 25; Dover, 12; Portsmouth, 9; Portland, 8; Devonport, 7; Milford Haven, 4; the Clyde, 6 hired paddlers fitting out. Other trawlers, and fast cross-Channel steamers intended to be used for minesweeping, had been sent out to the Dardanelles.

The figures quoted show that as yet the bulk of the minesweeping was in a more or less circumscribed area off the east coast of England.

The action of the Dogger Bank on January 28, 1915, led to the laying of a large enemy minefield on the eastern side of the Dogger Bank. It contained 480 mines, and was put down to trap any of our heavy ships which might be chasing the German battle-cruisers towards the Heligoland Bight after one of their raids on the east coast of England. The field was laid at a depth which should have been dangerous only to vessels of deep draught, and no British ship of any size was lost in it. But being in a fishing area the mines were soon discovered and dragged here and there in the trawls, incidentally becoming dangerous to any type of vessel. Sixty-nine mines were actually swept up in the area. The short seas of the winter gales probably parted the remainder from their moorings and dispersed them, though the supposedly mined area constituted an additional deterrent to U-boats crossing the North Sea.

Other fields containing 360 mines were laid off the Humber by German surface vessels on April 4, 1915. By May they had been located by our sweepers, which disposed of 127 mines in that month, and had cleared the whole area by the middle of July. These mines caused the loss of four British and five neutral steamers, in addition to three minesweepers.

Up to June, 1915, all minefields had been laid by surface ships; but in this month came an important development in the use of submarine minelayers by the Germans. Two new types of small submarines

[1] *Devonia, Brighton Queen, Cambridge, Westward Ho!, Glen Avon, Lady Ismay.*

had been ordered in November, 1914 – the coastal
U.B. boats of some 130 tons surface displacement,
and the U.C.'s about 40 tons larger. Built in Germany, they were taken apart, the sections sent by
rail to Antwerp and Pola, and there reassembled.
Manned by a crew of one officer and thirteen men
they were very simple in design, and were fitted with
heavy oil engines originally intended for small motor-
vessels. On the surface their speed was no more
than seven to eight knots, which was too slow for
chasing steamers. Submerged, they could do no more
than five knots, which made them useless in the six-
to seven-knot currents of the Dover Straits. It is said
that their batteries became almost exhausted after an
hour's run under water. Cramped, ill-ventilated and
all but uninhabitable, they went through the strangest
acrobatics when a torpedo was fired. One of the com-
manders likened his ship to a ' sewing machine ', and
it is nothing short of wonderful that they were able
to do what they did.

The U.B.'s carried a pair of torpedo-tubes, and the
U.C.'s had twelve cylindrical mines fitted in vertical
tubes built into the hull. They were the earliest submarine minelayers, and soon proved a thorn in our
flesh. The Flanders flotilla were the first in this new
field, their mines being discovered off the North Foreland on June 2, 1915. Further minefields laid by U.C.
1, 2, 3 and 11 were found off Harwich and Dover on
June 18. On the 30th the old destroyer *Lightning* was
blown up off the Kentish Knock lightship, though
whether or not by a submarine-laid mine is not quite
clear.

Other naval losses definitely due to mines laid by
U.C. boats in the Dover, Harwich and Yarmouth
areas occurred in quick succession during July, August
and September :

Trawler *Agamemnon II*, off Shipwash, July 15.
Yacht   *Rhiannon*, off Longsand, July 20.
Trawler *Briton*,   ,,   ,,   July 21.
   ,,   *Leandros*,   off N. Knock, August 6.

Trawler   *Ben Ardna,* off Elbow Buoy, August 8.
,,   *Worsley,*   off Aldeburgh, August 14.
,,   *Japan,*   off Shipwash, August 16.
,,   *Miura,*   off Yarmouth, August 23.
,,   *Dane,*   off Aldeburgh, August 28.
,,   *Nadine,* off N. Shipwash Buoy, September 1.
,,   *Malta,* ,,   ,,   ,,   ,,
Collier   *Churston,* off Orfordness, September 9.
Trawler   *Lydian,*   off S. Foreland, September 18.

An idea was prevalent at the time that all these new small minefields were laid by neutral trawlers, so much so that the Commander-in-Chief of the Grand Fleet is said to have requested that no neutral trawlers should be allowed to use British ports. On July 2, however, U.C.2 was accidentally run down and sunk off Yarmouth by the small coaster *Cottingham,* a vessel of 513 tons. The submarine was eventually raised, and was discovered to be fitted with twelve mines in six inclined tubes. It was an ingenious device. The mine carried 350 lb. of T.N.T. When released, it descended to the bottom on its sinker and rose to its proper depth after about half an hour, which gave the submarine time to get clear.[1]

This new method of minelaying threw a very heavy strain on the minesweeping forces at Harwich, the Nore, and Dover, which were the first areas to be affected. The small batches of mines constantly being discovered greatly hampered coastal navigation by the frequent stoppage and diversion of traffic.

How many U.C. boats were working from Zeebrugge during 1915 it is impossible to say, as their number fluctuated from week to week. But in that year the enemy laid from this base 54 cargoes containing 648 mines – 150 in the Dover area, excluding the French and Belgian coasts ; 180 off the Nore ; 306 in the Lowestoft area ; and 12 off Grimsby. Losses in the last six months of the year 1915 showed a

---

[1] For much of the information in this and the two preceding paragraphs I am indebted to *The German Submarine War,* by R. H. Gibson and Maurice Prendergast.

serious increase, a total of 103 vessels being sunk by mines – five supply ships ; one hospital-ship carrying wounded from France ; the two Trinity House vessels *Irene* and *Alert* ; 34 British steamers and 24 neutrals ; 10 fishing craft ; three destroyers ; 15 minesweepers ; and nine patrol vessels or drifters.

A useful form of night sweep came into use against this new menace. Known as the *Actæon* sweep, after the parent ship of the Sheerness torpedo school where it was evolved, it could be used by a single ship and consisted of a light wire, a depth float, a small kite and an explosive grapnel. One of these contrivances was towed on each quarter of a minesweeper, and on meeting a mine the explosive grapnel blew up and parted its mooring. The *Actæon* sweep was useful for *locating* new minefields, though not for sweeping them up, and had the advantage that it could be used at night. No really efficient method of *clearing* a minefield at night was evolved during the war.

The first mining offensive against the Grand Fleet was carried out on the night of August 7–8, 1915, when 380 mines were laid off the Moray Firth by the German auxiliary *Meteor*, a considerable portion of the Grand Fleet then being at Invergordon. This minefield was discovered by a trawler making a routine sweep the morning after it was laid. It caught no big ships, but was responsible for the loss of the destroyer *Lynx*, and the blowing off of the bows of the minesweeping sloops *Lilac* and *Dahlia*, both of which were saved. Sweepers were soon at work, and a clear channel was found along the northern side of the Moray Firth, which was at once used as an exit for the Fleet. Over 200 mines were swept away from the southern portion of the field to form an alternative channel, and the remaining mines were left in place to form a defensive barrier which the Germans would know was mined, and therefore need not be regularly patrolled or swept. As for the *Meteor*, which had laid this field, she was caught off the Horns Reef by Sir Reginald Tyrwhitt's Harwich force on August 9, and sank herself when capture was unavoidable.

By the end of 1915, however, the enemy minelaying had increased enormously, and 7,888 officers and men were employed in our Minesweeping Service. In that year 843 moored and 1,448 drifting enemy mines were accounted for in Home waters, together with 2,291 British and 587 unidentified 'drifters' – a total of 5,169.

In spite of the increasing size of our minesweeping force, and the better design of its ships, it was barely able to meet the demands put upon it by the increasing intensity of the German minelaying offensive, principally from submarines. Fifteen of the small U.C. minelayers had already been built, of which two had been lost and 13 were still at work. More dangerous still, the first of a new and better class of submarine minelayers, the ten vessels numbered U.71 to U.80, were rapidly nearing completion. They had a surface displacement of 750 tons, a far greater cruising range than the U.C. boats, and carried a couple of torpedo tubes in addition to 36 mines.

The outlook at the end of 1915 was about as black as it could be.

2

Another large field of 252 mines was laid to the westward of the Orkneys by the raider *Moëwe* on the night of January 2–3, 1916, as that ship was on her way into the Atlantic. Laid in zig-zags between Strathie Point and Cape Wrath, and between three and seven miles from the north coast of Scotland, it was aimed directly at the Grand Fleet. The loss of the older battleship *King Edward VII* on the morning of January 6 was the first sign of it, and two neutral steamers were afterwards sunk in the same field.

An account of this operation was afterwards written by the *Moëwe's* commanding officer, Count Nikolaus zu Dohna-Schlodien. It was sufficiently exciting.

'At 4 p.m. a beautiful bright light is again sighted . . . . Now at any rate I once more know exactly where I am, and the success of my enterprise off this very dangerous, rocky coast is practically assured.'

Everything being ready, the ship made at full speed for her starting-point, to lay her first mine off Strathie Point at 6 p.m. Meanwhile the barometer had gone down with a thump. It began to blow and to rain, and very soon there were heavy showers of snow and hail. But the friendly light still appeared between the furious squalls.

The operation was carried out as planned, though the weather grew from bad to worse. A regular snow-storm set in, with a gale blowing with a force of from 10 to 12. The ship was smothered in breaking seas; but the men worked with energy.

'Every one of them knows that the wilder the storm, the more certain we can be of escaping publicity,' Count Dohna-Schlodien wrote. 'And everything depends on this; for if the enemy should get the slightest wind of what is happening here right under his nose, his minesweeping divisions would be at work the very next day, disinfecting the infected area after their own fashion. But, thank heaven, our dear cousins on their island have no suspicions. Unmolested, we proceed against the sea from 9.30 onwards. . . .'

The laying of the first portion of the minefield was completed somewhere off Cape Wrath at about 11.30 p.m. on January 2, 1916, after which the *Moëwe* was forced to heave to. Sea after sea broke over her. It was cold and wet, and dry clothes were but a happy dream. For a whole week, Count Dohna-Schlodien says, the ship had been hurled about, rolling and pitching madly. Their energy was concentrated on keeping her head to sea. It was impossible to steam against it, and they would have been glad to have got further away from the coast because of the danger of being attacked. This, however, was out of the question. It was lucky for the *Moëwe* that in those northern latitudes the winter days are very short – not more than six or seven hours of real daylight, if as much.

But British vessels were in close proximity. A Fleet sweeper going south for refit left Scapa at 4.45 p.m.

SINGLE SCREW SLOOP *PRIMULA*.
COMPLETED JANUARY, 1917.
(Notice the Mine-sweeping Gallows in the Stern.)

on January 2 and passed Cape Wrath about six hours later. She must have been within ten miles of the raider while she was laying her first lines of mines, and was afterwards hove to in the North Minch while the *Moëwe* was similarly situated further north.

The raider apparently remained hove to for several days until the weather moderated and she was able to complete her work. Then, approaching the coast for the second time, she sighted a large, grey-painted steamer, which looked like an auxiliary cruiser. The *Moëwe*, heavily armed, was disguised as a neutral merchantman, but refrained from attacking. To have done so would have betrayed everything. Her primary object at the time was to complete the mine-field. 'With very mixed feelings we watch the large steamer circling round astern of us. She is over four miles away. . . . Suddenly she turns away, having apparently satisfied herself about us.'

The raider steamed on at full speed towards the starting-point of her next minefield, the weather being fine and clear. Came darkness, and the first mine went overboard at 8.15 p.m., though on what date I am not aware.

Lights were sighted – the lights of British fishing trawlers, says the Count. He avoided them at first; but eventually they became so numerous that he only altered course to prevent collision. 'The mines splash into the water right in the middle of the trawler fleet.'

Minelaying went on through the night, and every moment those on the *Moëwe's* bridge thought they must be discovered. But nothing happened. 'Either they think we are one of their own patrol vessels, and pride themselves on the vigilance of their unsleeping Navy, or, like good fishermen, they have no thoughts whatever.'

The last mine was laid by 6 a.m. in the position ordered, and when daylight came the raider was steaming away from the coast in bright sunshine. 'We have been cruising in British waters for twelve days, and no one has molested us. We have sighted

8

only one auxiliary cruiser, and are not even positive about that one.'

There is no doubt that Count Dohna-Schlodien was a consummate seaman who deserved well of his country. His dangerous operation was performed in vile weather in hostile waters and with complete success. Having carried out a good many operations in enemy waters from a minelaying destroyer, I can well understand his anxiety and final jubilation.

Once located, the *Moëwe's* minefield was treated in the same way as the *Meteor's* in the Moray Firth, by clearing a channel through it. The work was greatly impeded by a succession of gales, but by May some 71 mines had been removed.

3

By the beginning of 1916 fourteen of the new single-screw Admiralty built sloops of the ' Flower' class had joined the Grand Fleet for minesweeping purposes, while others were based on the Humber for the regular sweeping of the War Channels east of the Dogger Bank which might have to be used for the concentration of the Fleet in the southern part of the North Sea.

Sweeping the south-eastern end of these channels was an unpleasant task, for the sloops had no escort of any kind and some of their ancient 4.7-inch guns had been used during the Boer War. Scouting Zeppelins were often sighted during the early morning, and working it out on the chart it was discovered that a German destroyer flotilla, waiting off Heligoland with steam up, had ample time to catch them before they could reach the shelter of the English coast at their best speed of about 16 knots.

It was on one of these excursions that the *Rosemary* was torpedoed by a submarine, and her stern apparently blown off. The *Alyssum* took her in tow, and proceeded with the rest of the flotilla at about five knots for the Humber. They reached harbour after two days' strenuous towing, and when the *Rosemary* was taken into the lock at Immingham it was found that the gates would not close. A diver was sent down, to discover that the stern portion of the ship was hanging down at right angles to the hull, and that the explosive anti-submarine sweep was foul of the lock gates. Luckily it was not primed, otherwise the explosion of the torpedo would have detonated it and destroyed the whole ship.

' The rottenest job of all fell to the lot of the mark boats attached to our flotilla,' an officer of one of these sloops writes. ' They were captured German trawlers, and we used to take them out, absolutely unarmed, and dump them down in the middle of the North Sea with a huge flag at the masthead, and instructions to go back into harbour if they saw nothing of us for forty-eight hours. They had no wireless.'

' On one occasion we were recalled from the far end of our beat and had to leave our mark boat to take her chance. Some three weeks later there was a great commotion at Immingham, as this particular mark boat was still missing. Nobody had any idea of what had become of her, except that we had seen her in the middle of the North Sea about twenty-one days before. The wires got busy to other bases, and after a lot of telegraphing she was discovered lying quietly in the Tyne, having been lying doggo there for eighteen or nineteen days. The wily birds apparently thought they'd like a rest, so got in without making too much bobbery and drew neither rations nor pay until they were bowled out.'

On February 10, 1916, four of the sloops, the *Buttercup*, *Arabis*, *Alyssum* and *Poppy*, had been sweeping to the east of the Dogger Bank, and when darkness came down marked their finishing point with a lighted dan buoy. The *Arabis*, Lieutenant-Commander R. R. Hallowell-Carew,[1] was detailed to stand by the buoy, while the other three ships steamed on and off. At about 11 p.m. they sighted strange ships without lights and the whitened tracks of torpedoes passing through the line, so turned away. Simultaneously, the *Arabis*

[1] Now Commander R. R. Hallowell-Carew, D.S.O., R.N. (Retd.).

was engaged by three German destroyers.   Her steam-
pipes were shot away and her wireless disabled.   Nevertheless, unable to move, she replied so fiercely with her
two 4·7's that the enemy were driven off.   A little later,
however, she was again attacked by six destroyers,
which sank her with torpedoes.

Her commanding officer and Surgeon Probationer
John Hughes, R.N.V.R., were among the survivors
rescued by the enemy.   They were treated with every
consideration, though Mr. Hughes succumbed to exposure.   He was buried in the Naval Cemetery at Wil-
helmshaven on February 23 with the usual honours.

The 'Flower' class sloops were heavy-looking ships for
their size with two upstanding funnels.   Unaware of
their existence or appearance, the Germans reported
the *Arabis* as a cruiser.

By the beginning of 1916 the sweeping force of hired
paddlers had grown to five units comprising 35 vessels.
Their success as sweepers had also led the Admiralty
to order 24 new paddlers of the 'Racecourse' class between September, 1915, and January, 1916.   Their
design was based on that of the *Glen Usk*, and they
were vessels of 810 tons displacement and 15 knots
speed, with a draught of 6¾ feet.   Nearly all were in
service in the principal danger areas before the end of
the year, being stationed at Dover, Lowestoft, Grimsby
and the Firth of Forth.

Though their light draught gave them a great advantage over trawlers which sometimes drew 14½ feet
of water, they had certain disadvantages.   For one
thing, there was a danger of mines getting under the
paddles.   For another, the paddles were not efficient
in anything like bad weather.

Another new type of minesweeper was designed by
the Admiralty in 1916, and the first twenty were laid
down between June and October of that year.   They
were known as the 'Hunt' class, and had a displacement of 730 tons, a draught of 7 feet, and a full speed
of between 16 and 17 knots, being capable of sweeping
at 12.   A further 56 vessels of similar type but slightly
larger dimensions were ordered before the end of the

war, and 27 still figured in the Navy List for July, 1934. Details of all war-built minesweepers will be found in Appendix 6.

The Burney paravane also passed its tests in 1916, and by the end of the year had been supplied to 180 of His Majesty's ships of over 12 feet draught. This appliance was the product of the genius of Lieutenant Charles Dennistoun Burney, R.N.,[1] and was really a type of underwater kite with a buoyant, torpedo-shaped body provided with planes. Towed by a wire, the ship's speed caused it to stand out at a considerable lateral distance from the ship's side, while it was kept at a certain distance beneath the surface by a rudder actuated by a hydrostatic valve and oscillator.

The anti-submarine paravane – known as the ' high speed submarine sweep ' – was an explosive contrivance. It consisted of two paravanes towed from each quarter of a destroyer, and with many other vessels, my own ship, the *Murray*, was provided with this apparatus in 1915. It involved the fitting of special winches, and small revolving gallows on each side of the stern to carry the paravanes themselves. They could be set to run at any depth below the surface, and were supposed to enable a destroyer to attack a submarine whose position was only approximately known. They could be fired by means of a hand switch if the ship wished to get rid of them in a hurry ; but exploded automatically if any obstruction came into contact with the towing wires or the paravanes themselves.

We hated the contrivance, which was difficult to use, and always going wrong. Moreover, the ship had to ease down when the sweep was being got in or out, which was always a risk if a submarine was in the vicinity. Added to this, no commanding officer really felt happy with two explosive objects towing from his stern. There was the chance that they might be forgotten in a sudden emergency. For instance, if the ship had to go astern to avoid a collision, the paravane wires might quite easily be wrapped up round the pro-

[1] Now Commander Sir C. D. Burney, Bart., C.M.G., R.N. (Retd.).

pellers, and the explosive fish bob up alongside. So far as it is possible to discover, only two U-boats were destroyed by this particular method of attack. The depth charge was a far more potent weapon which is estimated to have sunk 38 submarines during the war.

But as a protective device against moored mines, paravanes certainly came into their own. In this case they were about 12 feet long and non-explosive. A pair of them were towed from a ' shoe ' which slid up and down the stem of the vessel. Towed from the point where the stem met the keel, the paravanes stretched their wires rigidly out at an angle of about

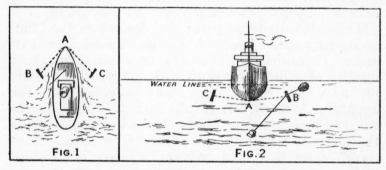

SKETCH SHOWING PRINCIPLE OF THE PARAVANE

A B, A C are the paravane wires covering the whole width of the ship, B and C the paravanes. In Fig. 2 the mooring of a mine has been caught by the paravane wire A B and deflected along the wire into the cutting jaws of the paravane. The mine mooring wire is severed and the mine comes to the surface clear of the ship's side.

50° to the fore and aft line of the ship. In this way the whole breadth of the ship was protected from mines, the mooring ropes of which, coming into contact with the paravane wire, slid along it until it entered a pair of steel jaws on the paravane itself, which immediately cut it. Mines then floated to the surface clear of the ship and could be sunk by gunfire.

A modified form of this apparatus known as the ' otter ' was fitted in merchant ships, and became compulsory in 1917.

One hundred and eighty men-of-war were fitted with the device, together with 2,740 merchant vessels. In the case of the former it cut 55 mine moorings during the war, while merchant ships cut between 40 and 50. Paravanes therefore saved many casualties, and are still in use in the Navy.

Another useful and simple innovation that came into general use in 1916 was the 'serrated' wire already mentioned on page 31. Its use certainly made sweeping from slow ships like trawlers far more expeditious and certain.

Apart from the mines laid by the *Moëwe*, all the other minefields put down by the enemy in 1916 were from submarines. Their cargoes gradually appeared further and further afield as more and larger U-boats were commissioned, some still working from Zeebrugge, and others, attached to the High Seas Fleet, operating from the Elbe. The flotillas were allotted separate areas for their minelaying, the High Seas Fleet submarines working north of Flamborough Head, and the Flanders U.C. boats being responsible for the coast from Flamborough Head to Dover, the English Channel, the Irish Sea and the Irish coast as far west as Waterford.

On the night of May 28-29, U.75, one of the larger submarine minelayers, laid her cargo of 18 mines close to Marwick Head off the west coast of the Orkneys. The operation formed part of the submarine activities off the British coast prior to the exit of the High Sea Fleet before the Battle of Jutland, and it is believed that U.75's mines were intended to be laid off Hoy Sound, the western exit of Scapa Flow, in the hope of catching vessels of the Grand Fleet as they emerged. The actual position of the mines had no strategic significance, and was not on any route normally used by British vessels. It is therefore probable that during the darkness of a misty night the submarine commander, Kapitän-Leutnant K. Beitzen, mistook the coast off Marwick Head for the very similar stretch of land about 12 miles further south.

His mines were laid at a depth of over 22 feet in a spot where the flow of the tide caused sufficient 'dip' to ensure them being harmless to even a deep draught ship except at low-water slack, and then only with the vessel pitching and thereby increasing her normal draught. The period of low-water slack was very limited, and it was sheer ill-fortune that caused H.M.S. *Hampshire* to be over this spot at this very period in a freshening gale and a heavy sea.

With Lord Kitchener on board on his way to Archangel, the cruiser sailed from Scapa Flow on the afternoon of June 6, 1916. At 8 p.m. she struck one of U.75's mines, foundering almost immediately with heavy loss of life and bringing Lord Kitchener's career to an untimely and dramatic end. There is absolutely no vestige of truth in the rumours that Lord Kitchener's embarkation was known beforehand to the enemy, or that the Germans were aware of the route to be taken by the *Hampshire*, which was decided only at the last moment because of bad weather. Moreover, it is sheer calumny to suggest – as it has been suggested in cold print – that there was disaffection on board the *Hampshire*, or that her loss was caused by internal explosion. The whole incident was fortuitous, and extremely unfortunate.

Fifteen mines were swept up on the spot when the weather moderated. Beitzen, the man who laid them, perished in U.102 when that submarine was blown up in the Northern Barrage on September 25, 1918.

Between May and October, 1916, the German submarine minelaying in the English Channel ceased as the result of an Imperial Order, dictated by the American note of April 18, to confine submarine warfare strictly to the terms of prize law. Indeed, on April 24, the German Commander-in-Chief ordered all the submarines of the High Seas Fleet to cease their operations against merchant shipping, while the U.C. boats from Flanders limited their activities to the laying of mines off Lowestoft, Harwich and the Nore.

In October, however, submarine operations against merchantment were resumed, and minelaying started afresh. Before the end of the year mines appeared off the Clyde and the Isle of Man, off the south-west coast of Ireland, and with considerable frequency off Ports-

mouth, Portland, Dartmouth and Falmouth. In 1916
a total of 195 groups were laid by German submarines,
the U.C. boats alone being responsible for 265 mines
off Harwich, 212 off Dover, 100 off Dunkirk, 100 off
Calais and 60 off Boulogne.

In Home Waters during 1916, 1,840 enemy moored
mines were swept up, and mines sank 131 merchant
vessels and damaged 36 more. Excluding foreign
waters again, one battleship, two cruisers, one destroyer, one torpedo-boat, one armed boarding steamer,
and 49 naval auxiliaries were sent to the bottom
through the same agency in the course of the year.
Of these 49, all but eight were hired trawlers or drifters.

These losses were hardly comparable with the far
heavier sinkings caused by the guns and torpedoes of
the U-boats. Nevertheless, the more or less promiscuous activities of the submarine minelayers were
putting an immense strain on the minesweeping resources of the Allies, and the brunt of it fell upon
Britain. On December 31, 1916, we had at work 93
fast sweepers, comprising sloops, twin-screw minesweepers, 26 gunboats and paddlers, and 430 slower
craft – trawlers, drifters and motor launches.

For anti-submarine and minesweeping purposes mis-
sions sent to Spain, Norway and Holland negotiated
the buying of trawlers. Competition between the different Allied Admiralties raised prices to such an exaggerated extent, that it was decided to centralise the
purchases by leaving it in the hands of an Inter-
Allied commission in London, which dealt also with
distribution.

Trawlers were worth almost their weight in gold,
though some of those acquired from abroad were so
old and unseaworthy, and of so poor a speed, that they
were useless for patrol work or minesweeping. One
French writer says that the programme of construction undertaken in Britain in 1916 did not consist of
less than 624 trawlers and drifters. I have no means
of verifying this statement ; but by December 31 in
that year we had completed or ordered since the beginning of the war 92 sloops of the 'Flower' class (not all of

which were used as minesweepers) ; 24 paddle minesweepers of the 'Racecourse' type ; and 20 twin-screw
minesweepers of the 'Hunt' class – a total of 136 vessels.

This large commitment was over and above a colossal building programme which comprised every type
of fighting vessel from battleships to coastal motor-
boats. Between September, 1914, and the last day of
1916, for instance, no fewer than 206 new destroyers
– apart from the pre-war building programme of
thirteen ships completing at the outbreak of war –
were added to, or ordered for, the Navy. In other
words, apart from trawlers and other hired vessels,
one minesweeper was laid down about every 6½ days,
and a destroyer every 4½ days.

4

The unrestricted submarine war of 1917 – of which
a few details are given in the opening chapter of this
book – was accompanied by a huge increase in submarine minelaying off the British coast. In April
515 mines were swept up, which far exceeded the
number for any previous three months of the war.

The reorganisation of the Naval Staff at the Admiralty had by this time led to considerable changes in
the Minesweeping Service. Rear-Admiral Hon. E. S.
Fitzherbert,[1] who as Rear-Admiral E. F. B. Charlton's
relief as 'Admiral of Minesweeping', had devoted much
time during 1916 to the perfection of the paravane and
other improvements in material, took over the department of Torpedoes and Mines, which included minesweeping devices. The control of minesweeping operations was delegated to Captain Lionel Preston, who in
October, 1917, was appointed to the Admiralty as
Director of the Minesweeping Division working under
the Assistant Chief of the Naval Staff. The whole of
the minesweeping, which by that time had become
greatly extended, was thus co-ordinated under one
central control, and with excellent results.

The increasing intensity of minelaying and the ex-

[1] Now Admiral Lord Stafford, K.C.B.

tension of minefields to distant areas during the first half of 1917 was exceedingly difficult to meet, a climax being reached in April with the loss of one minesweeper a day for the greater part of that month. Probably no section of the Navy – not even excepting the destroyers, submarines and Q ships – had a greater strain placed on their personnel than had the sweepers during April and the months immediately following.

Every available paddle steamer and motor fishing boat was commandeered, and those incapable of using the standard minesweep were fitted with a light one and employed for searching. Aircraft and motor launches were used for locating minefields at low water to reduce the losses of larger sweepers, while more and more attention was given to the organisation of traffic and co-ordination between adjacent areas. Protective minefields were laid to hamper the submarines.

Minesweepers were constantly being sent further and further afield as new minefields appeared, and by the end of the year over 1,000 miles of the coastal waters in Great Britain and Ireland were being swept daily for mines, the work starting at dawn by the different sections of sweepers stationed along the coast. At the same time, the 'War Channel' was extended to the Firth of Forth in the shoalest possible water, the great mass of shipping being only released from its night anchorages in the Downs, Black Deep, off Great Yarmouth, the Humber, and the Firth of Forth and elsewhere, when the channels had been swept and found clear. Thirty additional small paddle-steamers, 10 small tugs and 18 drifters were requisitioned, and orders were given for the building of 100 more twin-screw minesweepers of the 'Hunt' class, and 300 drifters. These latter were gradually to replace and release trawlers for patrol and anti-submarine work.

During the spring of 1917, the minelaying submarines of the High Seas Fleet had extended their operations to the Minch, and the routes off the west coast of Scotland used by destroyers and fleet auxiliaries. In the course of the year U.80 laid about 130 mines off Mull, Stornoway, Coll, Skye and Harris.

Eighty-eight appeared off Lough Swilly, Belfast and in the approaches to the Clyde, 72 of which were swept up after the loss of four steamers, one destroyer and four trawler minesweepers. One of the victims was the armed merchant-cruiser *Laurentic*, carrying specie to the value of about 5 millions to New York. She struck a mine off Lough Swilly on the wild night of January 23, and foundered in forty minutes. Her heavy casualty list of 349 dead was mainly due to the exposure of the boats' crews in the bitter, stormy weather.

In the Irish Sea, on February 15, the White Star liner *Celtic* was damaged by a mine, but was happily towed into Liverpool. This port, as the principal arrival base for the American troops after the declaration of war by the United States on April 6, was a constant source of anxiety. At the beginning of 1917 it had only two minesweeping trawlers. Mines were reported in the approaches on March 24. The Red Star liner *Lapland* struck one ; and on April 9, the *New York*, with the American Admiral Sims on board, was mined but reached harbour safely.

The area was particularly difficult to deal with because of the shallowness and narrowness of the ship channel leading up to Liverpool. Mines swept up and sunk without exploding remained on the bottom in close proximity to heavy-draught ships entering or leaving. Luckily, however, Liverpool was left unmined from the end of March until December, by which time the minesweepers had been reinforced. Of the 45 mines laid in the Mersey area, 33 were accounted for with the loss of 5 merchantmen and a pilot steamer in which 28 pilots were drowned.

Twenty-six mines were laid off the west coast of Ireland, but did no damage to shipping. It was one of these drifting ashore that was mistaken by the villagers for a new sort of liquor cask, with the results mentioned in the first chapter of this book.

But the south coast of Ireland was seriously and continuously mined, and the small tidal range and heavy swell made minesweeping particularly dangerous. A flotilla of sloops, under Commander G. W. H. Heaton, R.N., had been sent to Queenstown during February, and on March 17 and 18 the *Mignonette* and *Alyssum* were blown up with a loss of 14 lives in the first-named.

I have an account of the loss of the *Alyssum* from her commanding officer.[1]

' Our particular mine ', he writes, ' must have caught us just under the bridge. All I remember about it was an appalling shock, and looking up in the air to find it full of brickbats and wondering if any were coming my way. As soon as I collected my wits, I looked round to find the navigator and first lieutenant on the deck beside me. One poor fellow had been blown clean off the bridge, and we found him trying to drag himself along the boat-deck with his hands, both his legs being broken. Our foremost 4·7 gun and mounting were lifted clean out of the pedestal and were lying across the forecastle.

' We cut away the kite wire and slipped the sweep, when I'm blowed if another mine didn't come up out of the sweep. The after 4·7 and a 3 pounder were set to try and sink it, but failed to do so. I think a motor launch attended to it.

' In preparing to be taken in tow by the stern, I was very much struck by the way the crew worked. No panic or hurry. Instead of letting the gallows go with a run, the whole business was gone through just like an evolution and in extraordinarily quick time.

' Our consort first took us in tow, but the wire parted, and at the same moment a salvage tug appeared from a wreck nearby and gave us her hawser. As things were not looking too rosy and our fires were out, I transferred our crew to our opposite number and remained on board with the chief bosun's mate, carpenter and engineer.

' After being towed for about an hour we saw that there was little chance of our getting in after all. So I made a signal to the tug and she took us on board.

[1] Now Commander Graham Cunningham Glen, D.S.O., O.B.E., R.N. (Retd.).

Shortly afterwards the poor old *Alyssum* kicked her heels in the air, and went under. That was a Sunday. We got back to Queenstown that evening, and the officers and crew were put up at the Depot. I was invited to Admiralty House. On the Monday there was a Court of Enquiry, and in the evening we caught the passenger boat from Cork.

' On the Saturday we had seen the *Mignonette* go down in the same minefield, and as her skipper was in hospital I was told to take her crew along with mine. In addition, we took along with us the crew of a " Q " ship which had recently been sunk, and you never saw such a rabble.

' I was rigged up in the Commander-in-Chief's [1] uniform great-coat minus the shoulder straps, which he very kindly insisted on lending me, and was the best-dressed of the crowd. All the others seemed to have burgled a pawnshop. We had to cross London by underground on our way to Chatham, and our appearance created quite a sensation, though people were used to odd sights in those days.'

Commander Glen recalls other stories, including that of the ship's cook of, he thinks, the sloop *Gladiolus*. After sweeping up mines off Ballycotton the ship was sinking them by gunfire. All hands were on deck to watch the fun. Many rounds were fired at one mine without success, so the sloop closed it to make certain. The next shot had the desired effect, and the mine went up with a shattering explosion. Everyone darted for cover, the ship's cook diving behind one of the boats. Unfortunately, he was large and fat, and lying flat on his stomach failed to realise the amount of space he occupied. While his head and shoulders were in perfect cover, his nether regions were woefully exposed. A piece of the descending mine-case tore his trousers, and inflicted a slight cut on the then most protuberant portion of his anatomy. He was proud of his ' wound stripe ' as he called it ; but another inch or two and there would have been no ship's cook.

[1] Admiral Sir Lewis Bayly, K.C.B., K.C.M.G., C.V.O.

And among the *Alyssum's* crew at one period was a very old coloured gentleman from the West Indies with curly white hair who belonged to the Jamaican R.N.R. – ' I rather wondered how the stokers' mess would appreciate having him, but he was such a dear old man that he soon won his way, in spite of being able to speak very little English, and that almost unintelligibly. He could neither read nor write, so one of his messmates had to look after his correspondence.'

All went well until a regular bombardment of letters was opened upon the Commanding Officer by the Admiralty, the Vice-Admiral, and finally by the coloured gentleman's wife. They were all very trivial, but caused a lot of bother.

Why had the husband not come home the previous week-end? To this the C.O. replied that the ship had been at sea.

Why did he not write more often? The C.O. could only presume that the black gentleman's messmates had been otherwise employed.

Finally, the Admiralty informed Commander Glen that he was to stop the lady writing any more letters, but failed to suggest by what method!

The erring husband was interviewed on the quarter-deck, and told of Their Lordships' displeasure at the spate of correspondence. ' Well, sah,' said he. ' You know what dem women are.'

The climax came when the wife wrote to the C.O. asking him to engage lodgings for her in Grimsby. She, being white, had some difficulty in finding accommodation because of her dusky offspring. ' She never came to Grimsby,' Commander Glen adds. ' Shortly afterwards we moved to Queenstown and our correspondence ceased.'

In those days of war the captain of a minesweeper had more to do than to sweep up mines!

To revert to the mines off the south-west coast of Ireland in 1917, however, no less than 416 were laid in this area by submarines in the course of the year, 332 being accounted for with the loss of nine steamers and nine minesweepers. In one month alone, the sweepers from Queenstown disposed of 129 mines.

But the work was not entirely one-sided. Mines were laid with such regularity and punctuality, that the approximate date of appearance and position of fresh cargoes could be forecast with tolerable accuracy. Moreover, the submarines were aware that minefields were usually swept up the moment they were located. But not always.

On one occasion the sweepers merely *pretended* to sweep a certain area, and U.C. 44, commanded by an officer named Tebbenjohanns, arrived on the same spot to lay a new consignment in the certainty that the previous ones had been cleared. And at 10.30 p.m. on the night of August 4, 1917, there was a thundering explosion out at sea off Waterford. Patrols steamed full speed to the spot, and rescued Tebbenjohanns from the water. He had laid eight mines, and then blew up in the previous minefield laid by his compatriots which had been purposely left uncleared. Boiling with indignation, he is said to have complained most bitterly that the sweepers had not carried out their work with their usual thoroughness !

The Harwich sweepers were exceptionally busy during 1917, and their record must rank as one of the most notable minesweeping achievements of the war. At the beginning of the year the sweeping force based on this port had been increased to 4 hired paddlers, 2 hired turbine steamers and 29 trawlers. Between March and October 500 enemy mines were swept up in this area, the greater number in the War Channel, while the total record for the year was 629.

Another German mine barrage containing 400 mines at first, but constantly renewed, was also laid off the Dutch coast with the idea of interrupting the large volume of British shipping entering and leaving the port of Rotterdam.

The simultaneous mining of important points lying close together sometimes resorted to by the enemy increased the difficulties of sweeping, while submarines would occasionally follow the sweepers and mine an

PADDLE MINESWEEPER *ATHERSTONE.*
COMPLETED JUNE, 1916.

p. 116.]

area that had just been cleared. Minesweepers were also torpedoed.

The convoy system inaugurated in May, 1917, became general soon afterwards, and it again placed new burdens on the already overtaxed minesweeping service, the fast sweepers of which (sloops, gunboats, paddlers) increased from 93 to 122 in the course of the year, and the slow sweepers (trawlers, drifters) from 430 to 509.[1]

During 1916, 195 distinct groups of mines had been laid, chiefly on the east coast. In 1917 the number rose to 536 laid all round the British Isles, though mines were laid more thickly between Dover and Great Yarmouth than anywhere else to catch the huge volume of traffic using the regular War Channels. How great was this traffic may be deduced from the fact that 30,000 vessels passed Lowestoft in the course of the year.

In another chapter I have described the work of the raider *Wolf* which laid mines as far afield as off the Cape of Good Hope, Ceylon, Australia and New Zealand. Minelaying was also carried out by submarines in many areas in the Mediterranean, including the waters off Alexandria, Salonika, Brindisi, Genoa, Marseilles, Taranto, Bizerta, Oran, Syracuse and Malta. Taken as a whole, however, the Mediterranean was not very suitable for mines unless they were laid in the approaches to certain ports. Indeed, the number of enemy moored mines destroyed abroad in 1917 was only 301. Nevertheless, numbers of paddlers, trawlers, drifters and motor launches had to be sent out from England to deal with them.

The number swept up in Home Waters in the same year, however, was 3,989, at a cost of 170 Allied and neutral merchant vessels sunk, and 28 damaged. But the outlook was far more hopeful, for while the number of mines laid in 1917 was more than double that for the year previous, the loss in ships had only increased by nine.

---

[1] A census taken on July 11, 1917, established the fact that a total of 2,246 yachts, trawlers, whalers, paddlers, drifters, smacks and motor launches were employed in patrol or minesweeping services.

Thanks also to the increase and improvement in our anti-submarine methods, 63 U-boats – of which 33 were minelayers – were destroyed in the course of the year, an increase of 41 over the bag for 1916. They were being sunk faster than they could be built.

At the same time, the increase in the numbers and efficiency of our sweepers, the greatly improved mine-sweeping material, and the devoted work of officers and men, who, as has already been pointed out, were recruited from every different type of the seafaring community and included not a few landsmen, had virtually defeated the German mining offensive.

5

By the beginning of 1918, the toll of the German losses, and the difficulty of providing trained submarine personnel, was seriously affecting her mine-laying. Indeed, the total number of Allied and neutral merchantmen lost by mines in this year up till the Armistice fell to 27. This was largely brought about by closer co-operation between the Intelligence and Minesweeping Divisions at the Admiralty, the rapid distribution of intelligence, the firmer control of shipping, and the compulsory use of the Burney ' otter ', or modified paravane, by merchantmen.

One measure which contributed to the defeat of the German submarine campaign was the barrage of mines laid in the Dover Straits between Cape Grisnez and Folkestone which resulted in the loss of 14 or more submarines, and led to this route being declared ' practically impassable ' by the German Admiralty.

Another important step was the laying of the ' Northern Barrage ' by American minelayers between the Orkneys and Norway, which accounted for at least 6 U-boats.[1] Submarine activity was further curtailed by protective minefields laid off the east coast, and the intensive mining of the Heligoland Bight by British submarines and the 20th Destroyer Flotilla. All these measures, of course, were contributory to

[1] See p. 26 and footnote.

the ruthless offensive carried on in every area by hunting flotillas of destroyers and other craft.

An early appreciation of the failure of their mine-laying offensive on the east coast and in the Channel, coupled with their severe losses, led the Germans to concentrate their efforts in two directions only. The first was the gradual replenishment of the mine bar-rage off the Dutch coast directed against the regular convoys of British merchantmen voyaging across the North Sea to and from Rotterdam and Imuiden. It occasioned the loss of five destroyers and remained a grave source of danger, any minesweepers working there being liable to sudden destroyer attacks from Zeebrugge, barely 60 miles distant.

The second, and more grandiose, scheme was an attempt by enemy submarines to lay a semicircle of mines off the Firth of Forth. It was intended to menace the Grand Fleet, which was now using Rosyth as its main base, and also the Norwegian convoys which were collected off Methil in the Forth. Started in January, 1918, this barrage was completed, or supposed by the Germans to have been completed, towards the end of September. It consisted of batches of 36 mines laid at regular intervals 10 miles apart on a semicircle drawn 45 miles from the Bell Rock Light-house.

The existence of this minefield, or series of minefields, came to light in a peculiar way.

The first group was suspected through the report of a moored mine awash about 40 miles east of Montrose. A trawler subsequently brought up a mine in her trawl in the same area. Minesweepers were sent out and destroyed 32 mines.

After a regular interval, the second and third mine-fields were discovered, and were duly plotted on a large chart in the Minesweeping Division at the Admiralty. The rest of the story was told to me by Sir Lionel Pres-ton, at that time Director of Minesweeping.

The assistant Director, Commander Henry M. J. Rundle, was examining the chart with a pair of divi-ders in his hand. He noticed that the first three groups of mines were precisely 10 miles apart, and that they were on the arc of a circle precisely 45 miles from the Bell Rock.

Was it mere coincidence, or was it not?

He thought not. He said, in so many words – ' I'll bet we find the fourth batch of mines 10 miles from the third on the arc of the same circle. They'll probably be laid on such and such a date.'

His surmise was correct. After the necessary interval, sweepers were sent to the spot and duly found 36 mines, which they cleared up. They did the same with the fifth group, the sixth, and the others. Unaware how these minefields were located, the officers who did the actual sweeping could not imagine how it was they obtained a full bag of mines each time they were ordered to sweep in such and such a position. They were convinced that someone at the Admiralty was possessed of second-sight. However, within a very short time of each minefield being laid, it was as zealously removed. The Germans, who had spent nearly nine months on the job, finished their work in September – but their minefield was non-existent !

They never realised that all their labour had gone for nothing. After the Armistice, when a German cruiser, the *Königsberg*, came over with Admiral Meurer to arrange the preliminaries for the surrender of the German fleet, she was told what safe courses to steer on approaching the Firth of Forth. The course given her took her over one of the supposed German minefields, whereat she made a détour. On arriving late at the rendezvous she explained she had been delayed by being compelled to avoid a minefield which had been swept up months before !

In the Harwich area in 1918, 265 mines were laid of which 205 were swept up, with the loss of five steamers and four sweepers. The discovery of a moored mine off Walney Island, in Lancashire, on March 8, also led to special vigilance in that neighbourhood. The entrance to the Mersey was duly mined the next night ; but within 48 hours the unit of paddlers based upon

Liverpool had cleared the fairway for the large numbers of ships that had accumulated. The English Channel still received occasional visits from enemy minelayers, 44 mines being swept up in the Portsmouth area with the loss of two merchantmen and two sweepers.

A considerable amount of work was also done by British minesweepers during 1918 in removing British mines which had taken their depth too shallow, and were therefore a danger to surface ships. Over two thousand British moored mines were swept up in Home Waters during 1918, and 5,106 British ' drifters ' destroyed. The total of enemy moored mines swept up over the same period was 1,499 at home and 383 abroad. (See Appendix 2.)

For the Mediterranean, with its tideless waters, the enemy had devised a mooring system which made it possible for mines to be laid in depths of 100 fathoms, which had previously been out of the question because of the weight of the mooring wire pulling the mine too far beneath the surface. The clear blue water, however, lent itself to the use of aircraft for the rapid location of minefields, and greatly facilitated the task of removal. Thirty mines were swept up off Malta during the last year of the war with the loss of one steamer. The sweepers here were largely manned by Maltese reserve men who showed a gallant spirit and seamanlike competency in their dangerous work.

A cruiser submarine, U.151, appeared off the American coast in the latter part of May to sink coastwise shipping with gun and torpedo, and to lay mines off Cape Henry and in Delaware Bay which occasioned the loss of more vessels. Others followed in her steps, U.140, 156, 117, 155 and 152, submarines of a size undreamt of before the war which could remain at sea for 100 days and voyage 11,000 miles without touching the land.

But for the U-boats, minelayers as well as those other craft armed with guns and torpedoes, the campaign had already failed. And in British waters, long before the Armistice, British minesweeping had won the mastery over German minelaying. Day by day new vessels were joining the sweeping flotillas. As soon as Ostend and Zeebrugge fell into Allied hands, the minefields around them were swept up. And when Turkey made overtures for peace, a force of sweepers was waiting off the Dardanelles. Within 24 hours 600 British and enemy mines had been removed, and the Allied Fleet was on its way to Constantinople.

On the outbreak of war, as I have pointed out else-where, our regular minesweeping force consisted of a handful of old gunboats. At the time of the Armistice, it consisted of 726 vessels of various types. Two hundred and fourteen minesweepers had been sunk during the period of hostilities.

The Germans admitted to laying 10,237 mines off the coasts of Great Britain. Of these 8,316 moored mines were swept up, while the remainder probably broke from their moorings and were destroyed as 'drifters' – over 5,500 of which were accounted for in the last year of the war.

This in itself was a marvel of skill, endurance and organisation. But apart from that, a Minesweeping Service employing some thousands of officers and men had first been improvised out of nothing but fishing craft and excursion steamers manned by numbers of stout-hearted merchant seamen, fishermen and volunteers, and then was expanded into a magnificent highly trained and disciplined force which was a Navy within itself with customs and traditions peculiarly its own.

Our minesweepers were always in action, and, more than any other type of ship, bore the brunt of the war at sea. We should have been lost without them. All honour to those who swept for mines and lived through those four perilous years to see the hour of their triumph. All honour to those who perished so that the coastwise traffic and the fighting ships might pass in safety. Their names are engraved on the War Memorials throughout the length and breadth of Britain – indeed, of the British Empire.

And when the Armistice came, and men's thoughts turned to peace, demobilisation and the finding of a job, the minesweepers' work was not finished. For them there remained the prodigious post-war task of mine clearance.

CHAPTER VIII

SWEEPERS IN THE DARDANELLES

I

MANY books have been written about the abortive naval attacks on the Dardanelles in February and March, 1915, and still more about the subsequent campaign in the Gallipoli Peninsula. Admiral of the Fleet, Sir Roger Keyes, has recently added to their number in his *Naval Memoirs*.[1]

Throughout the whole of the Dardanelles operations and the Gallipoli campaign Sir Roger, then a Commodore, was Chief-of-Staff to the three Admirals successively in command of the fleet in the Eastern Mediterranean. He is a vigorous personality, a man who knows no fear, and, one may guess, more than a thorn in the flesh to those of his senior officers with whom he did not see eye to eye. Until the very last he did not give up hope that the Straits could be forced by the Navy after hard fighting, and, though a comparatively junior officer, did not hesitate to make known his opinions. Lord Kitchener is said to have referred to him as ' a very pertinacious young man '.

' I wish to place on record that I had no doubt then, and have none now – and nothing will ever shake my opinion – that from the 4th April, 1915, onwards, the Fleet could have forced the Straits, and with losses trifling in comparison with those the Army suffered, could have entered the Marmora with sufficient force to destroy the Turco-German fleet,' Sir Roger writes.[2]

---

[1] *The Naval Memoirs of Admiral of the Fleet Sir Roger Keyes. The Narrow Seas to the Dardanelles, 1910–1915.* Thornton Butterworth.
[2] *Naval Memoirs*, p. 186.

Again, writing of the time when the evacuation of Gallipoli had been decided upon : ' A most desperate effort was made to avert what I shall always regard as one of the most disastrous and cowardly surrenders in the Naval, Military and Political history of our country.' [1]

' In the light of our knowledge to-day ', run the last three lines in his book, ' can anyone doubt that the forcing of the Dardanelles would have shortened the war by two years, and have spared literally millions of lives ? '

Nobody who knows the facts can doubt it. It is idle, as so many people seem to do to-day, to regard the Gallipoli campaign as an expensive and useless ' side show ', or to condemn its originators in words similar to those used in the Australian official history : ' So through a Churchill's excess of imagination, a layman's ignorance of artillery, and the fatal power of a young enthusiasm to convince older and slower brains, the tragedy of Gallipoli was born.' [2]

The forcing of the Straits, had it come to pass, would have been incidental, a step in the passage of the Fleet through the minefields and past the guns of the inner defences into the Sea of Marmora and on to Constantinople. The landing of the Army on the Gallipoli peninsula and the desperate fighting there was a step in the same direction.

Constantinople was the eventual prize.

Its possession, combined with the command of the Sea of Marmora and the occupation of Gallipoli, would have cut Turkey's communications with Europe. Indeed, according to competent German observers who were in Constantinople at the time, the appearance of Allied men-of-war before that city would have brought about revolution and the end of the war so far as Turkey was concerned.

And far more than that. Allied command in the Black Sea would have eased the situation for the Russian Armies in the Caucasus which were heavily

---

[1] *Naval Memoirs*, p. 470.
[2] Quoted by Mr. Churchill in *The World Crisis, 1915*, p. 122.

beset by the Turks ; have enabled vast quantities of
wheat from South Russia to be exported to Allied
countries ; have provided an avenue for the import
into Russia of the munitions and weapons she sorely
needed ; and have given the Allies access to the
mouths of the Danube. Had these things occurred,
it is not too much to say that the Russian *débâcle* of
1917 might never have happened, and the Bolshevists
might never have assumed power.

Certainly a great feat of arms by the Allies in the
Near East would have had profound repercussions in
Eastern Europe. Greece, unable at first to make up
her mind, would probably have thrown in her lot with
the Allies. Bulgaria, which afterwards joined the
Central Powers, might have done the same. So would
Roumania. The effect upon Italy, which had not yet
joined in the war and still belonged to the Triple
Alliance, would have been stupendous.

With Turkey defeated and Constantinople in Allied
hands, the costly Mesopotamian campaign would have
come to an abrupt termination, Kut-el-Amara would
not have fallen, and there would have been no campaign in Palestine.

With Bulgaria fighting for the Allies instead of
against them, there would have been no Anglo-French
Army in Macedonia with their base at Salonika –
Salonika, which the Germans derisively termed their
' largest internment camp ' with over half-a-million
Allied troops locked away in virtual impotence.

The Gallipoli campaign was anything but an ill-
considered side-show. It was a sound and far-sighted
strategical conception that might well have altered
the whole course of the war. But the decision to
undertake further large military commitments in the
Eastern Mediterranean was not whole-hearted. There
was vacillation and procrastination, unwillingness to
divert troops from other theatres of war.

Most authorities agree that our failure was primarily
due to the abortive naval efforts to force the
Dardanelles, which gave the Turks ample warning
that landing was intended. Over a month elapsed

before the army was ready to land, and by that time the defenders were in a position to bring it to a stand-still. ' The only chance of success after that lay in very substantial reinforcements reaching the scene promptly. But neither the British nor the French would divert the requisite military resources from the main theatre of war at the moment, and when some additional troops were sent later, their numbers were insufficient and it was too late.' [1] The vital element of surprise had been lost.

But more than once we came, as Mr. Masefield has written, ' very near to triumph, achieved the im-possible many times, and failed, in the end, as many great deeds of arms have failed, for something that had nothing to do with arms, nor with the men who bore them.' [2]

2

In a book published in 1931,[3] I described a little of what the Navy – particularly the destroyers – did in the Dardanelles, and during the campaign ashore in Gallipoli. Very briefly, I wrote of the naval bom-bardment of the forts before the Army arrived on the scene, of how the troops were landed on the peninsula, maintained there, and finally carried away. In this book, where I am dealing primarily with the work of the minesweepers, some repetition is inevitable.

And here let it be said that it was not entirely the guns in the forts of the Dardanelles that prevented the Fleet from forcing the Straits. If guns alone had provided the defence, the fleet of old but heavily armoured battleships might have forced its way through the Narrows by accepting casualties. The primary defence of the Straits was ten lines containing 373 mines moored in the Narrows between Keplez and Chanak. These were the main obstacles to the success of the naval effort on the Dardanelles – these

[1] *Encyclopædia Britannica*, 14th edition, vol. vii, ' Dardanelles Cam-paign ', p. 56.
[2] ' Gallipoli ', pp. 3–4.
[3] *Endless Story*, Hodder and Stoughton. 7s. 6d.

and a little line of twenty mines laid on the night of March 8–9 by a small Turkish vessel called the *Nousret*.

The trawler minesweepers were not only inadequate in numbers, but wholly unsuitable for the work in hand. Their story, however, will be told later. Meanwhile, it is desirable to give a short résumé of the earlier operations off and in the Dardanelles.

Since the end of September, 1914, after the escape of the *Goeben* and *Breslau* to Constantinople, Vice-Admiral Sackville H. Carden had been in command of the squadron watching the Dardanelles. We were not then at war with Turkey, and the Admiral's sole duty was ' to sink *Goeben* and *Breslau*, no matter what flag they fly, if they come out of the Dardanelles '.

War was declared against Turkey on October 31, and on November 3 the battle-cruisers *Indefatigable* and *Indomitable*, with some French battleships, bombarded the Turkish batteries at the exit to the Dardanelles. About eighty rounds were fired in all, resulting in considerable damage to the forts and several hundred casualties to their defenders.

' The reasons for this demonstration . . . were simple but not important.' Mr. Winston Churchill writes : ' A British squadron had for months been waiting outside the Dardanelles. War had been declared with Turkey. It was natural that fire should be opened upon the enemy as it would be on the fronts of hostile armies. It was necessary to know the effective ranges of the Turkish guns and the conditions under which the entrance to the blockaded port could be approached.' [1]

Except for the gallant exploit of Submarine ' B.11 ' – Lieutenant Norman D. Holbrook [2] – which on December 13 dived through four lines of mines and torpedoed the Turkish battleship *Messudieh*, the Dardanelles remained quiescent during the rest of 1914.

Early the next year, after a naval attack on the Dardanelles had been decided upon, Admiral Carden

---

[1] *The World Crisis, 1911–1914*, p. 496.
[2] Now Commander, retired. He received the Victoria Cross for his services.

was reinforced. By the middle of February, 1915, his fleet consisted of the *Queen Elizabeth* and sixteen older battleships (four of which were French), the battle-cruiser *Inflexible*, five cruisers, sixteen British destroyers and six French, a seaplane-carrier, some submarines, and thirty-five minesweeping trawlers sent out from England.

From the first, the Admiral had said he did not consider the Dardanelles could be ' rushed ', though they might be forced by extended operations with a large number of ships. Asked to formulate his plans, he had mentioned the ships he considered necessary for the four successive stages of the operation. He visualised : first, the total reduction of the defences at the entrance ; second, the clearing up of the defences inside the Straits as far as Kephez Point ; third, the reduction of the defences in the Narrows ; fourth, the clearing of a passage through the mine-fields, the reduction of the remaining forts, and the final advance through the Narrows into the Sea of Marmora. The Admiralty concurred.

' We had undertaken ', Mr. Winston Churchill writes,[1] ' to begin a serious bombardment of the Dardanelles forts, and to attempt, without the aid of an army, by a new and gradual method of piecemeal reduction, to fight our own way slowly into the Marmora. But we believed we could withdraw from this operation at almost any stage if the difficulties and the Turkish resistance proved unexpectedly great. . . . We had undertaken this operation, not because we thought it was the ideal method of attack, but because we were told that no military force was available, and in response to the appeals for help from Lord Kitchener and the Grand Duke.'[2]

On February 19 took place the first serious bombardment of the outer forts at Cape Helles and Kum Kale. They were hit repeatedly and made an ineffectual reply ; but the operation was inconclusive

[1] *The World Crisis, 1915*, vol. ii, pp. 166–7.
[2] The Grand Duke Nicholas of Russia, Commander-in-Chief of the Russian Armies.

and showed that long-range bombardments were ineffective unless the ships could close in to decisive range and knock out the guns with direct hits.

For five days operations were held up by a gale. On the 25th, however, the bombardment of the outer forts was renewed with the ships gradually coming in to close range. The results were successful, and only the *Agamemnon* was hit with trifling casualties. The guns in the four outer forts were temporarily silenced, though not put out of action, and the minesweepers, covered by three battleships and destroyers, steamed into the Straits and began their sweeping. By the morning of the 26th they had swept a wide channel four miles up from the entrance and had found no mines.

Demolition parties were landed from the Fleet that same day to destroy the guns in the forts at Sedd el Bahr and Kum Kale, and on the night of the 26th–27th the trawlers, covered by destroyers, continued to sweep the Straits. They found and sank several range buoys, but discovered no mines. Meanwhile, some of the older battleships, steaming up into the newly swept area, had bombarded the inner forts at long range. The land guns made no effective reply; but the ships were considerably annoyed by the fire of mobile howitzers from either shore which could not be located.

Bad weather, with a strong north-easterly gale, heavy rain and low visibility held up the operations until March 1, when the work inside the Straits was renewed by six battleships engaging the inner defences. They were again annoyed by the fire of well-hidden howitzers.

During the night the trawlers continued sweeping up towards Kephez Point, covered by four destroyers and the cruiser *Amethyst*. By about 11 p.m., when within about 3,000 yards of the Point, and just short of the first lines of mines, they came under the rays of a searchlight. The minefield batteries on either side of the Straits promptly opened fire, and the trawlers were compelled to slip their sweeps and retire.

Steaming ahead, the destroyers made all the smoke they could, and fired at the gun flashes and search-lights. The action was kept up for over half an hour, and the trawlers, though the shells pitched thickly among them, retreated undamaged. Though the sweepers had not reached the minefield ' their con-duct ', says the Official History, ' had excited every-one's admiration, and in the morning Admiral Carden

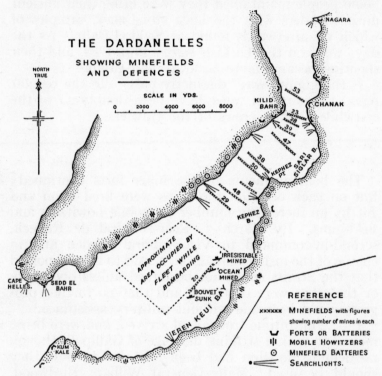

THE DARDANELLES

SHOWING MINEFIELDS AND DEFENCES

NORTH TRUE

SCALE IN YDS.
0   2000   4000   6000   8000

NAGARA

KILID BAHR

CHANAK

KEPHEZ PT.

SARI SIGLAR B.

KEPHEZ B.

APPROXIMATE AREA OCCUPIED BY FLEET WHILE BOMBARDING

IRRESISTABLE MINED

'OCEAN' MINED

BOUVET SUNK BAY

EREN KEUI BAY

CAPE HELLES.

SEDD EL BAHR

KUM KALE

REFERENCE

xxxxxx MINEFIELDS with figures showing number of mines in each
   ⊔   FORTS OR BATTERIES
  ╷╷╷   MOBILE HOWITZERS
   ⊙   MINEFIELD BATTERIES
  •⟨   SEARCHLIGHTS.

made the following general signal : " Minesweepers are doing fine work. Their perseverance and steadiness are excellent. Much depends on them ! " Indeed, almost everything depended on them, but how with their low speed they were to do the work in the strong current till means were found of mastering the mine-field defence was far from clear.' [1]

Under the protection of destroyers, the sweeping

[1] *Naval Operations*, vol. ii, p. 169.

operations on the Kephez minefield continued on the nights of March 2–3 and 3–4, though little or no progress was made in the face of the enemy's fire.

' It was distinctly nasty,' one of the destroyer officers wrote, ' and all calibres of Turkish guns let us have it. Occasionally there would be an enormous splodge quite different to the rest, with an unusual sound unlike that of an ordinary shell striking the water. Some people maintained they were firing their ancient muzzle-loaders with the huge stone shot, samples of which we afterwards found at Sedd el Bahr. As the days went on the Turkish *morale* improved, and their shooting became more accurate and galling.'

If the gunfire was ' distinctly nasty ' to the regular naval personnel, it must have been doubly so to the erstwhile civilian crews of the trawlers.

3

The bombardments of the inner forts continued ; but on each occasion the ships were fired upon and hit by an increasing number of mobile howitzers and field-guns. By March 3, Rear-Admiral de Robeck, second-in-command to Vice-Admiral Carden and in charge of the inshore squadron, is said to have reported that the Straits could not be forced unless one shore or the other were occupied, and that no further progress could be made without military assistance.[1]

In the meantime troops had arrived, and were being moved to within striking distance of Gallipoli, though no definite decision had been made as to how they should be used. Major-General William Birdwood, who was to command them, had arrived on the scene on March 1 and saw Admiral Carden the next day. As a result of his interview he reported that he did not believe that the Fleet alone could force the Dardanelles. Lord Kitchener, however, had no intention at that time of using troops to take the Gallipoli Peninsula unless the Navy found it impossible to get

[1] *Encyclopædia Britannica*, 14th edition, vol. xxiii, ' World War,' p. 783.

TWIN-SCREW MINESWEEPER *BELVOIR* ('HUNT' CLASS).
COMPLETED JUNE, 1917.

through without them. His instructions to General Sir Ian Hamilton, who had been appointed Commander-in-Chief of the Army and arrived off the Dardanelles in the cruiser *Phaeton* on March 17, contained the following paragraph: 'The Fleet have undertaken to force the passage of the Dardanelles. The employment of military forces on any large scale for land operations at this juncture is only contemplated in the event of the Fleet failing to get through after every effort has been exhausted.'

The naval operations continued with the *Queen Elizabeth*, with her 15-inch guns, bombarding the forts in the Narrows at Kilid Bahr by indirect fire over the peninsula from a position outside the Straits near Gaba Tepe, while some of the older battleships bombarded from inside the Dardanelles.

On the night of March 6–7 the sweepers, escorted by destroyers and with two old battleships and the cruiser *Amethyst* in support, made another attempt on the Kephez minefield. As before, they were shown up by the searchlights and came under the heavy fire of the minefield batteries. The ships and destroyers fired heavily on the searchlights, and once or twice seemed to have knocked them out. But the beams shone forth again after a few minutes' extinction, and the trawlers were once more compelled to retire.

The same thing happened the next night when French minesweepers made the attempt. Another effort made by British sweepers on the night of March 8–9 met with no better success, and resulted in the blowing up of the trawler *Okino* with the loss of all but five of her crew.

Experience seemed to prove that until the mobile minefield batteries could be suppressed, they could effectually prevent minesweeping operations in the Narrows. Moreover, until the minefield *was* cleared the ships could not close in to decisive range to demolish the forts. Indirect and long-range fire was comparatively useless.

Everything now depended on the sweeping of the Kephez minefields, and Commodore Keyes was becoming restive. ' I felt ', he writes, ' it was time to get on with the business, and that the minefields must be swept at all costs.' [1] At the Admiralty, too, Mr. Winston Churchill was beginning to doubt if ' there was sufficient determination behind the attack. In one of his telegrams, for instance, the Admiral reported that the minesweepers had been driven back by heavy fire which, he added, had caused no casualties. Considering what was happening on the Western Front and the desperate tasks and fearful losses which were accepted almost daily by the allied troops, I could not but feel disquieted by an observation of this kind.' [2]

Up to the present, the trawlers with their sweeps out had been able to make very slow progress against the current, which invariably ran out of the Narrows at speeds of between one and four knots. So for another attempt made on the night of March 10–11, they were ordered to steam up beyond Kephez Point, to turn, pass their sweeps, and sweep down with the current. The force detailed consisted of seven trawlers, with four destroyers for escort, and the battleship *Canopus* and the cruiser *Amethyst* in support. Two picket boats with explosive sweeps went with the trawlers. The *Canopus* was to go in first and to bombard the searchlights from just below the minefield.

Commodore Keyes was in the *Canopus* as a passenger, and describes the operation in his book. Five brilliant searchlights were at work, and on these the old battleship opened fire. They were extinguished now and then ; but only for a few minutes. ' For all the good we did towards dowsing the searchlights we might just as well have been firing at the moon,' the Commodore wrote.

Meanwhile, the *Canopus* was fired upon from all directions. There were gun flashes everywhere on both sides of the Straits, and the air was filled with the whine of shell, the bursting of shrapnel, and the roar of heavy projectiles which threw up great fountains of spray as they fell. But the shooting was wild, and the ship was not hit.

---

[1] *Naval Memoirs*, p. 210.   [2] *The World Crisis, 1915*, p. 208.

After a pause of about two hours to give the Turks the impression that operations had ceased for the night, the seven trawlers steamed up in line ahead. By great good luck they managed to get past Kephez Point while a searchlight was temporarily extinguished, and to pass their sweeps. The first pair, says the official history, at once caught two mines, which exploded and sank the *Manx Hero*. Her crew were saved by the *Koorah* (Skipper Woodgate) in circumstances of great gallantry.

When the explosions were heard ashore, the searchlights were switched on, and the sweepers were soon under a rain of shell. The escort, as usual, tried to put out the lights, but without success. The enemy's fire increased in intensity. Two sweepers were hit by 6-inch shell, and ' there was nothing to do but for all to retire as best they could under cover of the destroyers '.[1]

An officer who was in one of the trawlers gives a few more details. ' We were fitted with anti-shrapnel steel plate to protect the wheelhouses and the men working the sweeps,' he writes. ' These hampered the work and made our compasses absolutely useless. . . . However, on the night of March 10 we got past Kephez Point without incident and without the Turks becoming aware of us. But half an hour later, just as the leading pair were passing their sweep for the return journey, the *Amethyst*, who was stationed below the Narrows to support us, fired at the searchlight, I believe by order of the *Canopus*. Instantly the whole place was a turmoil of gunfire and shell splashes, and we had a thoroughly warm time for our trip out. One trawler bumped a mine and sank, but her crew escaped in their boat and were picked up by their sweep-mate. Several mines were exploded by the sweeps, and several hits were registered.'

Sir Roger Keyes, in the *Canopus*, tells a somewhat different story. ' The sweepers', he says, ' were so agitated that four of the six – the seventh is a leader – did not get their kites down, and so swept the sur-

[1] *Naval Operations*, vol. ii, p. 206.

face. The third pair exploded two mines in their
sweep. . . . A tremendous fire was opened . . . and
they and some of the destroyers in support were hit ;
but our only casualties were one trawler sunk by a
mine and two men wounded.' [1]

This same account says that the picket boats used
grapnels for creeping for the cables to which the mine-
sinkers were attached and blew them up with explosive
charges. This ' caused a great many mines to break
away ' which were ' destroyed in the morning as they
floated out of the Straits '.[1]

On the next night – March 11–12 – it was decided
to send another group of sweepers in without a battleship, as a big ship, some people thought, only warned
the enemy of what was coming. The results again
were discouraging. ' The searchlights were on the
alert, and as soon as the leading boat came in the
beams and the shells began to fall, she turned 16 points
and began to steam back. Her example infected the
rest, and nothing the *Amethyst* could do would induce
them to face the fire again. The behaviour of the
skipper was as surprising as it was depressing.' [2]

Commodore Keyes was furious, and told the officers
in charge that they had had their opportunity, and
there were plenty more to take their places. The
mines had *got* to be swept up, he added. It did not
matter if all seven sweepers were lost. There were
twenty-eight more to replace them. How could they
say they were stopped by heavy fire if they were not
hit ? [3]

It was evident that regular naval personnel would
have to be used. Any number of volunteers were
available. Somewhat tardily, orders were given that
every minesweeping trawler should have a commissioned officer in command, and a junior officer,
a petty officer and a signalman to stiffen up the crews.
The sweeping must be carried out regardless of cost.

Meanwhile, Vice-Admiral Carden was being urged
by the Admiralty to new efforts, and on March 11

---

[1] *Naval Memoirs*, p. 212.   [2] *Naval Operations*, vol. ii, p. 206.
[3] *Naval Memoirs*, p. 212.

had been told – ' the results to be gained are . . . great enough to justify loss of ships and men if success cannot be obtained without. The turning of the corner at Chanak may decide the whole operation and produce consequences of a decisive character upon the war. . . .'

The Admiral replied concurring, and in stating the position said that a final attempt was to be made to clear the Kephez minefield that night. If it failed, it would be necessary for the ships to destroy the minefield batteries before sweeping was continued. This would bring the ships under the fire of the forts in the Narrows, which must previously be silenced at long range regardless of the lack of aerial co-operation for spotting the fall of shot.

Everything depended on the clearing of a channel through the Kephez minefield.

4

On the night of March 13–14 the *Cornwallis* was sent into the Straits and spent an hour from midnight bombarding the searchlights and minefield batteries. At 2 a.m. the *Amethyst* and destroyers again closed in to engage the batteries with great vigour. Then, at 3 a.m., seven trawlers, commanded by naval officers and partly manned by naval ratings, steamed up in single line. They were accompanied by five picket boats commanded by young midshipmen and provided with explosive creeps. The minesweeping force was covered as usual by the *Amethyst* and destroyers.

The Turks were fully awake, and two powerful searchlights were illuminating the approach. They allowed the sweeping flotilla to get into the middle of the minefield on their way up, firing an occasional single gun. Then the searchlights were extinguished for a moment and flashed on again, which was evidently a prearranged signal. Instantly every gun that would bear opened fire on the trawlers, the dark shore sparkling with gun flashes and the water vomiting fountains of dazzling spray.

But there was no stopping the little ships on this occasion. Followed by the storm of shell, they steamed on to the point where the downward sweep was to begin, roughly two miles below the town of Chanak. It was a gruelling experience, carried through with the greatest gallantry and devotion to duty.

By the time they reached the turning-point, however, they had already suffered severely. Two of the trawlers had had their entire working crews killed or wounded. Hit by every type of shell from six inch to shrapnel fired by field-guns, kites were demolished, wires were cut, and winches smashed. Only two of the trawlers reached the turning-point with their gear fit for sweeping.

' I was in the leading boat of the first pair,' wrote an officer who was present. ' If anybody is in need of a few hours of intense excitement I can recommend minesweeping under fire as good sport ; but their nerves will suffer next day. You can judge of mine by my handwriting five days later. We were under fire for about half an hour on the way up, and three quarters on the way down. The most dangerous part was at the top, where you turned and stopped to get the gear out.

' It is about a mile and a half broad there,' he continued, ' with seven or eight splendid big searchlights and twenty or thirty guns a side, not counting pom-poms and Maxims, at ranges from 200 yards to a mile or so, and all sizes from 14-inch downwards. There is also a pretty fair chance of striking a mine. It was a proper show, regular Brock's Benefit, beat the Crystal Palace for fireworks hands down.

' Mine were the only pair of trawlers which succeeded in sweeping down. The others came out all right ; but they weren't able to sweep because of winches being hit, etc. The picket boats did all right, as they were too small to get hit. I was very lucky, because I managed to steer into a dark corner just at the critical time when we were getting out the gear. I was only hit once. . . . We must have swept through several lines of mines, and as none of them exploded we soon had so many that the sweep nearly parted and we could hardly tow them at all. I had the prospect of spending the rest of the night up there trying to tow them out, when the moorings parted. The next day over a dozen mines floated down; but I can't have had more than four or five of them. The picket boats with explosive sweeps must have got the rest. If the Turks had taken the trouble to defend their minefields with mooring buoys and chain cables, it would have been impossible to sweep through it at all.'

The enterprise was a very gallant one.

The volunteers for the trawlers had been provided by six of the battleships and the destroyer depot-ship *Blenheim*, and the trawler manned by the *Vengeance* was hit eighty-four times. She was commanded by Lieutenant-Commander E. G. Robinson,[1] who greatly distinguished himself on three separate and distinct occasions in the Dardanelles, and was awarded the Victoria Cross besides being specially promoted to the rank of Commander. Among others who were conspicuous in minesweeping on this and other occasions were Commander J. R. Middleton [2] of the *Albion*, and Lieutenant F. H. Sandford [3] of the *Irresistible*, both of whom were awarded the D.S.O. Sub-Lieutenant A. Bayford, R.N.R., and Midshipman J. C. W. Price, the latter of the *Ocean*, were awarded the D.S.C., while Mr. J. W. A. Chubb, the torpedo gunner of the *Prince George*, was mentioned for gallantry in bringing his

[1] Now Rear-Admiral Eric G. Robinson, V.C., O.B.E. (Retd.).

[2] Now Captain J. R. Middleton, D.S.O., R.N. (Retd.).

[3] This gallant officer had previously commanded the demolition parties from the *Irresistible* which landed to destroy the guns at Sedd el Bahr on February 25 and March 1. Sir Roger Keyes mentions having seen him some days after the minesweeping expedition of March 13 ' almost in rags, with clothes and skin discoloured by the fumes of high-explosive shell ' to be ' immensely impressed by his gallant, light-hearted bearing '. Lieutenant-Commander Sandford afterwards lost an eye during the premature explosion of one of a cargo of French mines that was being laid off Smyrna by a British trawler. During the memorable attack on Zeebrugge on April 23, 1918, this same officer again distinguished himself by taking a picket boat in under heavy fire to rescue the officers and men of Submarine C.3 – commanded by his younger brother – after that vessel had been blown up against the viaduct to the mole. His boat was holed in the process, but after transferring the wounded managed to return to Dover under her own steam.

trawler out in a sinking condition after his commanding
officer and three men had been killed.

No trawlers were sunk, but four of them and one
picket boat were put out of action. Thanks, however,
to the efficient protection of the steel plating fitted at
Malta Dockyard, their casualties were no more than
five killed and four wounded, including one volunteer
officer killed and another wounded.

The *Amethyst's* losses were more severe – 24 killed
and 36 wounded. While the trawlers went up to
sweep, this unarmoured, 3,000-ton cruiser had remained on the edge of the minefield to fire on the lights
and cover the retreat of the small craft. At about
4 a.m., she was unlucky enough to be hit by a heavy
shell which burst near the stokers' bathroom, where
the men of the middle watch were washing before
going below. There was no truth whatever in the
lurid accounts which appeared in some newspapers at
the time of the *Amethyst* having steamed through the
Narrows.

The failure of this minesweeping operation on the
night of March 13–14, made it perfectly clear that no
amount of fire from the covering ships could have any
effect in quenching the searchlights or the fire of the
minefield batteries. The defence, aided by the narrowness of the Straits and the configuration of the land,
was far too well organised.

At last it was realised that minesweeping from
trawlers at night and under heavy gunfire was an
operation that was virtually impossible. 'We must
now sweep by day under cover of the Fleet,' Commodore Keyes wrote in his diary. 'Fleet sweepers are
urgently needed,' the Admiral telegraphed to the
Admiralty on March 15. 'Meantime am fitting some
destroyers for this purpose with light sweeps.'

But not even fleet sweepers or destroyers could have
swept that Kephez minefield, by day or by night, until
the minefield batteries had been put out of action.
Of this I am fully convinced after consulting many
officers who swept for mines through protracted periods
of the war.

Admiral Mark Kerr knew the Dardanelles well, having been Naval Attaché in Turkey in 1903–4, and Commander-in-Chief of the Greek Navy in 1913–14, when, as there was war between Greece and Turkey, the Dardanelles was his principal business. In June, 1914, a Greek Admiral suggested that the Greek Fleet should go up the Dardanelles ; but the British Admiral reported to King Constantine : ' The British Fleet, backed up by all the other navies in the world, could not force the passage of the Dardanelles. This must be a Military operation assisted by the Navy. There are 17 rows of mines. . . . The batteries covering the minefields are built so that they cannot be destroyed by bombardment from ships outside the minefields. Therefore, both shores must first be taken and held by the Greek Army before the passage can be made.' [1]

Moreover, it is utterly unfair that the personnel of the trawlers should be accused of timidity on various occasions before the night of March 13–14 when they failed to do what was expected.

Too much was expected of them, for though the original fishermen crews sent out from England were accustomed to the risk from mines, they were wholly unused to sweeping at night under heavy, close-range gunfire in which even naval personnel were able to achieve little that was useful. It was not so much the human casualties that prevented the sweeping from being carried out, but the destruction of the winches, kites and wires without which sweeping could not continue.

Trawlers, being very slow with their sweeps out, were most unsuitable craft for the particular work in hand, and it is hardly surprising that their men detested it. Unlike the regular naval personnel, who had served for years under discipline in their battleships, cruisers, destroyers and submarines, and had been trained for war, and war alone, the trawlermen had

---

[1] Admiral Mark Kerr, C.B., M.V.O. The information in this paragraph is derived from the Admiral's letter in *The Times* of October 23, 1934.

received no real training before being sent oversea, and were a rough-and-ready crowd fiercely independent and conservative in their outlook.

Some men are naturally brave. Some men feel fear and do not show it ; but steadiness under shell-fire is largely produced by discipline, training and experience. Except in very rare cases it is not a natural human characteristic, and no General wishing to win a battle would put untrained and untried troops in the forefront of the engagement and expect them to comport themselves like Napoleon's Old Guard at Waterloo.

Yet this was what these rugged fishermen were apparently expected to do in the Dardanelles – to sweep minefields at night under the blinding glare of searchlights and heavy gunfire at ranges of 3,000 yards and less. These conditions are not wholly dissimilar to a fully trained destroyer flotilla carrying out a night attack on a battle fleet, except that destroyers have some chance of hitting back with their torpedoes, and can steam at eight or nine times the speed of trawlers with their sweeps out.

Nobody can say that a night attack by destroyers is not a risky undertaking that requires nerve and training, and that trawlers manned by fishermen were ever put into the position in which they were at the Dardanelles not only seems to imply a profound lack of imagination, but a lack of understanding of human nature. They were put there because they were the only sweepers on the spot, and the difficulties of sweeping the Kephez–Chanak minefields, and the impossibility of sweeping at night, were insufficiently realised.

It was a task which required high-speed sweepers and a highly trained personnel, and even with their agency its possibility may be doubted until the mine-field batteries had been suppressed. Moreover, the technical difficulties were greatly underestimated. It was regarded as a simple piece of work which any vessel fitted with a sweep could perform, and was attempted by a collection of slow trawlers.

The sweep used at this time, and throughout the war, was the 'A' sweep, consisting of a single 2½-inch wire towed between two ships steaming about 500 yards apart. Its depth below the surface was regulated by a water-kite twelve feet long weighing over a ton. The end of the wire had to be passed from one vessel to the other, and then the kites had to be streamed. The process was complicated enough in daylight. To carry it out at night under heavy fire required an exceptional combination of training, skill and courage.

Also, in the case of fast sweepers, the momentum of the sweep-wire through the water was usually sufficient to cut the moorings of the mines. But until serrated wire was brought into use in 1916, slow sweepers like trawlers were often compelled to drag mines and sinkers bodily into shallow water, when the mines came to the surface and could be sunk by gunfire. This made sweeping slow and deliberate work, and also meant that the 'A' sweep was really only efficient during daylight. In 1915 sweeping at night under heavy fire was all but impracticable.

5

Spurred on to renewed efforts by the Admiralty, Admiral Carden planned a naval attack and bombardment of the inner forts for March 18, by which time General Sir Ian Hamilton would have arrived on the scene. But the Admiral's health had been causing anxiety for some time. The constant strain and anxiety had had its effect, and on March 16 he was forced to haul down his flag and hand over the command to Rear-Admiral de Robeck, who had commanded the inshore bombarding squadron throughout the operations. The new Commander-in-Chief was given the acting rank of Vice-Admiral, Rear-Admiral Rosslyn Wemyss, in command of the base at Mudros, generously waiving his seniority and agreeing to serve under him.

During the next three nights trawlers were busily engaged in sweeping the area inside the Straits presently to be used by the ships for the attack on the inner forts and minefield. The general idea was to silence the defences of the Narrows and the minefield batteries simultaneously, and then for the sweepers to start clearing a passage through the Kephez minefield close to the Asiatic shore so that the ships could enter Sari Siglar Bay and engage the forts round about Chanak and Kilid Bahr at close range. So long as the minefield batteries remained silent, the sweeping was to be continued throughout the night. The remaining forts then having been silenced or dominated, the fleet was to pass through the Narrows and into the Sea of Marmora.

The preliminary sweeping operations inside the Straits in the area where the Fleet was to open its bombardment were carried on to within about 8,000 yards of the Narrows, and a few sweeps had been made along the Asiatic shore in Eren Keui Bay, resulting in the discovery of four moored mines on March 16. As no more were discovered in the vicinity, however, it was considered that these four were derelicts from the Kephez field which had floated down on the strong current until they were again anchored by their sinkers in the shallower and practically tideless water in Eren Keui Bay.

Seaplanes, which had been able to spot mines eighteen feet below the surface in the clear blue water of the Mediterranean, and also claimed to have located mines off Kephez, had flown over the region in which ships were to operate. They saw no mines, which seemed to corroborate the sweepers' report that the area was clear. Every allowance must be made for the difficulty of their task and the limited number of aircraft available ; but what the seaplanes had seen and reported off Kephez on various occasions were either mines very close to the surface, or buoys supporting some sort of anti-submarine net or obstruction.

It was not known until after the war that the four mines discovered on March 16 were, in fact, portions of a line of twenty mines laid about a mile and a half out from, and parallel to, the shore from Eren Keui

Bay. The forts had been bombarded from inside the Straits on March 6 and 7. And in the dark and windy dawn of the 8th, while the British destroyer patrol was withdrawing, a small Turkish vessel called the *Nousret* slipped down under the shadow of the land and laid her deadly cargo in the area from which the ships had been bombarding, and from which they might bombard again.

Four of the mines were swept up, but the rest remained undiscovered and unsuspected. There they still lay hidden beneath the calm water when, on the brilliant morning of March 18, the Allied Fleet steamed in to attack.

Those twenty mines, or the sixteen that remained, played what Mr. Churchill calls ' a recognisable part in the history of the Great War '.

6

The action of March 18 has so often been described that it is unnecessary for the story to be retold here in any great detail. Sir Julian Corbett's account in *Naval Operations*, volume ii, and that of Mr. Winston Churchill in *The World Crisis, 1915*, are, of course, based on all the available written material in the shape of reports and despatches. Sir Roger Keyes' description in his *Naval Memoirs* is valuable as that of an eye-witness who, as Chief-of-Staff to the Admiral, either saw, or was aware of, all that went on.

We are told how the four most modern ships, the *Queen Elizabeth*, *Agamemnon*, *Lord Nelson* and *Inflexible*, preceded by the destroyers *Chelmer* and *Colne* towing an improvised light mine-seeking sweep, went in first to bombard the forts at the Narrows at 14,000 yards. They were accompanied on the flanks, and slightly in rear, by the older battleships *Prince George* and *Triumph*, which were detailed to fire upon the intermediate defences round about Kephez and the shore immediately opposite.

The action started at 11.25. The forts immediately replied, ceasing fire, however, after the first few shots

as the ships were evidently out of range. The British
shooting was very good, the forts being hit repeatedly
and at least one big explosion being observed.   Unseen
howitzers and field guns soon opened a heavy fire on
all ships within range.   They were hit repeatedly,
though their armour saved them from serious damage.

The French squadron consisting of the *Suffren*,
Bouvet, *Charlemagne* and *Gaulois*, under the gallant
Admiral Guepratte, had been waiting in rear in accordance with the general plan, and at six minutes
past noon Admiral de Robeck signalled to them to
move in to engage at closer range.   They passed
through the British line in two divisions.   Their
approach woke up the enemy, who immediately opened
fire with every gun that would bear.   The French
replied, and the action became general.

The scene at this time was one of awful magnificence.
The sea was intensely blue and calm, just ruffled by a
light breeze from seaward.   The sun shone overhead in
a sky of almost cloudless blue, and the huge grey hulls
of the bombarding battleships wreathed themselves in
orange flashes and billowing clouds of tawny cordite
smoke as they wheeled and circled amid the forest of
dazzling spray fountains flung up by the enemy shell.

The *Chelmer* and *Colne* had been ordered to the
rear when the big ships came into action, but the
Wear remained close by the *Queen Elizabeth* to act
as a despatch boat.   Each ship was preceded by a
picket boat, armed with a 3-pounder and commanded
by a midshipman, for the purpose of sinking mines.
They were all under heavy fire from guns of every
size from 14-inch downwards, though the 8.2's and
5.9's of the new intermediate defences were the most
persistent.   The forts spouted great clouds of dust
and smoke, mingled every now and then with the
bright flashes of their guns and the redder glow of
exploding shell.   The roar of the terrific cannonade
rumbled across the water in a continuous ear-splitting
thunder, echoed and re-echoed from the frowning
greenish-brown hills on either side of the Straits.

The *Agamemnon* was hit twelve times in twenty-five minutes, though with no more damage than injury to one of her 9·2's and two of her 12-pounders. The *Inflexible* was unluckier. One of her 12-inch guns was put out of action through a hit from a howitzer shell, while a 4-inch projectile from a field gun had wrecked her control top, killing or wounding all but one of the nine officers and men up there. A heavy shell bursting close alongside had caused leaks in two compartments ; a 9·4-inch had made a hole in her starboard side just above the waterline, while another 9·4 passed through the foremast, burst, and caused a serious fire which enveloped the bridge and shot up as high as the control position, preventing the wounded aloft from being rescued. At the same time her picket boat was hit by a heavy shell, the crew just managing to bring her alongside and to make their escape before she sank.

Captain R. F. Phillimore, still heavily engaged, turned his ship so that the smoke and flames blew clear of the foremast, and continued in action until his fort had ceased to reply. Then he quitted the line for a short time to put out the fire and to restore communications.

The *Bouvet*, *Gaulois* and *Suffren* had also been heavily hit, but by 1.45 the forts were practically silent. In the Fleet not a ship had been put permanently out of action, while there were no more than forty men killed and wounded. ' The general impression was that the forts were dominated,' writes Mr. Churchill. ' Had there been no minefield, the ships could have steamed through the Straits, keeping the forts pinned down by their fire with little loss. It is certain, at any rate, that we had the measure of the forts.' [1]

At 1.45 Admiral de Robeck ordered the French squadron to retire, and their places to be taken by the *Ocean*, *Albion*, *Irresistible* and *Vengeance*, supported on the flanks, and slightly in rear, by the *Swiftsure* and *Majestic*. They were accompanied by the first division of minesweeping trawlers.

[1] *The World Crisis, 1915*, p. 226.

But at 1.54, as the *Bouvet* was following the *Suffren* out of the Straits, onlookers were appalled to see a great gout of black smoke shoot up at her side, which was at first taken for the burst of a heavy shell. But almost instantaneously it was followed by a rending explosion. Her magazine had blown up, and still moving very fast she heeled over, capsized, and plunged to the bottom. Of her company of about 670 officers and men no more than 35 were rescued.

She was the first victim of the *Nousret's* minefield.

The action was continued, the *Ocean* and *Irresistible* steaming up on the Asiatic side of the Straits, and the *Albion* and *Vengeance* on the other. Supported by the *Swiftsure* and *Majestic*, they soon opened fire, gradually reducing the range of the forts in the Narrows to 10,000 yards. The forts replied spasmodically, but none of the ships was badly hit, and then only by howitzer fire from the shore.

' By 4 p.m.', Admiral de Robeck reported to the Admiralty, ' the forts of the Narrows were practically silenced ; batteries guarding the minefields were put to flight, and the situation appeared to be most favourable for clearing the minefields.' [1]

Minesweepers were already at work, and had begun to sweep upstream. They had swept up three mines – evidently in the line laid by the *Nousret* – though the Admiral was not aware of the fact until next day.

At 4.11 p.m. the *Inflexible*, which had been manœuvring in or near the hidden minefield all day, struck and exploded a mine. Badly damaged, she left the line heeling over to starboard and considerably down by the bows. Her fore submerged torpedo flat had been flooded, killing or drowning the 27 men stationed there ; compartments below became filled with poisonous fumes ; all the electric lights were put out, and the ventilation fans stopped through the cutting of the electric main. Reaching Tenedos in safety, however, she was anchored in shallow water, where her injuries were patched up. She had to be sent to Malta, and then to Gibraltar, for repairs.

[1] *The World Crisis, 1915*, p. 227.

H.M.S. INFLEXIBLE.

Damaged by Mine Explosion in the Dardanelles, March 18, 1915.

At 4.14 the battleship *Irresistible* also struck a mine, and at once took up a heavy list and was unable to move. The old ship was slowly sinking, and seeing her stopped and heeling over, the enemy reopened fire. Unable to get any reply to his signals, Admiral de Robeck sent the *Wear* to find out what had happened. By 4.50 that destroyer was back alongside the *Queen Elizabeth* with her decks crowded with 28 officers and 582 men of the *Irresistible's* crew, the remainder having elected to remain on board their ship in case she remained afloat and could be taken in tow.

She was the third victim of the *Nousret's* small minefield.

The Admiral was now in a position of horrible uncertainty. It was not thought possible that moored mines had been laid in the water in which the fleet had been manœuvring throughout the day. Indeed, it was not known for certain until after the war. The *Bouvet* might have been sunk by a heavy shell; but both the *Inflexible* and *Irresistible* had been mined.

What mines were they?

Were they floating mines set adrift by the enemy higher up the Straits, or perhaps torpedoes fired from some concealed station ashore? This seemed quite probable. A number of floating mines had been seen and sunk during the day, while soon after the action started four vessels had been sighted in the Narrows. They speedily scuttled away when the firing began. They might quite well have been minelayers.

Whatever the new agency of destruction, it was sufficiently potent. The Fleet was in highly dangerous waters. Apart from the *Bouvet*, two more ships had been put completely out of action in almost as many minutes. The remaining ships might be destroyed piecemeal.

The two battleships detailed to cover the minesweeping during the night could not remain in the Straits, and, as some of the forts were still firing, the minesweepers could not do their work. The entire operation must be broken off, and at about 5 p.m. the

Admiral ordered a general retirement.   There was no alternative.

But the tale of casualties was not quite complete.

At 6.5 p.m., the *Ocean*, which was close to the sinking *Irresistible* and still in action and under fire, also struck a mine.   She at once took on a heavy list, and was abandoned when it was obvious that she would not remain afloat.   Her officers and crew were rescued under heavy fire by the ubiquitous destroyers.   Both the *Irresistible* and *Ocean* went to the bottom during the night.

And so the attack of March 18 failed, and was never renewed.   The forts in the Narrows, though severely battered, had not been put out of action, while the minefield, the key to the whole system of defence, was still virtually intact.

Preparations were made for a renewal of the attack. Officers and men of the *Ocean* and *Irresistible* volunteered in great numbers for service in the trawlers in place of their ordinary fishermen crews, and a sweeping force of destroyers was hurriedly improvised.   But never again were the trawlers to be used as mine-sweepers.

On March 19, Sir Ian Hamilton, who had witnessed the naval attack of the day previous, telegraphed to Lord Kitchener : ' I am being most reluctantly driven to the conclusion that the Straits are not likely to be forced by battleships, as at one time seemed probable, and that if my troops are to take part . . . it must be a deliberate and prepared military operation, carried out at full strength, so as to open a passage for the Navy.'

And three days later, at a conference on board the *Queen Elizabeth*, at which Generals Sir Ian Hamilton, Birdwood and Braithwaite were present with Admiral Wemyss, Admiral de Robeck stated he had abandoned all idea of renewing the naval attack until the Army was landed and sufficiently in occupation of the Gallipoli Peninsula to ensure the passage of the Fleet through the Dardanelles.

Henceforward the energies of the whole Fleet, and

its numerous auxiliaries, were to be concentrated upon landing, maintaining and supporting with gun-fire, the Army put ashore in almost incredible circumstances on the rugged peninsula.

A little more minesweeping with destroyers hastily fitted with improvised sweeps was done inside the Straits on the day of the landing, and the three subsequent days, to allow the heavy ships to come up on the right flank of the Army to bombard the Turkish positions with their heavy guns. That particular operation, which was not carried out without casualties, I have already described.[1]

Whether or not it would *ever* have been possible for destroyers fitted as minesweepers, together with other fleet sweepers that presently arrived upon the scene, to have swept a channel through that formidable mine barrier between Kephez and Chanak while the formidable minefield batteries remained in position, must remain for ever unknown. It seems exceedingly unlikely that they would have achieved any more success than the trawlers. They were faster ships, it is true. On the other hand, they offered better targets.

The mines that had proved the principal obstacle to success were not finally removed until Turkey gave up the struggle on October 30, 1918. And on November 12 the Allied Fleet, led by the battleship *Superb*, passed through the Dardanelles into the Sea of Marmora, and on to Constantinople.

But for the ill fortune of war, and a series of happenings which may well be regretted, they might have been there about three years and eight months earlier.

[1] *Endless Story*, pp. 66, 67.

CHAPTER IX

THE *TOTNES* UNIT

August–December, 1916.

NOTE. – *The following chapter has been sent to me by Captain C. C. Bell, D.S.O., R.N. (Retd.). It is printed with slight alteration.*

I

AFTER a short spell in the 10th Cruiser Squadron, where I served in H.M.S. *Teutonic*, I reported at the Second Sea Lord's Office at the Admiralty to find out what my next job was to be. My war service had up to then been in old ships, so I considered I was now entitled to something more modern, and asked for the *Glorious* or *Courageous* which were then nearing completion. I was informed that nothing could be promised, I being a First Class Navigator would have to go to the first job that was vacant. I was then told that a First Class Navigator was wanted for minesweeping ; would I volunteer for it. Here was a bolt from the blue, and I was given 24 hours to consider it.

I spent an anxious day trying to decide what to do. It was a job I knew nothing about. I did not know the Admiral in charge of minesweeping. On the other hand, if I didn't take it, what would my job be ?

I returned the next day, and said yes, I would take the job. So my name was sent up to Admiral Fitzherbert, who was then Director of Minesweeping. Later on I was sent up to him for an interview. He was extremely nice to me, and said, ' Of course I can guarantee nothing, but if you come to me I don't think you need worry about your prospects.' He told me I should be put

164

in command of six Paddle Minesweepers of the ' Race-course ' class which had just been built to Admiralty design to work under his direct orders from Lowestoft.

I was sent first for a week's instruction to the Sheerness paddlers, under Commander Sutton Smith, D.S.O. This gave me only about three days actual sweeping, just enough to get some idea of how the job was done, and to realise that minesweeping was not all ' beer and skittles ' ; in fact precious little ' beer ', and the ships employed looking very much like ' skittles ' when they came into contact with a minefield.

Sutton Smith gave me his blessing, and regretted he couldn't sweep any mines up for me, so away I went to Lowestoft, where I arrived on August 7, 1916, to find three of my unit, including the *Totnes* which was to be my command. The unit did not complete to full strength until August 27, and then consisted of the *Totnes, Pontefract, Gatwick, Cheltenham, Doncaster* and *Ludlow*.

A word about these vessels. They were Admiralty designed, somewhat akin to the mercantile paddlers that are so well known on the south coast and in the Bristol Channel. Unfortunately the *Glen Avon* was taken as a pattern, whereas if they had been modelled on the *Devonia* a much better sweeper would have evolved. The latter vessel is the finest paddle sweeper I have ever met ; she could sweep rings round any Admiralty paddler.

The ' Racecourse ' class had too small paddle wheels, and were of too low horse-power. Otherwise they were good seaboats, though most uncomfortable in a beam sea, or in fact any sea when there was a roll on. You never finished the roll – crash went the sponsons to check the roll when it was half through, squirting fountains of water over the whole ship.

In a strong head sea, sweeping was impossible, as ships would not steer with a sweep wire towing astern. The paddle wheels were on the same shaft, and could not be disconnected to work independently. And as there was no splash direct to the rudder as in screw vessels, the result was that ships became in mine-sweeping language 'Doggo', i.e. they lay helpless stern to stern. There was nothing left to do then but slip sweeps, and start again.

Our armament consisted of a 12-pounder gun on the forecastle, and an anti-aircraft 3-inch on the quarter-deck. We also carried lance bombs and four depth charges, and on the quarter-deck an enormous trawl winch with two drums, each with 750 fathoms of 2½-inch steel trawl wire.

Trawl wire is a vastly different wire to handle to the 2½-inch flexible steel wire used in the Navy. This was never forgotten by a luckless leading seaman, R.N., whose captain betted me that he'd splice wire against any man. Needless to say I accepted the bet, knowing my second hand of the trawler section R.N.R. would cut rings round him. And so it turned out. My man had finished before the other bloke had started tucking.

Right aft were the gallows for hoisting in and out the kite, the latter being twelve feet in length and weighing about a ton. It was the blessing, or more often the curse, of sweeping. A good kite, well balanced, with the slings adjusted correctly, would dive straight down and take up its depth and keep there. Perhaps for a week it would be a model of good behaviour. Then it would become possessed of a devil and behave like a bucking bronco, leaping a dozen feet out of the water, over the sweep-wire and down to the depths, then out again to turn over on its back and sulk, when nothing would make it dive. Finally it might have to be hove up, and hours spent in getting all the turns out of the wire.

When streamed again it would be a model of good behaviour, until the devil entered into it. It would cut its capers, until in sheer desperation we would condemn it and return it to store. I know nothing that can be so exasperating as an evilly-disposed kite. Fortunately the modern plunger kite, unknown during the war, is a far more tractable creature.

2

On joining the *Totnes* I found that in the whole six ships I was the only R.N. active service officer or man. My officers consisted of an R.N.R. lieutenant and two sub-lieutenants R.N.V.R. One of the latter, nephew of a famous composer, used to calm our shattered nerves with first-class fiddling.

I had a R.F.R. petty officer, first class, as Master-at-Arms and ship's steward, and a second hand R.N.R. trawler section. The seamen were either Mercantile Marine, R.N.R. or R.N.R. trawler section. Our two signalmen R.N.V.R. I nicknamed David and Jonathan. Two stouter volunteers I never met, devoted to each other, both Londoners. One, from an office in London, was very bad at flashing, so his mate used to come up to read his signals for him. Incidentally he was always very, very seasick. But even at his very greenest, if I asked him whether he wouldn't rather be on his office stool, he would smile wanly and reply, ' I wouldn't be out of this for anything.'

They were neither of them expert signalmen, and their hours were very long. When sweeping, it was always necessary to have them both on deck. They had to do all the signalling for a flotilla of six ships, and I'm afraid I was not always very patient with them. Still I put up with all their deficiences rather than get reliefs, as they were always so ready and eager to do their jobs despite bad weather and long hours.

My chief engineer was an R.N.R. engineer-sub-lieutenant, a pre-war chief engineer of one of Campbell's Bristol Channel paddlers, and an excellent man at his job. He was assisted by three mercantile marine officers, and several engine-men of the Mercantile Marine. The stokers were all merchant service ratings.

On joining I found Captain Walters in temporary command of *Totnes*. He stayed with me for a day or two to show me the ' ropes '. I should have been in sorry plight without him.

My first job was to sign on my crew, a thing entirely

new to me. If I remember rightly they were all signed on under T.124.Z, a special agreement with the Admiralty for this class of service, as it embraced all Mercantile Marine and Trawler ratings. My only trouble was with two young stewards aged about 20. By complement I was allowed one at a higher rate of pay, from a Service point of view a princely salary. Knowing nothing about either, I told them they were both to sign on at the lower scale, which they refused to do. However, I gave them 24 hours to think about it, and at 9 a.m. the next morning they both came up and said they wouldn't sign. So I told them to pack up and be ready to leave the ship by noon. During the forenoon I sent up to the police station to tell them two men were being discharged, and would they meet them and enlist them for the army. I never heard of them again, but trust they were enlisted at 1s. a day having refused to sign on at something like £2 per week.

Having completed my signing on, I had then to organise and produce written orders for the commanding officers of my flotilla. As all of them were R.N.R. officers, without service in the Royal Navy, I had to punish all defaulters, allowing C.O.'s limited powers to deal with small offences. Fortunately the number of defaulters was not large. Taking them all round, the men were very well behaved, considering that they were nearly all new to naval discipline.

I suppose the stokers were the most lawless. Unfortunately their mess deck was immediately under my cabin, and one day just before dinner-time a sustained roar came up ' 'Un-'ungry! 'Ungry! ' to be interrupted by my P.O. shouting down to them, ' What's the matter with you, you bloody cannibals ; do you want me to throw you down a Missionary ! ' He was possessed of a ready wit. On one occasion he was upbraiding ' Jonathan ', the signalman, who was not looking intelligent and was aimlessly scratching his head. The P.O. gazed at him with a horny eye and observed : ' Unless you want a splinter in your finger you'd better knock off doing that ! '

3

The flotilla was attached to the Lowestoft base, under Commodore Ellison. I received orders through him from the Director of Minesweeping for any special sweeps that were required. When not so required the flotilla did any local mine clearance work which was necessary.

To enable me to get the work done I used to anchor near my sweeping area, on occasion under the Leman and Owers Bank, knowing full well no submarine or surface craft would interfere with me.

Once I anchored within ten miles of the North Hinder Lt. Vessel, with six paddlers, three drifters and two destroyers, and I claim to be the only person to have anchored in practically the middle of the North Sea during the war.

On this latter occasion, September 25, 1916, I certainly got the ' wind up '. At 11 p.m. the wireless operator reported : 'German Telefunken W.T. signals very close.' I asked him how close. He replied less than twenty miles. Soon afterwards the general recall to all ships was made, which meant we had to close the land immediately.

I had as an escort the *Laertes*, Commander Malcolm Goldsmith, and *Llewellyn*, Lieutenant-Commander Geoffrey Nash. I dared not use flashing or sound signals, as I did not know how near hostile craft might be, so I ordered steam on main engines immediately, and at 11.45 p.m. weighed, closed and hailed all vessels including *Laertes*, placed sweepers and mark boats under the *Doncaster*, and ordered them to proceed with all speed and close the land with the *Laertes* as escort. Unfortunately, owing to thick mist and drizzling rain, I could not find the eastern mark boat, so hailed Nash in the *Llewellyn*, who was with me, and told him the circumstances, and said I must anchor, as it was like looking for a needle in a haystack. I knew I could not be far off our mark boat, so decided to anchor and await the dawn or the weather lifting, as I could not leave my little drifter all by herself. Needless to say

I spent an anxious night, but with the first streak of dawn, there, not two cables away, was my drifter. I weighed and closed her, ordered her to weigh, and be taken in tow. Then, accompanied by the *Llewellyn* I towed that drifter faster than she ever had gone in her life.

On return to Lowestoft I asked the Commodore if I had caused him any anxiety. To my relief he replied, ' Anxiety! Why should I worry about you? ' If he had known where I'd been, no doubt there would have been trouble ; but as I was in mined waters, I felt pretty safe anchoring where I did, though if we had been sighted by the enemy things might have been awkward.

The Lowestoft area was not too hospitable in any wind between north through east to south. We could obtain no shelter, and as we had to anchor four or five nights a week, it gave rise to many unpleasant nights. The worst I can remember was in September, 1916 – incidentally the 13th. I had anchored at 7.45 p.m. off Blakeney Overfalls, and during the night the wind veered to the north-west and blew a full gale. At dawn the ships were all dragging, so at first I thought it better to weigh and proceed to the south of Cromer. Unfortunately we were taking in green seas over the forecastle, and no one could live there, so I veered all the cable we had and dropped a second anchor underfoot, to spend a most uncomfortable day. Fortunately the weather moderated after a bit, and on the 15th we were able to carry on with our sweep.

On another occasion, when returning alone to Lowestoft, it was blowing a full south-easterly gale, so I anchored in Yarmouth Roads, where the banks gave a little lee, and reported to the Base I had done so, and requested to be informed when the weather had moderated sufficiently to enter harbour. To my amazement I received the order to proceed into harbour at once. I thought it was sheer lunacy, but I'd sooner be in than out. So I proceeded to make the most thrilling entry into harbour I've ever made.

There was a very heavy following sea, and a strong

tide across the entrance. A sea right astern is the worst possible for handling paddlers, as you have no wash from the propellers to help steering, and the rudder at times is almost right out of the water. However it was a case of do or die, so putting the telegraph to full speed I made for the entrance, the ship yawing horribly from side to side, heading first for one pier and then the other.

I well remember my officer of the watch literally gasping, ' You'll never do it, sir ! ' The next moment we charged crab-fashion through the entrance to be hailed by the pilot in agony : ' Stop, for God's sake, stop ! I'm coming on board ! ' As I put the engines to full astern I shouted ' Too late, George, you can't help now ! ' and just managed to bring her up short of the road bridge across the harbour without a scratch. Personally I thought the chances ten to one against our getting in unscathed ; but I resolved never again to come in in a S.E. gale whatever my orders !

During the first month we had as a unit swept up sixteen mines. This entailed many hours of hard work, and many fruitless days. I don't think the danger worried many people, and I know that it was a positive joy to hear a hail from aft, ' Mine in the sweep, sir ! '

Thanks to our trawler personnel this was hardly ever wrong. Used as they were to deep-sea trawling, they knew instinctively when an additional strain came on the sweep-wire. If the mine was caught in the cod of the sweep it was often fifteen to twenty minutes before the moorings were cut and up bobbed our black, evil-looking friend. Sometimes it was necessary to resort to a sawing motion, especially in heavy weather and when moving against the tide. In other words, one ship reduced to slow and the other increased to full speed. Then, when the leading ship was about four points on the bow of the rear ship, the latter would increase speed and the leader reduce. After doing this two or three times the mine moorings were sure to be cut by sliding to and fro along the sweep-wire.

Up to September 13, 1916, we had destroyed twenty mines. Then came a lean period until October 4, when one exploded in the sweep, one more on the 20th, another on the 21st. It is the lean periods which are the killing part of minesweeping, as it then becomes so deadly monotonous. They mean hours and hours of steady slog, at a speed of between six and eight knots, depending on the weather, up and down, up and down, but with station keeping still to be accurately kept, and continual parting, re-passing and splicing sweeps. I have parted as many as seven times in two hours.

The Lowestoft area was bad for its comparatively shoal water and masses of wrecks. When actually working on a minefield it was necessary to sweep up to a wreck both ways. Even then you had the possibility of dragging a mine up to a wreck and leaving it there when the sweep parted.

On October 23, 1916, we had our best bag in a day, four mines in the Haisborough channel and one drifting British mine. Two exploded in the sweeps, which I always thought a dull way of getting them, and the most nerve-racking. An enormous dull thud sometimes seemed to lift the whole ship. 'Heavens!' one thought. 'Is that us or one of the others hitting a mine?' Then an enormous bubble would rise out of the water and erupt, to break 100 feet or so into the air in a huge fountain and well clear of our stern, much to our relief.

We had one man who used to work in the minesweeping store aft, and whenever a mine exploded he used to shoot up the hatch with his hair on end, much to the amusement of the men at the winch. I regret to say they used to pull his leg, by dropping a five-cwt. sinker on the deck over his head, and yelling 'Mine!' Up he'd shoot in a dither only to see the grinning faces of the winchmen, and return again to his store muttering oaths.

Of the remaining two mines one was exploded by rifle fire. This meant hitting a horn, of which there were four, about one inch wide and six inches long.

This was the most satisfactory method of destruction. Not only did you see the mine and know it German, but you had a gorgeous explosion, sometimes like an enormous mushroom, 300 to 500 feet high, and knew that it would never serve the purpose for which it was laid. The other was sunk by rifle fire without exploding.

Our orders were to sink all mines by *gunfire*. My first mine I endeavoured conscientiously to sink with our 6-pounder A.A. gun. We were not allowed to fire nearer than 300 yards, and imagine a target two feet by ten inches, bobbing up and down, sometimes entirely submerged, and the ship rolling or pitching. How many shots would you take to sink it ? I gave it its chance. After twenty rounds, it was still there. ' Cease fire,' I said. ' Sink the damned thing by rifle fire.' I always kept a rifle and later a Lewis gun on the bridge, to keep my eye in, and generally after twenty or thirty rounds, with perhaps a dozen hits, the mine would slowly sink. I always maintained that a mine so sunk became innocuous after a month or two, though I never owned up to using rifle fire.

One of our paddlers, the *Cheltenham*, was towing a drifter mark boat, the *Ocean Plough*, off Lowestoft, on August 27, 1916. The drifter struck a mine, and when the smoke and water had cleared away there was nothing whatever of her to be seen except the usual wreckage floating on the water. Boats were lowered and survivors searched for, but of the crew of seven only two were rescued.

One of these was the skipper – Cutler, I think was his name – who had been blown clear through the window of his wheelhouse. He possessed a rather red and enormous nose, and save for a large gash on it he was otherwise uninjured.

Two or three days later I met him in Lowestoft with his nose plastered and bandaged. I asked him how he felt. He roared with laughter and said he was all right and that he had just been to the Naval Base to ask for another ship. His narrow escape and severe shock seemed to have had no effect upon him at all, and that he should be demanding to go to sea again after so short a time illustrates the courage of his class. He was quite indignant when he was told at the Naval Base that he *was* to take 14 days' sick-leave whether he liked it or not.

Speaking of skippers, however, reminds me of the man in command of another mark boat, the drifter *Eager*. As he was senior officer of drifters, I used to send for him and tell him to be in a certain latitude and longitude – miles out at sea – by such and such a time. He always asked for a bearing and distance from Lowestoft, and it was sometimes 50 miles out from land.

Never once did I fail to find him in his right position. Talking to him one day, I asked if he used a chart. No, he said. He didn't understand the blamed things, so when I asked him how he managed always to find the right spot, he just smiled and said : ' That's all right, Commander. I'll go anywhere in the North Sea if you give me its bearing and distance from some-where I know.'

I came to realise that these North Sea fishermen *did* possess some sort of homing instinct denied to us more ordinary people.

4

On October 24, 1916, we were ordered down to the Sunk Light Vessel off Harwich. We weighed at 5.30 a.m. and proceeded at full speed. There was con-siderable fog, and the visibility only 1 to 1½ miles. The aircraft patrol from Yarmouth apparently sighted us in the fog, and reported us as six enemy battle cruisers. We passed through Yarmouth Roads at about 8 a.m., and off Lowestoft had a very narrow escape.

The *Havelock*, a monitor with 14-inch guns stationed there for coast defence, had her guns loaded and crews closed up. Thirty seconds before she sighted us the aircraft report was amended. It was lucky, for the captain of the *Havelock* (Comdr. Guy Hamilton), told

me next time I saw him, that they were going to open
fire the moment we were sighted in the fog. However, I don't think they would have hit us, as they
had 10,000 yards on their sights, and we were only
passing at 5,000 at the most. We should have been
recognised before they could fire a second round.

We passed sweeps off the Sunk at 11 a.m., and by
noon had swept up three mines. We now had six
hard days' work, and had to return to Lowestoft for
coal on the 25th, with orders to sail again on the 27th.
Fortunately the weather was too bad to leave, so we
had a respite and did not go out till the 29th. Bad
weather then forced us to abandon sweeping and
anchor in Yarmouth Roads. We were out on the 30th
and 31st, but bad weather again prevented us doing
any real sweeping. We were sweeping on 31st with
a wind of force 7 and sea 6. In conditions such as
these it was quite impossible to sweep, the speed being
so reduced that it was impossible to keep the sweep-
wire off the bottom. After slipping, I anchored off
Aldeburgh. We were not popular for doing this. I
believe someone complained to the Admiralty.
Fortunately the request that we should not anchor
there was refused. The contention was that we
would draw an attack. We were really a protection. We gave them the protection of six 12-
pounder guns, and submarines had a rooted objection
to paddlers as they could not hear the paddles. At
least we should have saved Aldeburgh from a submarine bombardment.

We continued sweeping on November 1st, 2nd and
3rd, but had to abandon it at noon on 3rd on account
of bad weather. As it was too bad to enter Lowestoft,
we had to spend the night in Yarmouth Roads, entering
harbour at 7 a.m. We had been out for 6 days, with
particularly bad weather, which reduced our sweeping
hours on every day we had been out except the 2nd.
Only one mine was swept up during the period. It
was quite the most unpleasant week we ever had.
Our night anchorages were never really sheltered, so
sleep was practically impossible.

We left Lowestoft again on the 8th, and on the
10th the *Totnes* proceeded to Grimsby for a ten days'
docking, making good defects, and cleaning boilers.
I managed to get away for a few days' leave. I had
had three very trying months, not only learning the
job myself, but training a flotilla of six vessels, and
endeavouring to produce a really efficient unit.

On November 28th, when in Lowestoft harbour at
about 6.15 a.m., a Zeppelin was sighted returning to
Germany. She had carried out a raid on some Mid-
land towns and I believe had been crippled. She
dropped no bombs in our locality and seemed to be
going slowly. Of course we opened fire on her with
our 6-pounder A.A. guns. At 6.40 she burst into flames.
Lowestoft rang with real full-throated cheers. The
Zepp. had been brought down by a seaplane from
Yarmouth. Cadbury and another man were the
heroes, which was rather disheartening for a drifter
which was on patrol. She signalled to the Lowestoft
base, 'Have engaged and brought down hostile
Zeppelin', thinking that her little 6- or 3-pounder had
done the deed, not knowing there was a seaplane up
aloft doing the damage.

I afterwards had to sweep for her remains, but
owing to her position being reported incorrectly, I
was ordered to abandon search. She actually came
down in the middle of the British minefield.

During our next six days out our bag of mines was
a little better. Two in one day and four the next.
As it was a flat calm day, I decided to salve one of
these, and a ticklish business it was. I took away a
boat and lassoed the mine with a length of light wire,
then towed it back to the ship, hooked a wire on to
the lifting bolt, and hoisted it with our seaplane
derrick. All was well so far. We now had a live
mine in our midst, and the next thing was to make
it safe.

I had no mining expert on board, but knew a little
about them myself and decided the only thing to do
was to remove the detonator. I had the mine swung
inboard and about four feet from the deck. Not

H.M.S. *TOTNES*.

9.40 A.M., FRIDAY, DECEMBER 29, 1916.

p. 179.]

quite knowing what might happen, I cleared everyone away, and armed with a tommy commenced operations by unscrewing the detonator plug. I thought I had it loose enough and then tried to withdraw it by hand. It was very loath to come out, but at last it came with a rush and all was well. To my horror on looking at the detonator, I saw a deep score down its side, and realised I'd had a very narrow escape.

The area I was working on was in the vicinity of the Sunk Light Vessel, a very favourite mining ground as the German submarines laid their eggs to catch the Harwich Force on entering or leaving. I presume that owing to this Force's activities the Germans were particularly anxious to damage it. Altogether I had accounted for six mines in this area, and I rather think the local forces from Harwich accounted for some more.

The inshore portions of this area were heartbreaking to sweep, on account of wrecks. On December 3 between 8.15 a.m. and 1 p.m. we parted sweeps fourteen times. The area had now been cleared of mines as far as was humanly possible. Our coal was nearly exhausted, our six days at sea were up. So we returned to Lowestoft for two well-earned days' rest, not all rest by any means, as we had to coal, clean ship, complete with stores, etc.

I do not think it was ever realised by the Navy in general what senior officers of minesweeping units had to do. I was the only R.N. officer in the whole flotilla, and it was like an Admiral running a fleet with no staff. All the organisation, correspondence, of my own and other ships of the unit, had to be done by my own hand, and I had to advise C.O.'s, and do the hundred and one things necessary to keep an efficient sweeping unit. In addition, I was constantly revising our signal book to make it simpler with fewer flags to hoist. I know I considered myself lucky if I had an afternoon off at all, it was also a great relief and joy to go over to the *Havelock* to dine with her Captain, (Guy Hamilton) with whom I also managed an occasional sail on the Broads far away from the war.

12

Our next six days out was the most fruitful we had ever had. Ten German and one British mines were accounted for on December 15. Again in the vicinity of the Sunk Light Vessel, and between it and a War Channel buoy my pair exploded two mines in the sweep. The second pair immediately swept up three more. Again they had two more in the sweep, one of which, after showing on the surface, slipped out and was subsequently swept up by trawlers. Seven mines in one forenoon was a record for us, incidentally bringing our total up to fifty-one in four months. Three of these were exploded by rifle fire, always a pleasing sight, and a satisfactory ending to their lives.

For the next fortnight we were employed re-sweeping this area, but found no further mines. It was a very necessary precaution because of the foul ground, caused by sunken wrecks. On December 28 I had anchored off Aldeburgh, and during the night received orders to sweep an area off the Sunk Light Vessel, where mines moored afloat had been sighted.

I despatched my two mark boats at dawn, and was following them out, when I noticed one of them, the *Eager*, blowing her whistle, and the signal ' Mine in sight ', flying. She reported she had sighted a moored mine awash, and had dropped a dan buoy by it. The position was, I think, about five to seven miles to the northward and east of Orfordness, and therefore right in the track both of shipping and destroyers leaving and returning to Harwich.

I hoisted the preparatory signal for sweeping, and shortly after passed sweeps. About ten minutes after we began sweeping there was a violent explosion astern of the *Ludlow*. I saw a huge column of water thrown up, and as soon as it cleared away I noticed that she had had her stern blown off. Naturally my first impression was that this was the mine marked by the *Eager* and that her dan buoy was dropped a little further away from the mine than reported.

I immediately slipped the sweep, and proceeded to the *Ludlow's* assistance, turning outwards to port. As far as I remember we had turned something like three points [1] and were still under starboard helm, when the officer of the watch reported a mine off the port bow. I immediately put the helm amidships, and then saw the mine myself. I realised at once that nothing could save us, but that by porting the helm and going full speed astern I could ensure being hit forward. This I did instanter, and then leapt to the fore-side of the upper bridge, and roared, ' Clear lower deck. Everybody aft ! '

Fortunately my P.O. was on the forecastle, and he seemed to realise that there was real urgency in my order, with the result that the fore-part was cleared. I am under the impression that between my first sighting the mine and the explosion could not have been more than 45 seconds to a minute. The officer of the watch, Sub-Lieutenant Tschaikovsky, R.N.V.R., asked should he stay. I said, ' No, fly for your life, and good-bye if I don't see you again.' I knew my feelings were that my number was up. I watched the mine bobbing up and down as it sank and re-appeared with the sea, which made it obvious that it was moored. Then it was hidden by the break of the forecastle. I knew within a second or two the crash would come.

I stepped back behind the standard compass hunched my shoulders and pulled up the collar of my British warm. Then the explosion. – It seemed to rend the whole ship and shake her to the very core. I fully expected to be hit by falling débris, but marvellous to relate, other than a shower bath, I was untouched. Afterwards I picked up a lump of twisted iron as big as my fist, which must have fallen within a yard of me.

I shall never forget my feelings. I know my heart was beating as fast as if I had run a mile, but con-soled myself with the thought that anyway my horrible past has not come up before me, as it is popularly supposed to when your number is up, so I suppose I shall be all right.

After the explosion I looked over the bridge screen and saw that the entire forecastle up to within twenty

---

[1] A point is 11° 15′.

feet of the bridge was wrecked. I left the upper bridge, and going down met the chief engineer, and told him to stop the engines, and see if the foremost stokehold bulkhead was tight. I also ordered the signalman to tell the *Cheltenham*, my minesweeping partner, to take us in tow by the stern, and the *Pontefract* to go to assistance of *Ludlow* and tow her to Harwich.

I then went down to the fore mess deck to inspect the damage. It was a mass of distorted metal, wrecked lockers, and mess tables ; but not the slightest sign of fire. So if the stokehold bulkhead was undamaged there was nothing to prevent us making Harwich.

Groping about amongst the wreckage I came upon one of the stokers, an R.N.R. man. He was in great danger, for the deck was cracking ominously, and afterwards carried away. I asked him what he was doing, and he replied : ' I left my jumper here and came to find it. It's got a picture of my young lady in the pocket ! '

I suspect, however, there was some money in the pocket besides the photo of the young woman.

I went up on deck again, and the first lieutenant came up and said, ' Shall I lower the boats ? ' ' What for ? ' was my reply. ' To abandon ship,' said he, and then I saw all the boats were manned ready for lowering. I must say I really did enjoy the next few minutes, and my language was hardly parliamentary. Under my abuse the boats gradually became empty, and the hands were sent about their work. My steward was running about with the ship's dog in his arms, so I bit him full and hearty and told him to go and clear up my cabin, which, being under the bridge, was a mass of broken glass and crockery. Entering my cabin soon afterwards, I was amazed to find him with two counterpanes on the deck, frantically clearing all the drawers of clothes, etc., and making bundles of them, and making worse chaos than before. Of course I told him to replace everything.

The *Cheltenham* had us in tow stern first in under five minutes, and headed for Harwich. Steering was bad, and we yawed considerably. However, we could use our paddles, so continued going slow astern, which eased the tow. We made three to four knots. When we got in to shoaler water progress was very slow, this, I think was due to the fact that the forecastle deck had collapsed, and it was quite possible our cables were dragging on the bottom. When off the Cork Light Vessel quite close in to Harwich a harbour tug came out to us. I told the *Cheltenham* to cast off the tow, and to return and assist with the *Ludlow*. We eventually arrived at Harwich at about 4 p.m. and made fast to a buoy for the night. There was no possible chance of the ship sinking.

We docked next morning, and found that the whole forepart had been blown clean away, the upper deck had sagged, and the breakwater was level with the keel. They trimmed us up by cutting away all loose metal with oxy-acetylene. As we had lost our entire crew accommodation, the ship's company were accommodated in the depot ship. The officers remained on board with a few ratings for watch keeping. The Court of Enquiry was held at Harwich, and afterwards we were towed by dockyard tugs to Deptford dock, where the ship was taken in hand for repairs. When I rejoined her some six months later, she was as good as ever, and showed no traces of the disaster.

To return to the *Ludlow*, her explosion had killed five and wounded seven others. She was taken in tow by *Pontefract* and eventually foundered off the Cork Light Vessel at 11 or 11.30 p.m., the wind and sea having greatly increased. The water gradually filled her engine-room. This was a bitter blow to me, as I thought the vessel should have been saved. Unfortunately I was too busy with my own affairs in *Totnes* and did not dare leave the ship until safely in port.

So ended the first chapter of the *Totnes* unit, which up to date had destroyed fifty-three German mines in under five months.

CHAPTER X

TALES OF MINESWEEPING

I

BEFORE the war ended, German submarines had laid mines all round the British Isles, in the North Sea and off the coast of France. Mines appeared off Lisbon, Cape St. Vincent and Sierra Leone, throughout the length and breadth of the Mediterranean, in the White Sea, off the east coast of the United States and Halifax, Nova Scotia.

Elsewhere, the voyage of the German raider *Wolf* gave work to minesweepers in many an unexpected part of the globe.

She was a disguised merchant ship of 6,000 tons, carrying 458 mines. Leaving Germany on November 30, 1916, she managed to slip through the blockade line in the northern part of the North Sea, and to get safely away to sea on a voyage lasting fifteen months. Rounding the Cape of Good Hope, she cruised in the Indian Ocean, and then proceeded south of Australia to New Zealand and Fiji. Thence she returned home by way of New Guinea, the Dutch East Indies and the Cape of Good Hope, arriving safely in Germany in March, 1918.

Her mines were laid all over the world : 25 off Capetown and 29 off Cape Agulhas, in South Africa, on January 18, 1917 ; 39 off Colombo and 19 off Cape Comorin, the southernmost point of India, in February, 1917. One of her prizes – the *Turritella* – laid a consignment of 25 mines off Aden, while this vessel, or the *Wolf* herself, laid another 68 off Bombay.

The Capetown minefield was swept up by four whaling steamers fitted out for the purpose ; but in the Agulhas field two ships were lost and only seven mines swept up in 1917. It was in the Agulhas field that a whale was killed, and was found floating, practically headless.

The Aden group was removed by small harbour tugs manned by Somalis with British officers within two months of its location and after the loss of one ship, while the Bombay consignment was dealt with by local craft manned by British officers and Lascars. Fifty of the mines had been swept up by June, 1917, with the sinking of five ships.

After the loss of two large ships, the Colombo minefield was swept up by six trawlers purchased in Japan. They were re-named the *Kumarhami, Lankdys, Lakshmi, Parvati, Ranmenika* and *Sarasvati*, and were employed until the end of the war in maintaining a swept channel from the harbour entrance to the 100-fathom line. Then they were sold to a Bombay firm. Tugs fitted out as minesweepers before the advent of the trawlers were not altogether successful.[1]

Continuing her voyage, the *Wolf's* next mining exploit was off Gabo Island, the south-eastern point of Australia, where she deposited 14 mines which occasioned the loss of one steamer. Then she proceeded to New Zealand, where 15 mines were laid in the Cook Strait between the North and South Islands, and another 17 off Three Kings' Island, in the north. These last three minefields were dealt with by the Australian and New Zealand naval forces.

The *Wolf's* last big batch of 110 mines was laid off the Anamba Islands, in the South China Sea, about 160 miles to the northward of Singapore, on September 4, 1917, and was not located that year. In all, this raider's mines were responsible for the loss of about fifteen ships.

How the Admiralty received news of her activities was romantic.

In the earlier days of her cruise she had captured fifteen merchantmen, seven of which were British.

[1] Information from the Master Attendant at Colombo, through the courtesy of Maurice Prendergast, Esq.

The crews were retained on board as prisoners for a considerable time, and one of the British merchant captains, at the risk of dire penalties, threw bottles overboard containing notes of the voyage. One of these bottles, picked up on December 9, 1917, by natives in Toli-Toli, in the Celebes, eventually reached the British Consul-General of Batavia, who informed the Commander-in-Chief in China of its contents. The details, which included an account of the raider's cruise as far as Australia, reached the Admiralty on January 15, 1918.

A second bottle, found this time off the Norwegian coast, had its contents dated February 10, 1918, at which time the *Wolf* was somewhere in the North Atlantic. It appeared by the note inside that the writer was able to state the exact position of the last 110 mines laid. He was ill in a hammock at the time, and, being a prisoner, had no access to a chart. But he believed the spot to be somewhere off Singapore, though he stated subsequently he was unable to identify the lighthouse on the last piece of land seen before the minelaying took place.

A long and fruitless search took place off Singapore,[1] but the position of the 110 mines remained a mystery. It was not until after the Armistice that they were discovered from German sources to have been laid off the Anamba Islands. Otherwise, the information contained in the bottle was entirely accurate, and the officer who took the grave risk of supplying it received due recognition.

Another interesting and not unamusing incident occurred in connexion with one of the *Wolf's* mines.

On January 26, 1918, Mr. Abraham Louw and his son Gert, farmers at Elands Bay, South Africa, dis-

---

[1] In view of the *Wolf's* activities, the British sloops *Geranium, Mallow, Marguerite* and *Hydrangea* had left Malta for Singapore on December 24, 1917. After clearing the minefield off Singapore, they were to proceed to New Zealand for the final clearance of the minefields in the Cook Strait and off Three Kings' Island.

Five hired vessels, the *Pangkor, Kedah, Trimuar, Tailee* and *Hocklee* assisted in the search for the Singapore minefield, as well as a number of Japanese torpedo-craft specially fitted out with minesweeps.

covered a peculiar cast-iron receptacle on the beach. Having brought a cart, they proceeded to dismantle the object by unscrewing what was locally described as the large brass cap on one side of it, and detaching the pulleys and some sort of catapult apparatus.

Lifting the receptacle on to the cart Mr. Louw noticed it was exuding 'brown tar'. Intensely curious, he lit it with a match, with results sufficiently disturbing to cause him and his son to retire in haste. So did the horse, dragging the cart after it.

The object, of course, was a mine, and the 'brown tar' T.N.T. softened by the sun. The T.N.T. did not explode, but blazed up to a height of 200 feet, frightened all the inhabitants from the coast, and caused them to take cover in the bush.

The flames having expired, the Louws fetched the local policeman to the scene. He, ' not very interested in the thing ', rolled it into some bushes and covered it with reeds.

The naval authorities were informed, and an officer was sent to investigate. He found that the Boer farmer and his son had dismantled the primer of the mine with a tin-opener, and, for convenience' sake, had cut off the horns with a hammer and cold chisel !

Mr. Louw, 'after much persuasion ', as said the official report, returned the various parts of the mine he had dismembered, and said he had mistaken it ' for a new kind of boiler used in the manufacture of wireless telegraphy ! '

2

Mines were salved for examination, and swept for, in various unconventional ways.

I am assured that after the Belgian coast was evacuated by the enemy, the Zeebrugge–Bruges Canal was carefully swept for mines by a wire towed between two *horses*, one on each bank. To impart a nautical flavour to the operation, the seamen who were present in case mines were discovered tied a small White Ensign to the tail of each horse !

I have already related the true story of the fisherman who recovered a floating mine and rendered it *safe* by removing the horns with a chopper. There were numerous other narrow escapes, for instance, that of the trawler *Plethos*.

Engaged one day in sweeping with her consorts, she passed directly over a mine and struck it heavily with the after part of her keel. The mine was caught in the sweep of the next pair of trawlers following astern and brought to the surface, when a deep dent was observed between the horns, which had not been touched. The *Plethos* had avoided destruction by an inch or less.

There was the case of a small boy walking along a cliff, somewhere in the Shetlands, I believe, who saw an unfamiliar spherical object on the beach beneath him, and amused himself by throwing heavy stones at it. Finally he succeeded in hitting a horn, whereat the mine exploded. The lad retired unhurt, but, as the report had it, ' considerably shaken by his experience '.

And late one Saturday afternoon, on the north-east coast of England, a miner who had been indulging himself somewhat freely, happened to be strolling along the beach. Feeling sleepy, he decided upon a nap. Noticing an iron, cylindrical-shaped object with certain strange protuberances which had been left stranded by the tide, he hoisted himself upon it and went to sleep. Some little time later somebody else with more knowledge saw mine and miner on the beach, and, much concerned, hastened to inform the police. The police in turn advised the local naval authorities, who suggested that nothing should be done for the time being. Any attempt to arouse a miner in liquor, they considered, was sufficient to cause an explosion. A blow of 50 lb. from a heavily-booted foot on one of the horns *might* be disastrous, for not *all* mines were fitted with the safety arrangements supposed to render them harmless when they broke adrift from their moorings and drifted ashore.

On this particular occasion, however, there were no unfortunate results. Waking refreshed from his sleep, the miner clambered down from his perch.   Until the situation was explained, he was at a loss to understand why a considerable crowd had collected at a respectful distance.

Probably one of the best individual and unpremeditated minesweeping efforts of the war was that carried out by S.S. *Greenisland*, a very small coasting steamer commanded by Mr. S. Davidson, who happened to be an ex-petty-officer of the Royal Navy and a leading torpedo-man.

On May 1, 1917, he sighted a mine seven miles east-north-east of Ailsa Craig.   He at once steamed towards it to investigate, and took steps to warn other vessels in the vicinity.   Then, being a man of ingenuity, he set about manufacturing an improvised sweep.   It consisted of a towed spar weighted with fire-bars, and veering it astern Mr. Davidson manœuvred his ship so that the mine would be fouled and exploded.   The spar struck the mine several times, actually catching under the horns, but nothing happened.

Foiled in his efforts, Mr. Davidson then sent a boat away with a wire.   It made a wide circle round the mine, and brought the end of the wire back to the ship, where it was shackled to its own part, thus forming a sliding noose.

The *Greenisland* then went ahead tautening the loop round the mine moorings, and with ninety fathoms of wire out towed the mine three miles into shallow water and clear of traffic.   There she stopped and lay fast to the mine moorings for the night.

The next morning a second mine bobbed up to the surface near the first, but disappeared again after a short time.   Patrol vessels then arrived on the scene and sank the first mine by gunfire.   There were no signs of the second, however, so the end of the *Greenisland's* wire was picked up by a naval drifter and the second mine towed into shallow water.   Here, when it appeared, it was sunk by gunfire.

The towing wire was then hauled in, but the running noose was still fast round the mine moorings. Six ends of wire were pulled to the surface, and after much difficulty a mine and sinker were eventually salved complete. It appeared that Mr. Davidson must have passed his running bowline round two or more mines, or else have towed one foul of the other. His plucky effort in towing the mines clear of the fairway with his hastily improvised apparatus not improbably saved other vessels from destruction. His action was rewarded.

German submarine minelaying in the approaches to the Clyde was apparently fairly frequent in May, 1917, possibly because the enemy was aware that the battleship *Ramillies*, which had been built by Messrs. Beardmore's of Dalmuir was due to sail for Liverpool. There had been a mishap during her launch in 1916, when she charged across the river, hit the opposite bank, damaged her bottom, cracked her stern-post, and smashed the most important of her two rudders. There being no dock on the Clyde large enough to take her, she had to be sent to Liverpool for the damage to be ascertained and repaired.

Because of the injury to her steering apparatus she was practically unmanageable, charging in all directions and describing wild circles besides running ashore on more occasions than one. Her various misadventures and delays, and her eventual erratic and thrilling journey to Liverpool with four tugs forward and four aft, and screened by eight minesweepers, eight trawlers and six destroyers, is well described in Commander W. S. R. King-Hall's [1] *A Naval Lieutenant, 1914–1918*, written under his pen-name of ' Etienne ' and published in 1919. He was serving in the *Ramillies*, and after four rather hectic days of mishaps writes on May 11, 1917 : ' There are rumours of a congregation of Fritzes outside ; perhaps they have got wind of this entertainment.'

It seems that the submarines must have had news of something unusual. At this period, Mr. G. E. Blackmore, whom we last met as the navigating gunner of the gunboat *Circe*, was in command of the *Marchioness of Breadalbane*, a hired Clyde paddle-

[1] Commander Stephen King-Hall. Well known to B.B.C. audiences.

steamer stationed at Troon with three others for sweeping the approaches to the Clyde.

And on the morning that the *Ramillies* was due to sail, the sweepers had news from a motor-boat patrolling in the fairway that mines had been seen coming to the surface at regular intervals. They were, in fact, actually being laid by a submarine with the wrong depth setting.

Every available ship was at once hurried out to search for the intruder, and drifters laid indicator nets between the Cumbraes and Bute. The hunt was carried on all day and no trace of the submarine was found. It continued through the night with searchlights. All the bays were closely watched, it being the idea to keep the U-boat submerged to exhaust her battery power.

'The next morning', says Mr. Blackmore, ' we had a bit of luck. The submarine had worked up close to the nets off the Cumbraes, and came to the surface right ahead of a trawler, which had an easy job to ram her. A small quantity of wreckage was recovered, and eventually we were able to sweep and locate her exact position. She was lying in about 30 fathoms. The Ailsa Shipbuilding Company was ordered to construct a heavy steel canister, which was filled with explosive, lowered over the submarine, and fired electrically from a motor-boat, which left no doubt as to her destruction.'

This only shows how deceptive such incidents can be in wartime. Neither the British nor the German official records contain any trace of a U-boat being destroyed anywhere near the Clyde during 1917. The trawler may certainly have rammed her and inflicted some damage. But what the sweepers located and blew up with the bomb made by the Ailsa Shipbuilding Company was probably some old wreck.

However, the sweepers set to work to clear up the mines, fourteen eventually being destroyed. The manner in which they were obtained at intervals of days left no doubt that they were fitted with delay-action gear.

At 11 a.m. on May 23 the *Ramillies* finally sailed on

her ticklish journey to Liverpool with her flotilla of small craft in attendance.

'At 1 p.m. we passed the Cumbrae Light,' Commander King-Hall writes. 'At 2.30 p.m., about six miles farther on, the trawler *Merse*, one of our inner screen, when distant about a mile on our port bow, struck a mine and was blown to atoms. There was a large cloud of white and grey smoke, a report, and in a few seconds this had cleared away and there was nothing left except an oily patch and a few pieces of wood. – She was the senior officer's ship of trawlers, and her two officers, including the captain, Lieutenant Fane, R.N.R., were in our smoking-room that morning. There were no survivors out of a crew of 15.'[1]

The *Ramillies* had a narrow escape.

3

When the German submarines first started mine-laying, it was desirable that a specimen of the new type of mine should be recovered for examination. Sighting one of these not far from Cape Wrath, an armed yacht towed it near the shore and succeeded in beaching it close to some houses. Here, when the tide fell, it remained high and dry with its detonator buried in the sand.

The only way of getting at the detonator was to roll the mine over, though if this were done in the ordinary way the horns would be fractured and the thing would probably explode. Eventually cork fenders were procured from the ship to form a cushion, a long line was attached to the mine, and it was pulled over on to the fenders by a party of men behind a convenient sandhill.

The detonator thread was then found to be badly burred, which meant that it could not be unscrewed in the ordinary way. A 'tommy' – or short iron bar – had to be placed in the detonator holder, the line secured to the end of it, and the holder unscrewed inch by inch by the party behind the sandhill. This mine was one of a group laid very shortly after the death

---

[1] *A Naval Lieutenant, 1914–1918*, pp. 193, 194.

of Lord Kitchener in the *Hampshire* on June 5, 1916, became known in Germany. Painted on it was ' Kurfels Kitchener.[1]'

One of the most outstanding cases where a mine was rendered safe, and a ship and her crew saved by the gallantry of two men, occurred on December 12, 1917, off the Nab, at the east end of the Isle of Wight. I have details of the incident from its chief participant.

On the afternoon of December 6, 1917, minesweeping trawlers attached to Portsmouth discovered enemy mines in the War Channel between the Isle of Wight and the Owers Lightship. Soon afterwards Lieutenant F. W. Moody, R.N.R., in charge of the group, was killed with several others when his ship, the *Apley*, was blown up and sunk.

The officer of the other division of trawlers happened to be ill in hospital, and Mr. George E. Blackmore, the chief gunner in command of the paddle minesweeper *Marchioness of Breadalbane*,[2] was ordered to prepare all available trawlers for clearing the new minefield. They proceeded to sea next morning, with Mr. Blackmore, in command of the trawler *Manx King*, in charge of the division normally commanded by the officer in hospital. The work occupied two full days, several mines being swept up and destroyed under the direction of Commander R. Salmon, D.S.O., R.N.R., who was acting as Port Minesweeping Officer.

On December 12, it was decided to carry out a final sweep over the area to make quite certain it was clear, after which a Memorial Service was to be held over the spot where the *Apley* had been lost. This was to be conducted by a lieutenant R.N.V.R. in command of the coastal motor-boat attending on the sweepers, who in civil life happened to be a clergyman.

The sweep was carried out without incident. No more mines were found, and shortly after noon the order was given to slip the sweep-wires and haul them

[1] This particular mine, no longer dangerous, is to be seen in a garden at Emsworth, Hampshire.

[2] With the other paddlers from the Clyde, she had been sent to Portsmouth in September, 1917.

in. While this was being done Mr. Blackmore was amazed to see a mine come up in the kite of the *Manx King*. Because of its resemblance to the rounded end of the plunger kite, it was not noticed until it was hove up to the head of the arched steel gallows on the ship's side.

There was a choppy sea and considerable motion on the ship. And as the mooring-wire of the mine was wrapped in bights round the kite, the mine fell upside down as its mooring, still attached to the heavy sinker on the bottom, tautened out and anchored the trawler by the stern.

'Thank God!' Mr. Blackmore writes. 'The horns just cleared the gunwale as the mine fell over.'

Even so there was imminent danger of an explosion. The mine, swinging to and fro with the movement, had one of its horns within a few inches of the gunwale. Another, already dented, was no more than half an inch above the heavy kite. If one of them struck and collapsed, and a blow of fifty pounds was sufficient to do it, the ship and everyone in her would go sky-high.

Mr. Blackmore's first anxiety was for the safety of his crew. First, he ordered steam to be shut off. Then he told his men to abandon ship by jumping overboard. This they did, to be picked up by boats from the other trawlers close by.

But Blackmore was not leaving the ship himself. As he says: 'I retained only the second hand on board with me, a fine type of trawler-man called Edward Dollin, of Fleetwood. The mine couldn't be slipped without risking explosion, so in its upside-down position we first lashed it as securely as we could, and then removed the horns.'

As the safety-plug was against the ship's side it was impossible to get at the base of the mine and remove the detonator, so having removed the horns, with Blackmore standing on the mine to do so, they lashed it again so that it could not possibly move, and re-embarked the crew. 'We were exceedingly lucky to be able to do the job without an accident. Even then the crew didn't feel too happy.'

H.M.S. *TOTNES.*

1.30 P.M., DECEMBER 29, 1916.   TUGS TAKING SHIP INTO HARWICH.

p. 181.]

Little wonder !

There being no tools on board to complete the work, the motor-boat was sent in to Portsmouth to bring them out. She got back again at about 5 p.m., when the detonator was removed, and the mine and sinker were salved. ' It was a long job in the dark, and we didn't get back into harbour until nearly midnight.

' I am afraid we got more praise than we really deserved for this job,' Mr. Blackmore adds. ' All the same, it was quite my most hectic half-hour during the whole of my five years' minesweeping.'

For an example of cool courage and persistence in the face of horrible danger, this incident is difficult to beat. The bravery of Edward Dollin, who remained on board to help his commanding officer, was officially recognised by the award of the Distinguished Service Medal and promotion to skipper R.N.R. Mr. Blackmore, besides being mentioned in despatches, was specially promoted to lieutenant for gallantry.

He served nearly five years in minesweepers during war and the dangerous post-war mine clearance, and besides his well-earned special promotion and ' mention ', received the Distinguished Service Cross and the French Médaille Militaire. His O.B.E. came later, and he finally retired from the Navy as a lieutenant-commander in 1933, having begun his career as a bluejacket boy in one of the training-ships forty years before.

4

The salvage of German mines was always desirable in case improvements or modifications had been effected. It was invariably a dangerous operation, as it was common knowledge that the only thing about a German mine which was inefficient was the safety device *supposed* to render it harmless when it broke adrift from its moorings.

On the night of August 7–8, 1915, the German auxiliary minelayer *Meteor*, as already mentioned, laid 380 mines in the approach to the Moray Firth. The first notification of their existence came from a trawler

13

minesweeper carrying out a routine sweep on the morning of August 8. The same day the destroyer *Lynx* was sunk in the new minefield with heavy loss of life, and the sloop *Lilac* had her bows blown off. After a ten-mile channel had been cleared on either side of the Firth, in the course of which 222 mines were removed, the rest of the field was left unswept as a protection against similar attacks.

In the course of sweeping in this same area in September, 1916, a mine was caught and buoyed. The next task was to get it into shallow water for eventual recovery and examination. This was accomplished by two pulling boats, which passed a wire and a long loop of chain round the mine and brought it to the surface. Then, with great risk and no little skill in the heavy swell, the mine was cut adrift from its moorings and towed into Burghead Bay, where it was re-moored for the night. By this time it was dark, and throughout the night the paddle minesweeper *Glen Usk* kept her searchlight on the dangerous object and warned off approaching vessels.

The next morning the mine was towed inshore by the boats of the *Glen Usk* and *St. Elvies*, where it was safely beached, and rendered harmless. This operation was exceedingly risky, more especially because the detonator was jammed. However, the mine and its sinker were recovered complete, and the experts were able to carry out successful experiments.

Commander Gervase W. H. Heaton, R.N., was in charge of the paddlers. 'I beg to bring to your notice', he wrote in his report, 'the magnificent work of the individual boats' crews, who, when within a few feet of the mine, carried out their work jokingly – and especially the names of Temporary Lieutenant W. Highton, R.N.R., of the *St. Elvies*, and W. Westborough, Chief Petty Officer of the same ship. This officer and petty officer never left the mine for a moment, and by their resource and endeavours were mainly responsible for the safe accomplishment of the task.'

'Much ingenuity, pluck and good seamanship were shown,' Admiral Sir John Jellicoe wrote to the Admiralty. 'The general tone of those present', reported Captain Preston, who was in command of the Fleet Sweepers at the time, 'struck me in the light of a picnic party.'

What a picnic !

5

One wishes it were possible to obtain the names of many brave men hidden in official records – the trawler skipper who picked up a drifting mine in the dark and towed it clear of Eastbourne pier ; the young signalman who, after his vessel had been mined, took off his own lifebelt, put it on his unconscious captain, and went down with his ship ; the man who amputated a comrade's leg jammed in some wreckage after a ship had been mined ; the survivor on a Carley float who resuscitated his friend by artificial respiration, during the course of which the float twice capsized.

These gallant fellows, and many others, must perforce remain anonymous. For every really courageous act that reached the ears of authority, there were hundreds which passed unnoticed.

In June, 1915, the Germans had extended their minelaying to the White Sea, where Archangel was being used as a port for supplying our Russian allies with munitions and stores. At the request of the Russian Government British trawlers were sent thither to assist in sweeping and in keeping open a clear channel until the sea became frozen over.

Six trawlers were fitted out at Lowestoft with a couple of supply ships, the latter carrying stores for three months. Each of the trawlers was armed with a 12-pounder gun, and one, the leader, had wireless telegraphy. They were the *Bombardier*, *Sir Mark Sykes*, *T. R. Ferrens*, *Granton*, *Lord Denman* and *St. Cyr*, commanded by Acting-Commander Leopold A. Bernays, R.N., in the first-named.

Now Bernays had retired from the Navy before the war and was living in Canada when it started. Returning at once to England he had served in minesweepers, and had helped to clear the Scarborough and Tory Islands minefields. He was strictly unconventional in his methods, and had what is popularly known as ' a way with him '. Utterly fearless, he invariably steamed his own ship first over a minefield to show the others how easy it was. He had succeeded in infusing something of his own enthusiasm and contempt of danger into his fishermen crews. They understood and respected him, and would have followed him to the death, if need be.

The little flotilla left Lowestoft on June 22, bound first for Lerwick, in the Shetlands. Thence they steamed across the North Sea, and reached Alexandrovsk, on the Murman Coast, on July 6. They began work at once, and in three days several mines had been destroyed.

On July 13 the trawler *T. R. Ferrens* was mined ; but within twelve days of the expedition's arrival fifty mines had been swept up. By August 10 the little force had been augmented by a collier and two more trawlers from England. As yet, however, no Russian patrol craft had appeared to help in the work, only one miserable little steamer being engaged in stopping ships off Sviatoi Noss.

The enemy had skilfully laid the mines off headlands and across the tracks taken by shipping going to Archangel. The work of clearing them was carried out with the greatest difficulty in vile weather, and the Russians gave little or no help. Indeed, furious at a Russian Admiral's refusal to send his ship to sea in bad weather of which the British trawlers thought nothing, Bernays, forceful and unconventional as ever, emphasised his displeasure by pulling the Allied beard !

In October when the armed yacht *Aegusa* arrived in North Russia with Rear-Admiral Phillimore[1] on board, this officer reported that 150 mines had been destroyed by our White Sea trawlers and a few by the Russians. It was impossible to sweep up all the

---

[1] Now Admiral Sir Richard Phillimore, G.C.B., K.C.M.G. In the autumn of 1915 he was on his way to Petrograd as the head of a Naval Mission to Russia.

rest before the ice set in for the winter, which it did in November.

Commander Bernays, instead of being court-martialled for tugging the beard of an Allied Flag Officer – which was the literal fact – received the C.M.G. for his services. He afterwards volunteered for ' Q ' ships, and in command of one of these he was killed in action with a German submarine.[1] He was a great loss to the Service.

6

The closing of the Black Sea and Baltic brought the northern route to Russia into great prominence. During 1917 huge quantities of munitions, stores and fuel were sent to Murmansk, which was free of ice all the year round and was connected by rail to Petrograd in 1917, and to Archangel, which was open from July to October.

When the Russian débâcle came in this same year, Allied ships and troops were sent to North Russia and remained in occupation until September, 1919. The main object was to prevent Germany from using the ports as submarine bases, and to keep open a line of communication for supporting the Anti-Bolshevik forces under Admiral Kolchak.

It is unnecessary here to describe that unprofitable Arctic campaign which was one of the numerous side-shows of the Great War ; but, until after the Armistice, British minesweeping trawlers were employed in keeping the approach channels clear of the mines which were constantly laid by German submarines.

They worked in the most terrible conditions of fog, gales, snow and ice on an iron-bound coast that was practically unlit and unbuoyed.

Captain R. S. Gwatkin-Williams, C.M.G., R.N., who commanded the *Intrepid* in the Arctic in 1916 and

[1] Commander Bernays' ' Q ' ship was the 1,016 ton *Vala* with a speed of no more than eight knots and an armament of four 12-pounders. She sailed from Milford Haven on August 19, 1917, and her last reported position was in the Bay of Biscay at 3 a.m. on August 20. It was not known until after the war that she was sunk with all hands by one of the larger U-boats on August 21.

1917, has described the work in his book *Under the Black Ensign*, written soon after the war.

There was no dry-dock available if trawlers came to grief through touching a rock and damaging their propellers.   Until a rough-and-ready method was devised of replacing these necessary adjuncts under water with the help of divers, damaged minesweepers had to be beached on the only known strip of sandy shore in the neighbourhood.   It was only partially sheltered, and 100 miles away from the mother-ship.   Here, nevertheless, trawlers were put ashore at high water, fires were built under their sterns when the tide fell sufficiently, the damaged propellers were dragged off the shaft when the heat had expanded them, and new ones keyed on in place.   Throughout this operation the beached ships were exposed to any sudden blow that might come in from seaward.   There was always the chance that they might be pounded to pieces by the sea before the job was finished.

On August 7, 1916, the trawler *John High*, commanded by her skipper of the same name, was blown up on a minefield laid by an enemy submarine.   A heavy sea was running at the time, and of her crew of sixteen men there was only one survivor, the mate. When the explosion took place he happened to be standing in the bows with his lifebelt on.   Blown overboard, he was rescued by another trawler with no injury beyond the shock caused by his immersion in an icy sea.   In less than a week from August 6, however, the trawlers had swept up and destroyed 29 mines out of the submarine's possible cargo of 36.

Because of the strong tide, which dragged the mines to a depth of forty or fifty feet when it was running, and, when it slackened, allowed them to float up to the surface, the trawlers were in constant danger of being blown up.   This of course applied in other cases besides the Murman Coast and White Sea ; but on more than one occasion sweepers found themselves in a regular nest of trouble with half a dozen mines breaking surface all round them.

' Heavy gales with snow were becoming increasingly

frequent, greatly hampering the trawlers in their work,'
Captain Gwatkin-Williams writes.   Nevertheless, the
shipping was organised in convoys, each convoy being
conducted through the most dangerous waters in the
wake of a group of trawler sweepers.   The weather was
often such that the trawlers were unable to keep their
kites out in the mountainous seas, and more than once
had them swept back on board by particularly heavy
waves.

7

Another true tale of the minesweepers in the White
Sea is told by an officer who served there in the *Iphigenia* [1] in 1915 and 1916.

Potatoes had run out.   Men were becoming discon-
tented.   Officers from the trawlers came on board the
Iphigenia to complain, and were shown the telegrams
demanding potatoes that had already been sent off.
Everything that could be done had been done.   They
must pacify their men, and possess their souls in
patience.

The trawler officers replied that they were quite
satisfied that this was so, but was the captain [2] of the
Iphigenia aware that there was a Russian ship with a
cargo of potatoes lying in the harbour whose crew had
refused to sell them ?

' Well, if they refuse to sell, that ends the matter,'
said the captain, to which the reply was a somewhat
doubtful affirmative.

The subject was then adroitly switched over to
the question of one of the trawlers in the group which
had been under repair.   She had done a steam trial
that day, and was due to go to sea at daylight on the
morrow.   The group officer – a lieutenant R.N.R. –
and the skipper of the trawler, however, professed to

[1] The old *Iphigenia* and her sister-ship, the *Intrepid*, started the war
as minelayers.   Both afterwards served in the White Sea as mother-
ships for the minesweeping trawlers.   Both ended their useful 28-year
lives as block-ships during the well-known attack on Zeebrugge on
April 23, 1918.

[2] Now Captain Kenneth A. F. Guy, D.S.O., R.N. (Retd.).

be dissatisfied with the result of the trial. Could
they have another ' run round ' just to see all was
well before going out minesweeping? After some
discussion permission was given for the trawler to
slip and to steam round the harbour that evening.
This she did, finally to return alongside the *Iphigenia*
late at night after that vessel's captain had gone to
bed.

The trawlers went to sea early next morning. When
the *Iphigenia's* captain came up from his cabin some
time later, it was to see sack after sack of potatoes
piled on his upper deck. He scratched his head and
wondered. He asked a few judicious questions. Nobody seemed to know very much. Later in the day,
he received a wireless signal from the group officers'
trawler, miles away out at sea – ' Hope you are enjoying the spuds.'

Having been out at sea for their allotted time, the
trawlers returned to harbour and went alongside their
parent-ship. Then the truth of what had come to be
known as ' the spud mystery ' came out.

The evening the trawler had been allowed to do her
wholly unnecessary steam trial, she had cruised about
until after dark. Then, putting out all her lights, she
crept slowly and silently alongside the Russian ship
laden with potatoes.

The Russian discipline was somewhat lax. Every
man except one was ashore, and the solitary watchman was fast asleep upon his potato bags. Approaching him cautiously from behind, the visitors fell upon
him, pulled a convenient sack well down over his head
and shoulders, and securely lashed him. Then they
got busy and hoisted out what potatoes they required
into the trawler waiting alongside.

The next part of the programme required a certain
amount of strategy.

After waiting a decent interval, the pirates ' started
up a racket on board with lots of shouting', and released the watchman, who naturally wanted to know
what was happening.

' We are the British patrol,' the trawler officer explained. 'We saw lights over here and came to see what was happening.'

The Russian could only state what had occurred – that he had been surprised and lashed up in a potato sack, while some persons unknown had robbed the ship. In a terrible state of alarm, he declared he would be shot for neglect of duty.

The officer in charge of the 'British patrol' admitted the serious nature of the outrage. It was dreadful to think that thieves had visited the ship while the watchman was asleep. But still, as the watchman *had* been slumbering while he should have been alert . . . well, things looked rather bad for the watchman.

What should be done, the Russian wanted to know.

The British officer pretended to consider the matter. Finally, he advised the watchman to say nothing of the affair, and to trust to luck that the potatoes would not be missed. And if he would hand over six bags of potatoes as a little – er – present, the 'British patrol' would refrain from making a report and would see that the watchman was kept out of trouble. What about it ?

The watchman willingly agreed, and proceeded to hoist out six more bags of potatoes in addition to those already stolen. There the incident closed, and the trawlers and the *Iphigenia* got their spuds.

The pirate-in-chief on this occasion was Lieutenant A. E. L. Rudd, R.N.R., who was very ably assisted by all the hard cases in his group of trawlers.

Arthur Rudd, who had joined the Royal Naval Reserve as a young sub-lieutenant at the outbreak of the war, was enterprising and utterly fearless. On his return from the White Sea, he was put in command of a group of minesweeping trawlers working from Lowestoft, his 'flagship' being the *Bracklyn*, a fine Fleetwood vessel whose skipper, Radmore, was described by a senior officer who knew him, as 'one of the finest in the Service'.

The sweep for which the *Bracklyn's* group was responsible was on the Smith's Knoll section, and just before

dark on the evening of May 10, 1917, they picked up
a mine near one of the buoys marking the Cross Sand
– Smith's Knoll Channel.

The usual sweeping formation was as shown in the
diagram, and it was Rudd's invariable habit to station
his flagship on the inside of the second pair of trawlers,
which facilitated signalling and gave him more complete control. In other words, he occupied the position marked X.

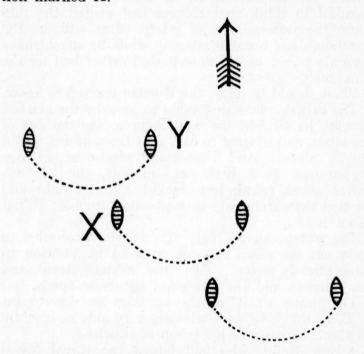

On the morning of May 11, when sweeping was recommenced, he adopted his usual formation and swept
up nearly to the buoy where the mine had been found.
Then, to the surprise of all the skippers, he turned the
group round and swept back. Next, for the first time
on record, he changed the order, putting his own ship
in front on the inside of the channel in the position
marked Y.

He then turned again and swept right up to and past
the buoy where the mine had been found the evening

before. The *Bracklyn* struck a mine and sank, the gallant Rudd and Skipper Radmore both being lost.

As writes Captain W. M. Bruce, who was Port Minesweeping Officer at Lowestoft at the time – ' Rudd had swept up *hundreds* of mines before, and had never shown any signs of nerves.   If there is anything in the Scots word " fey ", I think this is a wonderful example of it.'

Rudd *must* have had some premonition that the risk of being blown up was greater than usual, and put himself and his own ship in the most dangerous position.

CHAPTER XI

A LIEUTENANT-COMMANDER'S STORY

NOTE. – *The following chapter has been sent to me by Captain H. T. Baillie-Grohman, D.S.O., O.B.E.   It is printed after slight alteration.*

I

WRITING now after a lapse of more than sixteen years, it is not perhaps surprising that my chief memories of minesweeping should be their re-action on myself. So, if the first person singular is unduly to the front in these few pages, please excuse it.

My minesweeping experiences began with my appointment to the command of H.M.S. *Gentian*, a new ' Flower ' class sloop just completing at Greenock in January, 1916. My previous ship had been the *Ghurka* in the Dover Patrol, which was being fitted with new water barrels to her boilers at Portsmouth. As this was to take two months, the officers and most of the men were soon distributed amongst other ships.

Although the *Ghurka* had been a good command for a young lieutenant of 6 years seniority, being a 1,000-ton ' Tribal ' destroyer in the Dover Patrol, I felt that a sloop was more of a ship, and was very pleased to go to the *Gentian*. I stood by her for fourteen days while she was being completed, when she was intended to go to the Mediterranean. The day before commissioning, however, we were informed she was to join the Grand Fleet Minesweepers at Scapa Flow.

Our crew numbered 96 all told, of whom 24 were Able and Ordinary Seamen, 6 of the latter being absolutely green, and nominally there for instruction. Of the remaining 18, nine were Royal Navy, or Fleet

Reserve men. The remaining nine were 'Hostility Only' men who had done no more than a few months sea time. They formed a rare mixture, and among them were a young schoolmaster, a bookmaker's clerk, a jobbing gardener, and a man who called himself an engineer. It transpired later that he was the stoker of a central-heating apparatus at a lunatic asylum.

There were no fishermen in the ships of the 1st and 2nd Fleet Minesweeping Flotillas of that time, these flotillas being formed of sloops. The fishermen were generally retained in minesweeping trawlers, and later in paddle minesweepers. There, as is well known, they did excellent work.

The proportion of inexperienced men among our stokers was about the same as the seamen. This was soon brought home to me, for on our trip from the Clyde to Scapa to join the Grand Fleet in March, 1916, we could not maintain revolutions for even six knots. We took off from Rathlin Island at dark, with the revolution indicator ordering ten knots, and next morning should have sighted the Outer Hebrides. But nothing of that sort occurred. It then transpired we had hardly been doing revolutions for six knots since sunset the night before, due to sea-sickness and inexperience. One soon got accustomed to such surprises, and learned to take them in a philosophical manner, with the mental reservation that one must not get too accustomed to taking such faults as standard, when there was no sufficient reason for it.

I was new to minesweeping, the sum total of my experience having been to see the contractors' men test the winch and the heavy wooden kite – quite 12 foot long and weighing about 25 cwt. – by towing it for a few minutes during our trials, and hoisting it on board again, an operation which nearly caused a bad accident owing to an inexperienced winchman.

On my first arrival at Scapa late at night I was sent to coal alongside a collier, and then reported on board the Senior Officer's ship, Captain Lionel G. Preston in H.M.S. *Hollyhock*.

He told me the best way for me to learn the job

was to plunge straight into it.   So far, he added, every ship but one had had an accident and damaged a man or officer during the first week or so.   He hoped I would avoid this, and said that he had arranged for me to sweep the first week with his second-in-command, Commander H. H. Holland.

I then repaired on board Commander Holland's ship.   This officer, whose sweeping partner I eventually became, gave me my first and only theoretical lesson in minesweeping – how to reeve the wires, when to put the kite down, and how to avoid a few of the many pitfalls.   The lesson lasted twenty minutes, and with half a page of notes, I made my way back to my ship to instruct the first lieutenant in the intervals of coaling.   The only text-book in those days applied to the *Skipjack* class gunboats, which hardly applied to new ships.

We left harbour early next morning, and by the Grace of Providence and good luck, my pair was the first to pick up and pass the sweep, for which piece of good fortune, we received 'Manœuvre well executed' from the S.N.O.   That day, helped by the fact that the sweep did not part, we acquitted ourselves unexpectedly well.   However, our pride was soon to receive a fall.   For the next three days we could do nothing right !

Because of our ignorance, our upper deck and forecastle was a mass of wire for three days, a kite was lost through hitting the sea bottom, and the time spent in wire splicing – we still tried the old-fashioned long slice in those days – was very great.   Nevertheless, no one was hurt.   During that period we made every mistake that could be made.   After it, I think I can say we settled down to be a fairly creditable and reliable sweeper.

It was fascinating work in many ways.   To be a good sweeper many people had to play their part efficiently day after day.   One good officer or petty officer would not make a ship good at sweeping. From the captain, who had to handle his ship at very close quarters, often in a heavy sea, to the A.B.

who let go the hangers, each one had to do his job. Co-operation was the very essence of the work.

My first lieutenant and second-in-command was an acting sub-lieutenant, just promoted from midshipman. The other officers were two R.N.R. (temporary) sub-lieutenants, one with a master's certificate, and the other with a mate's; a chief warrant mechanician R.N. of the old type, and a Scotch probationary surgeon, R.N.V.R. The elder of the two R.N.R. sub-lieutenants (he was five years older than I was) I made the navigator. Neither of these officers had been afloat in a ship flying the White Ensign before. The first time I went down to the wardroom, before dinner, I found it empty. Enquiry showed that the R.N.R. officers preferred to eat in 'their rooms', as they called their cabins in Merchant Service style, while the first lieutenant and chief engineer had followed suit. However, very soon there were no more enthusiastic followers of the mess idea than these two reserve officers. It was one of them whom I overheard referring to me as the old man! My age at the time was 28.

Just as the officers in the ship were a mixed crowd (using this term in no opprobrious sense), so were the captains of the sixteen sloops in the two flotillas. Lieutenant-Commander P. D. R. West, a survivor of the *Victoria* disaster in 1893, was about the oldest of us, while Lieutenants Hermon-Hodge, R. A. Clark, Gilbertson, Dillon and myself were the youngest. There was considerable good-hearted competition between us five in various ways, which led to greater efficiency all round.

The sweepers themselves were not all of the same class in the first half of 1916, there being two or three of the old gunboats still working with us. When I arrived in the flotilla there had recently been two ships damaged by mines, but during the eighteen months I was there, only one ship – the *Carnation* – hit a mine. This occurred while we were steaming in single line in a fog, sweeps having been slipped some time previously.

The mine, which was submerged, was seen close under the chains of the leader, the *Godetia*, and by the next astern (myself). It struck the sixth or seventh ship. The S.O.M.S. had hastily made the ' Mine close by ' signal, but there was no time for combined action, as in the low visibility it was a case of each ship for herself. So far as I remember, there was only one death caused by this mine, although the *Carnation* was out of action for some time. She was safely towed into Kirkwall.

There was one curious accident to one of the *Carnation's* crew. At the time the mine was hit, a man was in the stokers' bathroom forward, near where the mine struck. He was found shortly after the explosion outside the ship, hanging half-unconscious on to a piece of bent plating. He had been blown through the side of the ship with no further injury than a severe shock !

The ' Flower ' class sloops proved themselves sturdy ships. After the Armistice, it took two mines to sink the *Gentian* in a gale of wind.

2

The Grand Fleet Sweepers were responsible for keeping open certain defined approaches to Scapa Flow for the use of the Grand Fleet. This meant constant work, leaving harbour two hours before daylight during most of the year, and continual searching during daylight hours. After dark, we usually returned to harbour, while every third day we coaled on our return. Gales sometimes made it impossible to sweep, and these gave us an occasional day in harbour. In the summer, however, we sometimes spent as many as thirty-three consecutive days out sweeping, coaling every third day on our return to harbour.

While I was in the flotilla, Captain L. G. Preston went to the Admiralty to become Director of Minesweeping, Captain H. H. Holland becoming S.O.M.S. at Scapa. It was generally agreed that Captain

p. 192.] GERMAN MINE HOISTED ON BOARD H.M. TRAWLER *MANX KING*, OFF EASTERN APPROACH TO SPITHEAD.
DECEMBER 12, 1917.

All three photographs show mine as it eventually came to rest after being capsized by the strain on the mooring wire. In centre photograph
is Mr. Blackmore and in background Commander Salmon, R.N.R.

Laid by U.C. 200. Mine Mark V. Serial No. 10,214. Laid at depth of 18 feet. Charge 360 lb. T.N.T.

Preston had made a very great success of his job, and he was as popular as was his successor.

It is interesting to remember that in about 1916, an order came out that all minesweeping sloops were to fit strong nets immediately before and abaft the bridge, the idea being to catch the personnel on the bridge before, after being blown up into the air like acrobats, they came down on anything hard. Experience had shown that many casualties occurred in this manner. They also had sweeping mess decks, on the upper deck, where the men could mess during sweeping. But they were only used when sweeping over known minefields.

Most of the work in the Grand Fleet Sweepers was searching for mines, and making certain that certain channels were clear. Up to August, 1917, we did not find many mines in the regular Fleet channels off Scapa Flow, and those we did find were cleared with remarkable speed and efficiency.

In the *Gentian*, as in most of these ships, our work was our hobby too, and that we should never fail our partner or S.O.M.S. was a matter of honour for us all. I remember meeting one of the few active service leading seamen of the *Gentian* eleven years afterwards. As all men do, he looked upon his time in the ship as a happy memory. I remembered he was the P.O. in charge of the sweeping gear, and consequently had the privilege of sleeping in the minesweeping storeroom. He said he well remembered that on joining the *Gentian*, I had sent for him and told him his job, and then said – ' You understand that the efficiency of all this material is in your hands. You have not only to think sweep-wires, and to sleep amongst them, but have to dream about them as well.' He added with a grin that that was the sort of talk he liked.

In August, 1917, after serving eighteen months in the *Gentian* as a Grand Fleet Sweeper, I was appointed to relieve Commander C. C. Bell in the command of a flotilla of paddle minesweepers based at Newcastle. This flotilla was known as the ' *Totnes*

14

Unit ', and consisted of six Admiralty Paddle Mine-sweepers. H.M.S. *Totnes*, the Senior Officer's ship, had lately had her bows blown off, but was now afloat again with a new bow fitted.

It was a strange sensation to take a paddler to sea for the first time, for her beam of over 60 feet over the paddle-boxes was very large for her length of 240 feet. She was like an old duck, and I wondered how on earth I would manage. They were clumsy ships to handle. Both paddles were on one engine, and there was no putting one paddle ahead and the other astern. Both had to go one way or the other. I only remained a short time at Newcastle, and was then ordered round to Oban with the flotilla. Here I found Commander Eric Harbord commanding a flotilla composed of the old *Skipjack* class gunboats. I was under his orders for operations at first, though I gradually came to be directly under the Director of Minesweeping at the Admiralty.

It was a great pleasure to be under such a fine officer as Harbord. His sweeping ground consisted of certain channels between the latitude of Oban and Stornaway, while mine was from Oban down to the Cumbrae, afterwards extended to Liverpool, and including the N.E. coast of Ireland. My job was to hold my ships ready to proceed at short notice to any spot in this area where mines might be found, and to find a channel for merchant traffic. When no mines were about, I carried out certain routine sweeps of channels usually used by ships coming to the Clyde from the North.

In the spring of 1918, when the Convoy System became more general, a weekly convoy used to as-semble in Lamlash and I had to sweep ahead of it to the Mull of Cantyre. In the weather usually pre-vailing it was not an easy job to keep my ships in constant readiness whilst carrying on the other duties. One of my handicaps was the attitude of certain local S.N.O.'s who objected to giving out stores, etc., out of working hours. However, I was having no nonsense. The magic words, ' I am here under the

direct orders of the Admiralty', used as a last resource, *eventually* opened all storeroom doors at
whatever time we required them, whether at Oban,
in the Clyde or in the N.E. Ireland area.

Owing to defects, the flotilla was seldom at full
strength. The chief causes of weakness were the
paddle boxes, which were not sufficiently robust to
withstand the strain, while the special metal mixture
for the float brushes (of which there was a large
number) was often not up to standard. It was a
long job to put them right. Very often one of the
Skipjack class would be lent me by Commander
Harbord for a few weeks at a time, while some of
the new 'Hunt' and 'Town' class minesweepers, directly
after being completed on the Clyde, were attached
to my flotilla for short periods. This was not a
very satisfactory arrangement, and often caused considerable delay owing to the new ships not having
got into their stride.

The captains of the ships in my flotilla were, with
one exception, all much older than myself. One old
gentleman, who had been a Hughli pilot, was old
enough to be my grandfather. But they all worked
together, and with me, with utmost willingness.

The youngest C.O. was a New Zealander called
Holm. His father had been owner of several sailing
ships and the son had been brought up in sail in
consequence. This young officer handled his ship
in a magnificent manner.

I should mention that most of my sweeping area
was shallow with a rocky bottom. This meant frequent parting of sweep-wires, and the amount of
sweeping carried out depended very much on the
manner and speed with which sweeps were picked up
again after carrying away. This again depended
on the handling of the ship by the captain.

One C.O. we used to call 'Grandfather' was a
source of some trouble to me, especially from the
administrative point of view. He once had eight
leave breakers who, in spite of previous warning,
missed the ship when sailing. It was decided to

punish them by warrant, but bad weather prevented communication between ships for a few days or so. I eventually sent a boat over to collect the names and certificates of the men for their warrants to be made out, preparatory to submitting them to the S.N.O. ashore. Grandfather wrote to me that he had already made out the warrants and read them on his own. He had no power to do this, and the resultant tangle took months to clear up.

There was one officer who re-discovered a liking for strong liquor. I had to speak to him several times about it. However, I had noticed that whenever his wife, a very masterful type of woman, was in the port, he was a model of good behaviour. It was only when she was away, or he was in another port, that he broke out. Thinking that to get on with the work was my chief object, and not courts martial, I addressed him seriously, and gave him the option of bringing his wife down to any port where we were to be based for more than a week, or of being court martialled on the spot for his last outbreak. He selected the wiser course, and for a few months there was no more trouble.

At the end of this period, he was, by order of the Admiralty, detached from my flotilla (we were at Troon at the time) and instructed to call in for orders at Ardrossan, about eight miles up the Clyde from Troon, and thence to proceed North-about to the Firth of Forth. He left harbour the next morning early, and I happened to be on deck. After banging his ship twice against other ships in the harbour at full speed, and as much like a streak of lightning as a paddler ever could be, he scraped out of the small entrance. But he did not reach Ardrossan without trouble. He piled his ship on some flat rocks just outside that harbour on a perfect June morning, in full view of all the unco' guid going to Chapel.

When the local S.N.O. came on board some time later, he was found sitting on the telegraphs, with these still indicating full speed ahead. The ship got off without much damage, but it was recommended that the C.O. should be at once removed to another sphere of activity. For some reason, however, he was allowed to proceed to Oban, where his officers called on the local S.N.O. in a body and protested against going on with him in command, as he was again the worse for liquor. The final result was a court martial as soon as he arrived on the east coast. He was a gallant fellow who had every excuse to serve ashore on account of his age alone ; but he liked minesweeping and stuck out the bad weather of that whole winter in the west coast of Scotland. To appreciate what that meant, one had to experience it.

CHAPTER XII

SOME SKIPPERS' YARNS

I

AS I have complained elsewhere, the greater number of trawler skippers – at any rate those of them who swept for mines during the war – seem strongly averse to putting their experiences on paper. They are essentially men of action, not of the written word. To a score or more of letters, I have received only two replies.

Earlier in this book I have quoted the opinions held by certain naval officers of the trawler personnel under their command during the war. Here I cannot refrain from quoting the words of Commander (now Captain) C. H. G. Benson, D.S.O., R.N., who was minesweeping for nearly three years, and the Mine Clearance Officer in the Northern Area during the post-war period. He writes:

'I cannot allow the opportunity to pass without expressing my admiration for the skippers and men of the R.N.R. (T) with whom it has been my good fortune and privilege to have served. By association with them I have learnt something of the qualities of seamanship with which those who earn their living in small fishing craft are imbued. Two incidents occur to me as typical.

'In the first case a trawler skipper, during the influenza epidemic, had eight men down out of his total complement of twelve. The remaining four managed to take their ship to sea, pass sweeps, and carry out the day's work. A trimmer was running the engines, a deck-hand fired the boiler under his direction, the cook worked on deck, and the skipper was at the wheel.

'The second case was on an occasion when, endeavouring to comply with an urgent signal to search the eastern channel on the morrow, the flotilla proceeded at their best speed from Cape Wrath to Freswick Bay. As night fell, they were caught in the Pentland Firth in a dense fog. The tides were strong and the currents erratic, and with great difficulty and taking every precaution, I managed to get into Freswick Bay about three hours later to find the other ten trawlers, under their own skippers, anchored before me.

'Many were the occasions, in open anchorages in mid-winter, at night, when the vigilance and good seamanship of the skippers and crews extricated their ships from dangerous positions. It was a liberal education to see them handling their little ships when passing sweeps in a gale of wind. In these days of rapid changes and new inventions *it is apt to be forgotten that it is principally upon the men that real success and efficiency depend. While there are such men to man the auxiliary forces of the Navy, there need be no anxiety for the future.*'

The italics are mine.

All the more is it to be regretted, then, that the number of our fishermen tends steadily to decline year by year. As an Aberdeen trawler skipper wrote to me in 1932: 'Our business has been such a heart break these last few months that it is almost impossible to take an interest in anything. What with weather, slack fishing, and if we got home with a decent catch we have got nothing for it. It has just been a case of set your teeth and bear it.'

But if the trawlers are hard hit, the herring fishermen in their drifters are strangled. Large numbers of the drifter-men and others ashore dependent on their labours have been thrown out of work, few new drifters have been built, the fishing often has to shut down before the season has ended, while quantities of herring, valuable as food, are thrown back into the sea or converted into fertiliser at prices which do not pay for their catching.

In more prosperous times about 80 per cent. of

British-caught herring went abroad in one form or another – sometimes fresh, but usually pickled or salted. Russia, Germany, Poland and the Baltic States were the chief markets, but their demand has now shrunk to the most modest proportions. About 66 per cent. of the British drifter fleet is over twenty years old, and their owners cannot afford to replace them.

It is a surprising fact that not more than 18 per cent. of British-caught herring find their way to British consumers. The total catch in 1933 was only about 40 per cent. of that for 1913, while the home consumption has dropped 55 per cent. in the same twenty years. In the words of a report [1] on the herring industry presented to Parliament by the ' Sea Fish Commission for the United Kingdom ' : ' If the housewife came to realise their ' (the herrings') ' vitamin content and could rely upon their quality, price would be partly offset by value.'

The standard of living in Britain has increased, and it is surprising to think how little the average household spends on fish. Out of every £100 spent upon food, £34 goes upon meat ; £22 on dairy produce ; £11 on cereals ; £8 each on sugar and fruit ; £7 each on vegetables, and eggs and poultry ; £3 on fish. Thus 34 per cent. of the national housekeeping money goes on meat, which is largely imported, and only 3 per cent. on British-caught fish !

The fishing industry is a story in itself. What should be emphasised is that if it be suffered further to decline, an important auxiliary to the Navy declines with it.

2

Here is the war story in brief of Mr. John E. Harwood, now a Skipper R.N.R., and, at the time of writing, in command of the Aberdeen trawler *Hannah E. Reynolds.*

' I joined up about the beginning of '15, and had been trawl fishing before then. At this time we had

[1] Cmd. 4677. 1934.

to produce two years' deep-sea fishing discharges before they would have us ; but it wasn't very long after that practically anyone could wangle their way into the sweepers.

' I left Aberdeen on board the trawler *Rose IV*, official number 1183. I was over eighteen months in her, and I believe it was about my happiest time in the whole of the war. We commissioned at Pompey ' – Portsmouth – ' and left there with orders to take part in a submarine chase going on outside. After that we had to open sealed orders and carry on to our new base. Our orders were for Holyhead, but the funny thing was there wasn't a soul aboard who knew where Holyhead was.

' About Christmas, 1916, we were sent to Portland. I was a signalman about that time. We were put on to patrolling off the Casquets. My word, but we had some weather to contend with. We worked fourteen days out and seven days in. From Portland we were sent back to Pompey, and then we really knew what the trawlers were doing.

' We were put into a section of sweepers, and used to sweep daily between the Owers and the Nab light-ship. One day we were sweeping and got seven mines laid by a German submarine. Seven again next day in exactly the same place. A third day we were getting them again, when the signalman in our opposite number, the *Apley*, sent me the signal – " This is the last lap for England, home and beauty. Give her hell ! " meaning to get some more power into our sweeping.

' Then, bang ! Off goes a mine under our port quarter, which parted our sweep-wire and kite-wire. The *Apley* was blown up a few weeks later, and there were only two or three survivors. Then we were put on to the French Coal Transport, and went across to France with convoys every night. It was just a case of hell-for-leather all the time from St. Helens to Havre. It was a monotonous job, though the sub-marines were active and took a fair toll.'

From about October, 1917, Harwood spent a couple

of months ashore at Portsmouth qualifying as a gun-layer and for promotion to ' second hand ', otherwise second-in-command of a trawler. And at the beginning of 1918 he was sent to join H.M.S. *Hannibal* at Alexandria, doing some of the journey by train. He spent eight or nine days in one train, and ' could nearly have walked it as quick '. Then on to Alexandria in an Australian troopship escorted by two Japanese destroyers.

There he joined the trawler *Margaret Duncan* the same day as Lieutenant Beckett, ' ex-skipper of a private yacht and a proper little toff. The first job we were on was escorting from Alexandria to Bizerta. It was some run – over 1,000 miles – and I think the way that it was carried out was simply marvellous. The last few months of the war our lieutenant was Senior Naval Officer on the Palestine coast. We had all sorts of jobs to contend with, sometimes on patrol, sometimes sweeping, then convoying and carrying stores and mails. We also took down the Egyptian Labour Corps as the troops advanced.

' After the Armistice we were told off to sweep up the mines off the coasts of Egypt and Palestine. At Alexandretta we met a British sweeper called the *Robert Drummond*, which had just picked up the survivors of a French sweeper called the *Pavot*. We got the plans of the minefield from the Turkish Consul, and the mines were laid in the form of an arrow with the point directed at a low-lying sandy beach, which nobody in his senses would have approached in a ship. They were only about 18 inches below water, so we located them first by sweeping with our small boats. It was hard work with four oars, and one had to be very careful not to dig too deep with an oar, or else it would have been " Ta ta, Bella ! " After marking the spots where we found mines we dropped small buoys. Then our trawler connected up a wire to her opposite number, the *Gloria*, and brought them to the surface. A drifter followed behind and sank them by gun fire.

' The natives heard all the explosions, and when

we got back to our anchorage they used to be all out
in their boats to meet us dressed up in their Sunday
best. – Afterwards, we were one of the first ships to
go to Beirut, and got in there on October 2, 1918,
about two days after the Turks and Germans evacuated
it. What a sight met our eyes ! Starvation was
rampant. The population was nothing but living
skeletons. The only decent-looking persons we saw
(by that I mean people who seemed to have had any
food at all) were the girls, who had been kept for the
enemy's own convenience. We were welcomed with
open arms wherever we went. "Vive L'Angleterre"
was their cry there, and there seemed nobody like
a Britisher to those poor souls.

'Britain wasn't very long in getting ships loaded
with food for them, and everyone lent a hand at unloading them. The people seemed to be dead to all
surroundings before that.

'After we had cleared up all the stray mines, all
the trawlers and drifters were sent to Port Said, where
they were docked and painted and sent home in convoys. The drifters were in a very poor state of repair
down below, and couldn't do more than about 6 or
7 knots, while the trawlers carried more coal and
could steam 9 or 10. So we put the ends of our sweep-
wires on to the drifters and helped them along.

'We left Port Said about the beginning of April,
1919, in beautiful weather, and went off with whistles
blowing and long paying-off pendants flying from our
masts. Our first port of call was Malta, and we got
a pretty stiff westerly breeze before we got there, the
result being that one of the drifters had to be con-
demned as the stem was practically pulled out of her.
We spent about $2\frac{1}{2}$ days coaling and watering, and
then went on to Gibraltar, where we were kept 9 or
10 days as they were making smaller convoys and
letting us out in relays.

'From Gib we went to Corcubion in Spain. We
were going to Ferrol, but some of the ships ran short
of coal or stores. The Spaniards didn't half charge
us for them – 10*d*. a lb. for potatoes, and everything

else correspondingly dear. We had a splendid run across the Bay, slipped the drifter at Falmouth and carried on to Portland, where we were put to anchor for a few days in quarantine before being allowed alongside the quay. We only parted our thin tow-ropes five times during the whole long journey which took 6 weeks.

' After the spell of quarantine most of the crew were sent home. We were left with a skeleton crew of 6 and took the ship to Fleetwood, and then on to Liverpool where we handed her over to her owners. I was there about a fortnight awaiting demobilisation. I got my orders about 11 a.m., and was up before the doctor, paymaster and everything cleared up and off home by 1 p.m.'

Thus ended Mr. Harwood's war, during which he saw a good deal of the world he might not have seen otherwise.

' Please excuse bad writing and paper,' he adds. ' I am writing this while my ship is dodging a westerly gale. We are working now away down below the Bressay shoal (off the Shetland Islands), and the sea is just boiling. We have a mine-cage (American) on our fore-deck at the present time. I haven't half cursed the Americans since the war, I can tell you. The sea bottom down this way, near the old Northern Barrage, is smothered with old mines ; but thank goodness they are all duds. But they play havoc with our gear, and give us a lot of extra work and trouble.'

3

Here is the tale of Chief Skipper Martin Fielding, who joined the R.N.R. in 1911, and has since served, as he says, ' in battleships, cruisers, minesweepers, ammunition carriers and as a temporary naval warder ashore. I was an A.B. in H.M.S. *Cæsar*, *Implacable*, *Hogue* and *Brilliant*, rather an old lot, but they all had their stories. I was blown up by a mine in the paddle minesweeper *Fair Maid* on November 9, 1916, off Lowestoft, and was wounded in the right leg by falling wreckage while swimming about in the water.

'When the war started,' he continues, 'I had served in three men-of-war and was more or less a fully trained man.   I had passed the Board of Trade signals, knew a little about torpedo work, and could strip a gun of the 12-pounder size. . . .   Just before it started I had shipped as mate of a trawler called the *Victory*.   Our destination was Heligoland, and as we steamed peacefully on a course E. ½ N. none of the crew thought about the rumours of war that we'd heard before sailing.   But I did.   I was the only reservist on board, and in my bunk was a copy of Erskine Childers' *Riddle of the Sands*.   I simply couldn't leave it alone. – Anyhow, this was four days before war was declared, and we steamed off 280 miles in fine weather.   Our skipper was nicknamed Mad Pooley, and had no use for war scares in newspapers.

'We were after soles and turbot, and arriving at our destination shot our trawl off the Amrun Bank lightship.   During our fishing operations German warships were passing in and out of the Bight and often quite close to us.   One night we saw a great Fleet quite near, and the lightship didn't seem to be functioning.   We imagined we'd got too far from it, but I think the Germans had withdrawn it.   I laughingly remarked that we must be at war, but little did I realise how true it was.

'Anyhow, there wasn't enough fish for us, so we steamed about 80 miles west.   A good job too, for all the British trawlers in that area were captured, and their crews spent a dreary four years in Germany.

'By the time I got home my calling-up papers as a reservist were at my lodgings, and I was soon on my way to Chatham.   From there they sent me to join the S.S. *Indrani*, of Glasgow, carrying ammunition for the Fleet.   Our first destination was Scapa Flow . . . and was there when a German submarine was thought to be lurking about.   As we had about 600 tons of 12-inch, 6-inch and other ammunition on board, we were ordered to weigh anchor !

' We eventually steamed half-way round the United
Kingdom calling at different places to discharge our
cargo to various ships. . . . The *Indrani* was returned to her owners and I went back to barracks.
I put in a request to go to minesweepers, but the
reply was " Not granted ". Instead, I was sent to
H.M.S. *Brilliant*, Captain Harold Christian in command. She had been a gunnery training-ship previously, and it was dark with a drizzling rain and a cold
wind as I humped my bag and hammock up her
gangway.

' We coaled ship next day, and as the commissioned
gunner said – " We're going to get a medal or two
to-morrow. We bombard the Belgian coast." Away
across the Channel we steamed, and went into Dunkirk.
Just before dawn next day we prepared for sea and
cleared for action, and were soon under way for the
Belgian coast. Ahead of us was a group of minesweeping trawlers – no man-o'-war grey on their sides,
but just as they came from the fishing ports, all the
colours of the rainbow. Their fishing numbers and
port letters were boldly displayed on their bows and
sterns – G.Y. for Grimsby, H. for Hull, A. for Aberdeen,
etc. We also had several old gunboats, torpedo-
boats, the old battleship *Revenge*, and, I think, a few
French war-vessels as well.'

Mr. Fielding goes on to describe the first day's bombardment, which passed off without incident. The
Brilliant returned to Dunkirk at dusk, and that night,
having money to burn, some friends and himself
decided to break out of the ship ' and see what France
was like '. When the sentry was out of sight, half-
a-dozen of them slid down a mooring rope and got
ashore, to find themselves in a railway siding and
mixed up in a maze of fences and barbed wire. They
soon became separated, and the problem was how to
get out of the dock into the town.

Fielding found one of his companions crawling on
his hands and knees, and presently they reached some
white cattle-pens and ' climbed dozens of these fences
while steering straight for a faint light in the distance '.

Then they were suddenly challenged by a sentry. Neither of them knew a word of French, so they put their hands up and waited. A figure with a rifle and fixed bayonet 'about a yard long' appeared out of the gloom, muttering something as it came. 'The point of it was all but touching me, so I nervously said *Brilliant*, the name of my ship.'

'The result was astonishing. "Ah! The *Brilliant*!" said the sentry, as he grounded his rifle butt. Then he started to talk in almost good English – What did we boys want? – I told him he spoke very good English, and he said, "Of course I do. I was a chemist's assistant in London for ten years!" He told us we'd had a narrow escape of being shot, and then he put his arm in mine and piloted us out of the dock. . . . We wandered out into the town, and while I was looking at the statue of Jean Bart in the square, I felt a tap on my shoulder. I turned and found myself face to face with a French soldier of the Foreign Legion – or he said he was. He spoke English perfectly, and turned out to be an American. We went into a café near by, and while we were there a Belgian armoured car stopped at the doorway and the crew all came in yelling and shouting. Apparently they'd just returned after a skirmish with a German cyclist patrol somewhere near Dixmude, during which they swore they had scuppered the lot. Things got a bit wild and hilarious . . . we decided to get back to the ship before we were missed, and eventually got on board by simply walking up the gangway. Nobody spotted us.

'The next morning we were off again at dawn to bombard, and this time we didn't have it all our own way. We fired right into the different towns and hamlets along the coast in the vicinity of Nieuport and Ostend. We were so close in that one could almost see the people on the beach. The after 6-inch gun, manned by marines, let out a vigorous cheer during the firing, and on enquiring what it was all about, they said they had sunk a submarine. But our captain, as cool as ever, discovered it to be a

wooden box, and remarked that half of us had submarines on the brain, etc., and that we were getting
panicky. In fact he brought the *Brilliant* out of
range, mustered nearly all of us near the after part,
and told us the tale. It was rather a long speech ;
but addressing the officers and men, especially those
survivors of the *Hogue, Cressy* and *Aboukir*,[1] of which
we had quite a few, he said, " Let's have no more
of this nervousness because of submarines, etc." [2]

' At about 11 a.m. we ceased firing and were ordered
aft. It was decided that we should lower our boats,
and with rifles and machine guns storm these places
under cover of the big guns. This may not be official,
but it's true. I don't profess to know whose orders
they were. " Volunteers for the boats to go ashore ! "
was the cry. Of course everyone wanted to go. I
was to be part of a machine-gun's crew. We were to
row like hell to the beach and dig ourselves in, and
then meet half the German artillery emplaced in the
town. The zero hour was about 12 o'clock. We had
rum served out, and I was soon busy filling or feeding
cartridge belts for the Maxim gun with a kind of coffee
machine. While doing this our guns opened fire.
So did all the ships assembled, and for an hour hell
was let loose.

' Then Jerry started in earnest – whizzbangs, coal-
boxes and other things bracketed the old *Brilliant*,
some three yards over and some three yards short.
Then they began to hit. Our port 4·7 inch was put out
of action and the gun's crew killed or wounded ; boats
were smashed, and the fire control was put out of use.
It became necessary to use independent firing, with
someone on the bridge shouting the range through a
megaphone. Everyone seemed to be shouting – " More
lyddite ! " " More common ! " more this or that,
" Stretcher bearers ! " " Fire party ! " Captain
Christian, his cap on at a 45° angle, was asking the
gunners what they were firing at. Some fired at the

---

[1] The *Hogue, Cressy* and *Aboukir* had been sunk on September 22.
[2] Rear-Admiral Hood's reports of October 24 and 28, 1914, stated that
submarines had been sighted and attacked.

A TYPICAL MINESWEEPING TRAWLER, THE *IRENE WRAY*, COMMANDED BY LIEUTENANT RUDD, R.N.R.

lighthouse, and when that piece of masonry toppled over like a pack of cards, they cheered lustily.

'By dusk we were returning to our base to lick our wounds. A day or so afterwards we buried the dead at sea, and a very impressive ceremony it was. . . . Soon after that the *Brilliant* went to the Tyne, and then to Immingham for repairs. While we were there Admiral Ballard came to inspect us. I put in a request to see him, and told him about my unsuccessful efforts to get into minesweepers. He apparently got things going, for in 48 hours I was on my way to join the depot, H.M.S. *Pekin*, where I reported to Commander Pollen, R.N.,[1] a perfect gentleman. However, instead of minesweeping I was promoted to petty officer and put in charge of a sort of gaol – catching deserters, leave-breakers and drunks. He told me I was just the man for the job. I had two marines and four seamen under my orders, and one night a prisoner escaped by hitting the sentry under the jaw. We used to take parties of prisoners up to the gaol at Hull. This was in March, April and May, 1915. In the meantime I was studying for my skipper's certificate at the night school for fishermen. Then I was relieved in my gaoler's job by a sergeant of marines, and was sent to sea as mate of Minesweeper 452, a trawler.

'Three days afterwards I saw my first mine floating near the mouth of the Humber. Three or four sweepers stopped to sink it by rifle fire, and several of our men were on the bridge watching their efforts. Although warned not to get closer than 200 yards, our ships were gradually drifting nearer as the mine seemed to be having a charmed life. Suddenly it became covered in a flame of fire like a Christmas pudding. It looked quite pretty. – Crash ! – Three of us in the wheelhouse were almost knocked off our feet. We hadn't seen a mine go up before, and for a moment we thought it was an earthquake, or the heavens had dropped.

'Well, I personally saw very few mines in this area, though there were plenty about. I passed for my

---

[1] Now Captain Francis H. Pollen, C.B.E., R.N. (Retd.).

15

skipper's certificate and was transferred to the *Lord Ridley*, and after a month or so to the paddle minesweeper *Fair Maid* at Lowestoft. The week I left the *Lord Ridley* she was blown up off Whitby with all hands.

'I must tell of an incident, comical, while I was in the 452, the *Vindelicia*, minesweeping in the Flamborough Head area. The signalman sighted a submarine bearing S.W. On the horizon were a cruiser and two destroyers. The sub. was reported to the skipper, H. Skinner, and the signal was soon hoisted – "Submarine bearing S.W." Meanwhile the cruiser was fast approaching. Said our skipper, "There's a boat alongside it ! " – the submarine. By now every ship was on the alert, and our skipper was heading for the cruiser. – We had no gun, of course. – But he shouted to the cruiser through a megaphone what he saw. No reply from the man-o'-war, but a flutter of flags at her masthead which read : "Investigate strange object bearing S.W. ! "

'Away we all steamed in formation getting our rifles ready, for none of the sweepers in our section had a gun at that time. Well, we arrived to find it was a huge whale, which had been a long time dead, by its smell. I wrote a bit of doggerel about it at the time :

'Now gather round, my hearties, and listen to this tale.
How the 452, a minesweeper, was diddled by a whale.
'Twas off the Point of Flambro' a submarine we spied ;
It looked a very large one, upon our starboard side.

Now submarines are funny things, and this one was a Hun.
The 452 was eager ; but we hadn't got a gun.
So we gave the information to the captain of a sloop
Who had a good quick-firer a-mounted on his poop.

The sloop sent up a signal, which gave us quite a rub,
"Investigate strange object, and *see* if it's a sub."
Our skipper got his pistol, getting ready for the fray,
"Remember it's promotion, also lots of extra pay ! "

Away we steamed toward it, all out to give it hell,
And were about to ram it, when we smelt a fearsome smell.
He hadn't got no gas-masks, and the look-out calmly said,
"Why, it's a blinkin' whale, sir. It's been a long time dead ! "'

4

To continue Mr. Fielding's story :

' Broken sweep-wires were at first a great trial to the fishermen. They became foul of the sea bottom or carried away because of bad station keeping. I can remember having to splice a wire as often as six times in six hours, and some ships did more than that. The majority of fishermen had never spliced wire in their lives, and some thought a knot would do. But that was too dangerous as it caught the mine mooring. So we *had* to splice them, and I have seen arms and faces and hands badly scratched and lacerated in the process. Soon they were able to splice them in less than ten minutes.

' Well, I joined the *Fair Maid*, as second hand or mate, on October 23, 1916. I had had my skipper's certificate since March of that year, and was expecting to be promoted at any time. I had done a lot of sweeping off the N.E. coast of England. It was soon evident that paddle sweepers were just the ideal vessels for use in shallow water owing to their light draught. Also they were faster than trawlers and covered more ground. Their disadvantages were they were no use in rough weather, they had a pretty heavy coal consumption, and if lost they were more costly and difficult to replace. The casualties, too, were heavier than trawlers, for the paddlers had a crew of 40 or 50.

' The *Fair Maid* had very few fishermen. We had quite a mixture of merchant seamen and youths who hadn't much sea service. My duties were to rig up sweep gear and tend the paying-out of sweep-wires on orders from the bridge. I also had to splice all broken ends, and we had plenty. Now and again I took a watch on the bridge. We carried two R.N.R. commissioned officers on deck, and two below. Our C.O. was nicknamed "Hurricane Bill ", and he was all that and some more.

' Up anchor early one morning, and away to the Cross Sand light-ship. "Prepare for sweeping ", etc., and while superintending this work aft, I had occasion to correct one of the seamen for not turning up at his post at the proper time. This led to a bit of cursing and swearing, the discipline of some of our men not being all that it should be. The time was about 8 a.m.

'Then fate took a hand in the argument – just a sort of dull booming crash and oblivion as far as I was concerned. – I was unconscious, and travelling in an express train talking to my wife (I can never forget it), with a baby on her knee – my son. It seemed a glorious day, sun shining – lovely. We were moving at a great speed. (Now I'm no copyist in any of my writings or drawings. In describing this I tell you the truth.)

'The next sensation was delightful music as from a church organ. Then reality, and I opened my eyes. I was under water. I felt as if my lungs would burst. I was trapped amongst wires and wreckage. I kicked and struggled, and it seemed an eternity before I reached the surface. How far down I was I don't know, but it seemed a long way. On the surface men were screaming and shouting.

'The *Fair Maid* seemed to be about 100 yards away almost broken in two, but still upright and afloat. I was always a strong swimmer and tried to make for the ship, but found I couldn't move my right leg. It was numbed, like cramp ; it was freezing at the time, and little did I think I was badly hurt. Boats were being lowered by the *Duchess of Buccleuch*, the *Devonia* and other paddle sweepers. My eyes were getting dimmed. I was unknowingly bleeding to death.

'Anyhow, by a superhuman effort I got alongside the *Fair Maid*, and grabbing some rope hanging over-side pulled myself on board. The only man aft was a deckhand named Vandervoord, of Dutch descent. The man I had been rating for unpunctuality was killed outright, and his body was lying across the winch. Vandervoord pointed to my leg and yelled at the top of his voice. My sea-boot had been cut through and trouser leg torn off. I made a rough tourniquet from my tie.

'Boats were fast approaching us. There was a huge hole in our ship from the bridge to the after-well deck. Both engineer officers had lost their lives, and the magazine and after gun had gone sky-high. Soon it was seen that the *Fair Maid* was settling down, and by the time the boats were near we had to jump in the water. We were soon rescued, and I was hauled on board the *Devonia*, Commander Rice, R.N. He personally tended the wounded, speaking a cheery word to each of us as we sped our way back to Lowestoft Hospital. I was stitched up by the surgeon of H.M.S. *Havelock*, the monitor at the base there. He told me I was very lucky I did not bleed to death. The cold frost had congealed my blood.'

This account of Mr. Fielding's is borne out by the official 'Hurt Certificate' subsequently granted to him:

'This is to certify that . . . Martin Fielding O.N. 3564 A. was wounded. His ship striking a German mine at 8 a.m. he was blown in the air and fell clear of the ship into the water; and while swimming to the surface was hit by falling wreckage. He sustained severe contusion and wound in the right popliteal space of right leg, and lacerated wounds on right thigh. . . .'

After spending some time in hospital he was sent on the usual sick leave, and then to the R.N. Barracks at Chatham.

'Again I put in a request to see the Commodore, having also written a personal letter to the Admiralty, risking the consequences. . . . When I went up before the Commodore I asked to be promoted to skipper, which was so unusual that everyone stared. However, having heard my story and seen my Hurt Certificate and three good references, the Commodore was most considerate and sympathetic. "Well, young man," he says, "I'll see what I can do." A navigating officer interviewed me next day, and 48 hours later I was sent for to the Barracks and informed I had been promoted to skipper. I was sent to the warrant officers' quarters, and next day to a local tailor to be measured for uniform. Thus, in February, 1917, I became the temporary gentleman.'

After a fortnight's course at the Signal School, Fielding was ordered to Lowestoft, and on arrival reported himself to Commodore Ellison and Commander Bruce, R.N.R. – " You will be Commodore of Group 12 and take command of the trawler *Earl of Buchan*," they told me. " Excuse me, sir," said I. " I've never been in command before, let alone Commodore." (This was promotion with a vengeance.) " That's all right, skipper," they said. " Carry on." – So I carried on and next morning was a regular bundle of nerves at the head of a section of sweepers feeling our way through the Pakefield Gat and the various channels. My mate had been on the job quite a while, and had much local knowledge. At least, that's what he said.

' I found out that I was only to be in the ship for that one trip, the other skipper having gone on a fortnight's leave. Of course the whole group was in charge of a Lieutenant R.N.R., but the Commodore's ship took the lead and kept the courses for the different channels to be swept. No one can have looked at the chart more than I did that ten days. Mines were continually being swept up and exploding from different pairs of vessels. I can assure you my knees knocked, as I hadn't got over my experience in the *Fair Maid*. Anyhow, I kept as brave as it was possible. A life-jacket was continually worn by all hands.

' On the ninth day I was ordered to return to harbour next morning, being then at anchor off Sheringham. During the night it came down a thick fog, and knowing I was the leader, I was getting the wind up about the morning. Well, I for one was getting my anchor up. I flew the signal to the others to weigh anchor next morning, although I couldn't see a ship in sight. I had the mate on the lookout forward, and away we started slowly ahead. Then the fun started. You must understand I imagined the rest of the section would surely find their way home, as they were acquainted with the place. And I, the Commodore, would have been laughed at if I couldn't locate the harbour.

'Presently we came to Yarmouth Roads. It was chock-a-block with shipping, for they daren't leave the anchorage till the channel was swept by our relief group. The fog was still as thick as ever, and coming down on the flood we narrowly escaped ramming the monitor *Marshal Soult*. We just missed her by inches. Sighting a buoy soon after, my mate kept singing out – " Keep her going, skipper. You're all right ! " But we weren't all right by a long chalk. If we'd kept going we should have been ashore. It was the Scorby Sands buoy. So after that I took little notice of him and proceeded slowly S. by W. We kept the lead going continually, and eventually sighted the gasometer near Lowestoft. We could hear someone shouting, and assumed it was the harbour master. Hard-a-port ! Keep going, and hey presto ! we found ourselves in the harbour.

'As the leader of the outfit, I had to report to the base. Commander Bruce looked up at me and barked – " Where's the rest of the group ? " " Well, sir," said I, " I thought they were here ! " " No," he smiled. " They're not. But how on earth did *you* find your way in here in this fog ? I thought you told me you didn't know this locality ? In any case you should have had a pilot." I didn't like to admit my getting in was a sheer fluke, or else I shouldn't have been the blue-eyed boy any longer. Anyhow, Commander Bruce gave me my papers and sent me on leave for a week, and the group didn't fetch up until next tide.

'So I became relief skipper and had various trawlers until I took over the *Strathmory* permanently. My first week on her was enough to almost break my nerves. Mines had been reported outside the entrance of the channel to the south of Yarmouth Roads, and it was necessary to join up sweeps as soon as we weighed anchor. We weren't long before a couple of mines exploded in our sweep. They were going off like a dozen

bombardments.   I was in the second pair, keeping behind the flagship – Lieutenant Young, R.N.R., in the
Vitality.   Our sweep parted, of course, and a new
sweep was quickly got out.

'I had just taken up my station again for about ten
minutes when a column of water about 300 feet high
shot up about 200 yards ahead of us.   Then a shattering roar, and up went the *Vitality*.   It shook us
nearly out of the water.   We were quickly on the spot
and lowering our lifeboat, but were astonished to find
no one was lost.   There was a regular nest of mines in
this area, but by nightfall we had swept the channel
clear.

'One afternoon, with the sea calm and everything
apparently quiet, we were sweeping the Smith's Knoll
Channel.   I was working as "A boat" with the *Coadjutor* – Skipper Worledge – which meant I kept a steady
course while she kept station on me at about 400 yards.
We felt a pull on the sweep-wire, and when this happened, we generally increased speed if possible, and by
slacking out and heaving in, cut through the mine mooring wire.   Only one ship could do that, that is the "B
boat", in this case the *Coadjutor*.   So I kept my course
and speed, and hoisted the signal, "Mine in sweep."
But the *Coadjutor* was dropping astern and getting outside her distance.   I signalled to increase speed.   This
he apparently couldn't do, so I had to equalise my
speed to his to prevent the mine running along the
sweep-wire towards him and blowing him up.

'Looking through my glasses I saw great activity
on board the *Coadjutor* – people running forward, etc.
So I signalled by semaphore – "What's wrong?"   He
replied, "The mine is in the kite."   Now this was a
dangerous position.   They had apparently slacked
away all their kite wire in an effort to clear it, but the
chain and mooring of the mine was foul of the chains
on the kite.   Had the mine exploded in that position
nothing on earth could have saved her, and the skipper
had sent all his crew forward, leaving one hand at the
winch.   This rough sketch explains the situation,
though of course it's not drawn to scale.   You can

imagine the anxiety and fear of this crew at being in such a dangerous position.

'Then a miracle happened. The mine suddenly became clear, and jumped out of the water like a rubber ball, though that wasn't the end of the story. *I* was ordered to slip sweep and salve the mine. Why? Well, on hauling in his kite wire the *Coadjutor* found the detonator fitting jammed in his kite gear, and had signalled that information to the senior officer. I was

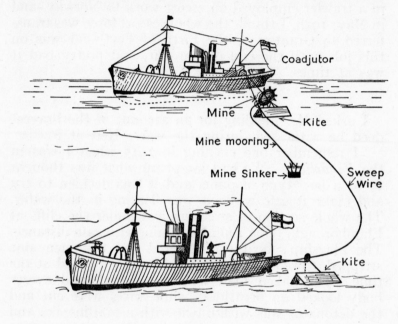

From a sketch by Chief Skipper
MARTIN FIELDING R.N.R.

unaware that the detonator was out and that the mine was safe, so when I got the signal "Salve mine", I thought the S.O. must mean "Sink mine". Meanwhile, the section had carried on and I was left alone with my German dumpling, which I sank by rifle fire.

'I returned to the group and signalled what I'd done to the S.O.'s ship, and he said, "Report to me on finishing sweeping operations." So that evening I boarded him at anchor, and went down to his cabin. "What the hell did you sink that mine for?" he demanded. "It was quite safe. I wanted you to pick it up so that our experts could have a look at it." I could only reply that I was unaware the damned thing was safe, and of course I was reported and got a strafing from the C.O. of the Base. Well, this is the end of my story of minesweeping, for nothing much else happened in that line. I was a kind of sub-divisional leader later in a trawler employed on escort work to Norway, and in May, 1918, I think, the whole escort force was transferred to Granton in the Firth of Forth. I was on this job until the end of the war, and pretty bad it was at times.'

5

I asked Mr. Fielding for an account of the bravest deed he witnessed during the war. Here it is.

'I remember one evening in 1915 when I was in the *Vindelicia*. We had swept up what was thought to be a new type of mine, and it was decided to try and make it safe while it was floating in the water. The whole section of sweepers was under the cliffs at Flamborough, lying round the mine at a safe distance. The Flagship's boat was lowered and two men, one stripped, rowed to the mine. It was very cold at the time. The naked man went overboard, and everybody looked on breathless while wires were cut and the detonator was withdrawn with a marlinspike and other tools after a long struggle. When it was done the boat returned to the trawler, and the trawler picked up the mine and brought it in to Grimsby. It took some doing, I can tell you. I believe the man who went overboard got the D.S.M.'

'While we were minesweeping,' he adds, 'we often anchored off Aldeburgh, near Orfordness. Here some kind people used to send us off woollen clothing and parcels of food, which were a godsend. I wish I could thank these people in some way, for they sent these things off to every minesweeper that anchored there, winter or summer. These kind and strange friends

have my best wishes and thanks. I also received a
parcel from a Miss Irene Wilson while I was in the
Brilliant. It was not sent to me personally, but what
I got contained her address in Southsea. I wrote and
thanked her, and we corresponded right till about 1920.
I went to see her while I was at Portsmouth when I
was just promoted to skipper, and she was a lady of
72. I am just telling you these things to show how
much we appreciated the efforts of these kind people
who looked after us so well.'

'And if you are writing a book,' Mr. Fielding goes
on, 'just say something about the engineers and black
squad cooped up below. They had very little chance
of being saved when the trawlers bumped a mine.
Their job was the most dangerous of all, and I never
knew them to fail when anything was asked of them.
They deserve all the honour and praise it is possible
to give them.'

We can agree.

6

Even after hostilities ceased the fishermen still had
to be on their guard against mines.

In December, 1919, Mr. Fielding was in command
of a steam trawler called the *Elk*. He was outward
bound and well out in the middle of the North Sea,
when, coming on the bridge as dawn was breaking, he
sighted a group of mines close ahead floating just
awash. The engines were immediately reversed, and
the ship stopped.

In all, about ten mines were sighted, and as trawlers
still carried rifles for sinking them and received a bonus
for each one destroyed, the next hour or so was spent
in disposing of them. Another trawler was engaged
in the same congenial occupation about half a mile to
the southward of the *Elk*.

The position, depth of water and a description of
the mines were entered in the official log, and having
sunk them Fielding steamed on another eighty miles
or so and shot his trawl. Eight days later he returned
to Grimsby with a 'good voyage of fish', and on re-

porting the mines received a bonus of about £20 which was shared out among the crew.

Sailing again the next day the *Elk* again returned in a week with a good catch. ' But here was stark tragedy. Opening my evening newspaper, I saw that a trawler had been blown up with all hands. It appears that the *Uvalaria*, while fishing in company with several other trawlers in the position in which we had sighted the mines the voyage before, was hauling her trawl, when a terrific explosion took place. She was blown to pieces. There were no survivors, only a few pieces of broken wreckage.'

Even thirteen years after the war mines were still occasionally being fished up in trawls. ' I got two in 1931,' our skipper says. ' Though they were very much rusted and apparently safe, it isn't much catch playing about with them. I simply clear them from the trawl, put a sling round them and carefully dump them overboard, then steam a couple of miles away before shooting my net again. I send a rough sketch of one incident, which shows the difficulty and danger of clearing the beastly things. Sometimes we got as many as three a voyage soon after the war. It became necessary to lower away the trawl again and tow along until the mine exploded or broke free. In any case the trawl was destroyed.'

In 1926 Mr. Fielding took command of the trawler *Gurth*, which had returned from sea with the skipper and mate badly injured.

The little ship had trawled up a mine, and having been in minesweepers during the war, the skipper knew how to render the mine safe. Having safely extracted the detonator, he put it on one side and dumped the mine overboard. After a day or two at sea, however, the skipper in an idle moment thought he would extract the explosive from the detonator, so he and the mate started operations in the cabin beneath the wheelhouse.

The man at the wheel was suddenly roused out of his day-dreams by a crack like a rifle-shot, and looking through the hatch into the skipper's cabin saw a sickening sight. The detonator had exploded, blown the skipper's hand off, and almost shattered the mate's face. The place looked like a shambles. The ship had to make speed for port at once. Everything was done that could be done for the two injured men. The skipper to-day has an empty sleeve. His arm is almost off by the arm-pit.

A boy on board a trawler for his first voyage was picking fish out of the fish pound on deck one night

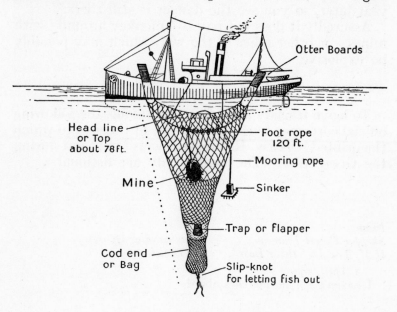

From a sketch by Chief Skipper
MARTIN FIELDING R.N.R.

MINE FOUL OF A TRAWL

when he saw something bright amongst the mass of oyster shells and seaweed. Knowing nothing whatever about mines or detonators, he slipped the shining brass thing into his pocket, thinking he would take it home.

He left the trawler on reaching harbour and later got work on a little farm just outside Grimsby at a village called Holten-le-Clay. He still had the brass detonator, and thought it would make a cigarette-lighter or fountain-pen. One day, while digging up potatoes, he stopped for a rest and examined the brass thing he still had in his pocket. Boylike, he got his pocket-knife and started to take it to bits.

' A loud report brought the farmer and his servants, to find a badly injured boy lying on the ground,' my informant writes. ' To-day he walks about the docks with all the fingers off his right hand, looking for a day's work when he can get one. He told me this a year later, so you see the danger is still there.'

Assuredly it does not pay to ' monkey around ' with mines – or other relics of the war, which may possibly be explosive.

7

To leave tragedy and come to humour, the following official correspondence shows some of the uses to which the printed Service ' Reference Sheets ' were put during the Great War. The names only are fictional.

I

From
Skipper Robert Johnson
H.M. Trawler ' Polar Bear '.

To
Commanding Officer
Y Division.

1 *April*, 19 – .
I haven't got no matches abord.

II

2nd *April*. *To S.N.O.*
Submitted – Forwarded herewith request for matches made by Skipper of Trawler ' Polar Bear ' under my command.

ADOLPHUS BROWN,
Lieut. R.N.R.

III

To Naval Store Officer, Granton.
Forwarded, concurring in supply.

JOHN TRAVERS,
Captain R.N.,
Senior Naval Officer.

IV

To Senior Naval Officer.
 Noted and returned.
 It is pointed out for your information that matches are not included on the list of establishment stores. Instructions are requested.

ANDREW FLANNIGAN,
N.S.O.

V

To N.S.O., Granton.
 Please take steps as necessary to supply.

JOHN TRAVERS,
Captain R.N.,
Senior Naval Officer.

VI

April 15th.
MX.224.75/3317/62.
To Naval Store Officer,
H.M. Dockyard, Rosyth.
 It is requested that matches, safety, boxes, 12 in number, may be forwarded as soon as possible for Armed Trawler ' Polar Bear ' stationed at this Base.

ANDREW FLANNIGAN,
N.S.O.

VII

TO N.S.O., Granton.
 Returned, observing that matches, safety, are not included in the establishment of stores for Armed Trawlers. Request duplicate pattern of article required in order that communication may be made with Director of Stores, Admiralty.

JAMES MITCHELL,
N.S.O.,
H.M. Dockyard, Rosyth.

VIII

1st June.
To N.S.O.,
H.M. Dockyard, Rosyth.
 Forwarded herewith pattern as requested. The matter is becoming urgent.

ANDREW FLANNIGAN,
N.S.O., Granton.

IX

Telegram.   July 3rd.
To N.S.O.,
H.M. Dockyard, Rosyth.
 Reference my MX.224. 75/3317/62 of April 15th, forwarding demand for matches, safety, boxes, 12 in number.   It is requested supply may be hastened.   0760. N.S.O., Granton.

X

July 8th.
To N.S.O., Granton.
 Reference from MX. 224. 75/3317/62 of April 15th and telegram 0760 of July 3rd, please state reasons for which these articles are required.

JAMES MITCHELL,
N.S.O.,
H.M. Dockyard, Rosyth.

XI

July 10th.
To S.N.O., Granton.
　Submitted – forwarded.

ANDREW FLANNIGAN,
N.S.O., Granton.

XII

July 11th.
To Commanding Officer,
Y Division.
　Note and return with your remarks.

JOHN TRAVERS,
Captain R.N.,
S.N.O.

XIII

July 13th.
To Skipper Robert Johnson,
H.M. Trawler ' Polar Bear '.
　Note and return with your remarks.

ADOLPHUS BROWN,
Lieutenant R.N.R.,
Commanding Officer, Y Division.

XIV

July 15th.
From Skipper Robert Johnson.　　*To C.O. Y Division.*
　Sorry. I made a bloomer. I meant mattress.

ROBERT JOHNSON,
Skipper R.N.R.

p. 201.]
LIEUT. RUDD, R.N.R., AND SKIPPER RADMORE.
Minesweeping trawler *Bracklyn.*   Sunk by mine off Yarmouth, May 11, 1917.
(Both these officers were lost with their ship.)

XV

July 17th.
To Senior Naval Officer.

Submitted – Skipper of H.M. Trawler ' Polar Bear ' reports he made a clerical error. The demand was for a mattress.

ADOLPHUS BROWN,
Lieutenant R.N.R.

XVI

July 21st.
To C.O. Y Division.

You are to caution Skipper of H.M. Trawler ' Polar Bear ' to be more careful in future. Mistakes of this nature entail much unnecessary work for all concerned.

JOHN TRAVERS,
Captain R.N.,
S.N.O.

XVII

July 23rd.

Submitted, Skipper Johnson has since been transferred to Archangel. Request instructions.

ADOLPHUS BROWN,
Lieutenant R.N.R.,
Y Division.

At the foot of this correspondence were further pencilled remarks, apparently in the Senior Naval Officer's handwriting. They are unpublishable.

CHAPTER XIII

THE EAST COAST AND THE NARROW SEAS

I

THE HUMBER

HULL and Grimsby are the two largest fishing ports in Great Britain, and immediately on the outbreak of war trawlers were requisitioned for minesweeping purposes. Thirty-four were fitted out within seven days of the opening of hostilities, and another 160 were added in about eight weeks. Some were retained for service in the Humber area, but the majority were sent to other ports. They were manned, as usual, by fishermen, and in those early days few trawlers were provided with guns, and none with wireless telegraphy. Carrier pigeons were often used for sending messages in from the sea.

The duty of organising the work in the Humber area was in the hands of Captain F. E. Massy-Dawson, R.N. (Retd.),[1] assisted by Commander F. H. Pollen, R.N. (Retd.),[2] the mobilising officer for the district. In all, Hull and Grimsby supplied over 9,000 men and 800 trawlers during the war, while a large minesweeping base and training centre was established at Grimsby. It acted as a source of supply for minesweeping personnel all over the world, the old Emigrants' Home being used as a naval barracks for accommodating men waiting to go to sea. Close by was the hospital, schools for wireless telegraphy, signalling, and navigation, together with a lecture-room, and storehouses containing every possible article of equipment required by minesweepers. During the last year of the

[1] Now D.S.O.
[2] Now Captain F. H. Pollen, C.B.E., R.N. (Retd.).

war much of the work in connection with stores and the fitting of minesweeping gear was in the hands of the 'Wrens', otherwise the Women's Royal Naval Service.

Captain Massy-Dawson, who was at Grimsby throughout the whole period of hostilities, had pleasant things to say of the many fishermen who from time to time came under his orders. Punishments were few and far between when the men once became accustomed to naval ideas and discipline. Loyalty, he said, was the motto of the Service, and he was proud to command a splendid body of deep-sea fishermen who carried out their arduous and dangerous work day by day, year in and year out, in every kind of weather. Serving under officers of the Merchant Service with temporary commissions in the R.N.R., their behaviour, discipline and devotion to duty left nothing to be desired.

As the war progressed and the enemy minelaying from surface craft was abandoned in favour of the more dangerous and intensive minelaying from submarines, which planted their 'eggs' in small batches wherever the traffic was thickest, different types of sweepers were based on the Humber. First came the trawlers, then the hired paddlers, next the war-built naval paddlers of the 'Racecourse' type, finally the twin-screw minesweepers of the Seventh Fast Sweeping Flotilla. At the time of the Armistice, however, 165 miles of the 'War Channel' up the east coast of England was being swept daily from Grimsby, while 160 miles of additional channel leading out into the North Sea was swept periodically every ten or fifteen days under Admiralty instructions. In all, Grimsby sweepers accounted for 1,029 enemy mines during the war, and a far larger number of drifting mines.

The Seventh Fast Sweeping Flotilla, formed towards the end of 1917, consisted of six of the new twin-screw minesweepers of the 'Hunt' class commanded by Commander Basil R. Brooke, D.S.O., R.N., first in the *Clonmel* and then in the *Penarth*. Lieutenant G. E. Blackmore, D.S.C., R.N., who had been promoted to

that rank for his gallantry in the *Manx King* described in Chapter X, became second-in-command of
the flotilla in the *Cupar* during 1918.

The flotilla was kept very busy in the War Channel
and as far east as Terschelling. When in harbour it
lay at buoys off Cleethorpes, and on one of the rare
occasions when it had a morning off duty, the *Cupar*
was responsible for a scare which reached the Admiralty and caused some flutter in the official dovecotes.

She was carrying out a wireless exercise to test some
new telegraphist ratings, and the senior man, not content with using ' buzzer ', took it unto himself to use
slight power. The exercise transmitted was made up
with the usual sort of wireless signals made at sea –
reports of progress in sweeping, latitude and longitude,
course and speed, etc.

To impart verisimilitude, however, the leading telegraphist went too far. He made – ' *Cupar* has struck
a mine ', followed by a position in the War Channel
and an ' enemy report ' which stated that two hostile
battle-cruisers and four destroyers had been sighted
off the coast.

The signal being picked up by the wireless station
at Flamborough Head was immediately passed to the
Admiralty. The Vice-Admiral commanding the east
coast of England at once sent all available craft to
the *Cupar's* assistance, though history does not relate
whether units of the Grand Fleet were set in motion
to deal with the mythical enemy battle-cruisers !
Neither do we hear what happened to the leading
telegraphist at the subsequent Court of Enquiry.

Just before the Armistice, the flotilla was ordered
to search for mines off the Terschelling lightship.
Mines had apparently been reported there, one of them
with six horns. This was thought to be a new type,
so the *Cupar* was ordered to follow astern of the
sweepers and to salve one for examination.

On most of these more distant excursions the
sweepers were screened or escorted by cruisers and
aircraft from Hull. On this occasion, however, on
arriving off Terschelling, they were surprised to find

that no covering forces were present. However, they carried on their sweeping, and the *Cupar*, following about a mile and a half astern of the others, was suddenly attacked by four enemy aircraft. Seven bombs were dropped, the nearest missing the stern by a few feet, before the unwelcome visitors were finally driven off.

Shortly afterwards a wireless signal was received by a vessel specially sent out ordering the flotilla to return to base with all despatch. German ships were apparently on the move, and efforts had been made to recall the sweepers during the previous night. But the wireless apparatus fitted was not capable of receiving the messages, with the result that the *Penarth* – with more up-to-date equipment – was sent down from Granton as senior officer's ship in place of the *Clonmel*.

Of the 56 merchant ships sunk by mines in the Grimsby area during the war, 38 came to grief through disobeying the Admiralty orders to keep to the War Channel. Of the 23 fishing vessels lost, ten were in prohibited areas. It took some time before the masters of merchantmen, and the skippers of those few fishing craft that still plied their normal business, could be induced to see that the shortest way to or from a port or a fishing ground was not necessarily the safest. Many casualties were caused by sheer ' cussedness ' and the dislike of official interference.

In this area, as elsewhere, it is difficult to select individual acts of gallantry or devotion to duty.

On January 2, 1916, the trawler *Mediator* struck a mine off Hornsea. The weather was bitterly cold and blowing hard with a rough sea. The ship was badly damaged and likely to sink at any moment, but the skipper, R. Pool, and four men remained on board in a gallant effort to keep their ship afloat. They worked at the pumps and stopped every accessible leak, but in vain. The water gained upon them, though they did not relax their efforts until the *Mediator's* deck was awash. She foundered a few minutes after they had left her.

Then there was the case of Chief Skipper Arthur Fletcher. The sweep-wire of his trawler carried away while sweeping was in progress, and the ragged end whirled over the deck, mangled his hand, and broke his arm. The mate asked if the ship should return to harbour.

'No,' said the maimed skipper. 'Finish the job.'

They tied up Fletcher's bleeding arm as best they could and carried on, contenting themselves by sending a wireless signal into Grimsby to say that the skipper would require hospital treatment on arrival next day !

I have already mentioned the minesweeping trawler *Night Hawk*, which was blown up off Whitby on Christmas Day, 1914.[1] Six men were lost in the explosion, and her commanding officer, Lieutenant W. E. Senior, R.N.R.,[2] after being some time in the water, reached a floating raft, which he managed to scull towards the other men struggling for their lives. He was able to drag some of them on board his crazy ark, and kept them there until boats came to the rescue. It was blowing fresh at the time and freezing hard. The sea was icy cold. Senior's action undoubtedly saved several lives.

Then there was Chief Engineman Bateman, of the trawler *Cuirass*, who, when his ship was in the midst of a minefield with mines exploding all round her, calmly went about his work below searching for leaks, and keeping his engines running, while the *Cuirass* was 'constantly shaken by violent detonations'. Bateman hadn't a chance of being rescued if his little ship struck a mine. His nervelessness was typical of that always displayed by the men of the engineers' department.

When the hired paddler *Lady Ismay* was sunk in a minefield near the Longsand lightship on December 21, 1915, her mate, William Carter, swam to a raft. He was floating about in the dangerous area when a man named Bell appeared on the surface calling for help. Carter dragged him on board, and, though him-

[1] See p. 104.   [2] Afterwards D.S.C.

self exhausted, tried to revive his comrade by artificial respiration, with the seas washing over them. Bell succumbed, and Carter was more dead than alive when rescued with the corpse of the man he had risked his life to save.

On April 14, 1916, the trawler *Alberta* was blown up off Grimsby while sweeping a large enemy minefield. Undeterred by the explosion, the skipper of her sweeping mate, the *Orcades*, at once took his ship alongside the sinking vessel. While there the *Orcades* was also blown up with a loss of twelve out of her fourteen men, including the gallant skipper.

Lieutenant Crossley, R.N.R., has already been mentioned in connection with his work in the Scarborough minefield.[1] On another occasion, when the trawler *Courtier* was sunk in a minefield off Kilnsea on January 6, 1916, Crossley steamed in over the minefield and rescued some of the crew, for which he was rewarded with the D.S.C.

Once again this same officer was in charge of a section of sweepers when, in the middle of a large minefield, two of his trawlers were blown up in as many minutes. Again he took in his ship and saved the survivors. After this incident he was ordered to discontinue sweeping in this particular area. Within a fortnight, however, he had reorganised his section and was again at work in a spot where a large number of enemy mines were being swept up. 'In spite of injuries and shocks,' said the official report, 'Lieutenant Crossley always volunteered for the most dangerous and arduous work.' This gallant officer's death through natural causes in 1918 was a great loss to the Minesweeping Service.

It was in the bitterly cold month of January, 1916, after the blowing up of the *Courtier*, that a young deck-hand of the *Varanis* called Huntingdon, jumped overboard to rescue a badly wounded man named Barber. He reached and supported him until help came, though it was only with the greatest difficulty that both men were eventually saved. Huntingdon

[1] See p. 99.

was awarded the bronze medal of the Royal Humane Society.

One might cite case after case of heroism and gallantry – deeds performed not only by officers and men of the Royal Navy who had been brought up to the idea of war and its attendant risks, but also by seamen of the Merchant Navy, men of the Fishing Fleets, and, in many cases, by civilians who had volunteered for service at sea.

At Grimsby, as elsewhere, their conduct was wholly admirable.

2

HARWICH

Harwich –

To those of us who served there during the war, as I did for two and a half years in command of a destroyer, the mere sound of the name must conjure up ineffaceable memories of one of the most strenuous periods of our lives.

We must have steamed past the town and ancient seaport of Harwich some hundreds of times on our way out to sea and back again. We saw it every hour of the day and night, and in every possible state of the weather. One remembers it from the northward as a cluster of grey-looking buildings huddled on the tip of a low peninsula. In the foreground was a little basin enclosed by jetties and a pier, once used by the railway steamers going to the Hook of Holland, but in our time by the ferry-boats plying to Felixstowe and Ipswich, and an occasional Trinity House steamer. A red lightship sometimes lay moored alongside one of the jetties.

Beyond, across the roadway, stood the solid, square block of the Great Eastern Hotel, and in the background, over an irregular outline of roofs, a conspicuous church spire and the slender tower of the old high lighthouse.

With the blue smoke curling from its many chimneys, the little town had rather a pleasing silhouette against the rosy sky of the dawn to the eastward. It was more pleasing than ever when we saw it on our return to harbour, and felt one's ship slipping smoothly through the calm water after three or four days buffeting in a fierce welter outside. It blew great guns sometimes.

On the foreshore to the eastward of the town, facing the entrance to the harbour, lay the black, dismasted hull of a wrecked sailing ship – a small coaster from the look of her. She was a trivial object enough, but I remember that old wreck for a peculiar reason. She lay stranded immediately opposite the spot where the duty destroyers swung at their buoys off Felixstowe, and from where, on a calm May morning in 1916, we cleared lower deck to watch a little procession of tugs, motor-boats, a destroyer, and a salvage ship slowly wending its way up harbour.

It was a sight of unusual interest. A submarine flying the White Ensign over the white, black-crossed emblem of the Imperial German Navy was lashed alongside the destroyer *Firedrake*. She was on her way to be put into the floating-dock off Shotley.

Commanded by an officer named Ulrich Mohrbutter, U.C.5 had been the first submarine minelayer to penetrate the Straits of Dover from Zeebrugge, and to lay her 'eggs' off Boulogne on August 21, 1915. Another consignment of her mines had been responsible for the loss of the hospital ship *Anglia* with about 80 lives on November 17. On the following April 27, she ran hard and fast ashore on the Shipwash shoal while about to lay mines in the approaches to Harwich.

The following extracts are taken from the log of U.C.5. (Times are one hour in advance on G.M.T.) :

5.15 a.m.   Dived to avoid minesweepers.

5.30.   Came to surface and steered west.

5.40.   Boat went violently aground. Full speed astern. Tide rising. Floated.

6.0.   Dived. Trimmed boat.

6.40.   Lay on bottom 16 metres (8¾ ftms.).

9.20.   Came up to 9 metres (5 ftms.).

11.0.   Came to surface. Boat ran aground 8 metres (26¼ feet).

It happened that the *Firedrake*, Commander Aubrey T. Tillard,[1] one of the destroyers attached to the submarine flotilla at Harwich, was out exercising with submarines. Having finished the exercises, Commander Tillard had sent the submarines back into harbour and was busy picking up their torpedoes when he saw what looked like a buoy in a position where no buoy should be. His suspicions were immediately aroused. The strange object *might* be a submarine, so he wirelessed in to Harwich asking if any British submarines were in the vicinity. He received the answer ' No ', so having recovered the torpedoes steamed towards the object, presently to identify it as the grey conning-tower of an U-boat. He soon saw the low deck, and men standing upon it apparently doing their utmost to push her off with spars.

Approaching, the *Firedrake* fired a gun over the submarine. The Germans ceased their efforts and held up their hands in surrender. Stopping within 500 yards, the destroyer lowered a boat, whereupon the Germans leapt overboard and were picked up, though not before Tillard had noticed a puff of smoke as though they had tried to scuttle their ship. Mohrbutter, indeed, had endeavoured to destroy his vessel and his confidential documents when he saw that capture was inevitable. As U.C.5 was already aground, she could not be sunk.

The prisoners were taken back into harbour, and for the next fortnight or so the salvage ship *Ranger* – Captain F. W. Young, R.N.R.,[2] – with the *Firedrake* guarding her, was at work salving the submarine. The task was difficult and dangerous. The twelve mines were still in their tubes. They had been released from inside the hull, which meant that they would fall out of their chutes and become dangerous the moment U.C.5 slid off the shoal into deeper water. Lieutenant Quentin H. Paterson,[3] the torpedo lieuten-

[1] Now Rear-Admiral Aubrey T. Tillard, D.S.O. (Retd.), who has kindly given me the details.
[2] Afterwards Sir Frederick Young, K.B.E.
[3] Now Commander Q. H. Paterson, D.S.C., R.N. (Retd.).

ant of the submarine depot ship *Maidstone*, had been able to make a few of the mines safe. The others had temporarily to be secured in their tubes by lashing collision mats and wire nets underneath the hull.

Dragged off the shoal when the damage had been repaired, U.C.5 was brought up harbour in triumph, though there was considerable anxiety lest her 'eggs' should fall out and mine the narrow fairway. However, all went well. U.C.5 was put safely into the floating dock, where Paterson made the rest of the mines safe and removed them. He received a well-deserved D.S.C. for his share in the business. Mines were no things to monkey with, particularly as these might have been fitted with some sort of device to make them explode when tampered with by the captors.

We all visited U.C.5 in turn, and so did thousands of other people when she was afterwards on view in the Thames. I still possess two brass cartridge cases for Verey lights discovered in a locker in her cramped and evil-smelling interior. One wondered how her crew of one officer and thirteen men ever managed to exist in the miserable accommodation of that coffin-like hull. We conceived a healthy respect for the work of the German submarine crews, enemies though they were.

To revert to Harwich, however, I doubt if I visited the town more than three times, at the most, during the thirty odd months I was based there in a destroyer. When the place is mentioned, my mind flashes back to Dovercourt, Parkeston Quay, and the wide estuary of the Stour, which in those days was uncomfortably crowded with vessels-of-war.

The lean grey cruisers, five or six of them, with Sir Reginald Tyrwhitt's [1] broad pendant as Commodore fluttering at the masthead of the *Arethusa*, *Cleopatra*, *Curaçoa*, or one or other of the ships from which he commanded the Harwich Force throughout the war, swung at their buoys between Harwich and Shotley. The destroyers lay in pairs at their trots off and above

[1] Now Admiral of the Fleet Sir Reginald Tyrwhitt, Bart., G.C.B., D.S.O., D.C.L.

Parkeston Quay, with a division of four off Felixstowe with steam available at half an hour's notice. The depot ships, with more destroyers and the submarines alongside them, lay at Parkeston Quay itself, while there were two or three oilers in mid-stream. An aircraft-carrier – a converted railway steamer – was moored off the Shotley shore, and at one time, when she did not often go to sea, the irreverent asserted that she was hard-and-fast aground on her own jam tins and bottles. There were trawlers by the dozen in Felixstowe Dock or round about the *Ganges* – the old veteran *Minotaur*, built as a five-masted ironclad in 1866 – which lay off Shotley as part of the boys' training establishment.

There was always movement in the harbour. The cruisers and destroyers were invariably slipping to sea at short notice, and at any time of the day or night. Sometimes it was a routine affair of two or three cruisers and a couple of divisions of destroyers going out to escort one of the convoys of merchantmen which ran regularly every three or four days to and fro between the Shipwash and the Maas lightship off Rotterdam. Since they brought back foodstuffs to a country sadly in need of them, we called it the 'beef trip'.

Sometimes we set forth for an air-raid on the Zeppelin sheds at Tondern or a sweep of the Heligoland Bight, operations which involved every available cruiser and destroyer in the harbour. Occasionally it was a real 'spasm', as the men called it, because enemy destroyers were at sea and we were required to intercept them off the Schouwen Bank or Terschelling. One never knew what was in the wind from one moment to another. Destroyer divisions were sometimes detached for weeks at a time for odd jobs from the Humber, and from Dover, Portsmouth, Plymouth – even Belfast.

We often returned weatherbeaten, with our oil-fuel running low, and the fore side of our funnels caked white with the salt of dried spray. Ships were sometimes battle-scarred, and more than once friends and flotilla-mates had been left behind in the grey, inhospitable shallows of the cold North Sea.

But regarding it as Home, we were always pleased to see Harwich again after being detached to some other port, where they never did things in quite the same way as ourselves, and we were strangers in an unfamiliar land. And one was glad enough to return after two, three or four practically sleepless days and nights on the bridge in weather that was often vile. Few destroyer captains managed much sleep at sea in war-time.

One remembers the submarines moving unobtrusively down the river on their way for their ceaseless vigil in the Heligoland Bight, some, alas, never to come back. Paddlers, trawlers, drifters, motor-launches and a host of smaller fry steamed fussily out and in on their way to or from their everlasting minesweeping and patrol work. There was always something on the move between the Guard and the Beach End buoys, and our old friend the Cork lightship bobbing about off Felixstowe.

The destroyer depot ship *Dido*, with the *Maidstone* and *Pandora* for the submarines, lay alongside Parkeston Quay, which had been taken over by the Navy from the Great Eastern Railway. Our *Dido* could supply us with anything from a teacup or a pair of seaman's undergarments, to a new 4-inch gun or a pom-pom – undertook anything from repairs to a leaky condenser, to fitting a temporary patch over a shell hole.

The railway sheds served as a sort of naval store depot, as well as a dump for all conceivable sorts of things that exploded, from war-heads for torpedoes and depth charges, to 6-inch, 4-inch, $2\frac{1}{2}$-pounder and small arm ammunition.

One recollects the Zeppelins overhead at night. They shone like silver in the questing rays of the searchlights, with the sky all round them sparkling with the red flashes of exploding shell, while the air trembled to the crash of anti-aircraft gunfire and the duller reverberations of exploding bombs.

Thank heaven the bombs never found Parkeston Quay! If they had, the explosion and the inevitable fire would have been mighty indeed. But the quay was straddled more than once when bombs fell and exploded in Parkeston village and in the harbour beyond, literally missing the danger spot by fathoms.

Bits of shrapnel from our own guns sometimes came thudding down on deck and plopping into the water all round us as we lay at our buoys. But could we keep the ship's company down below under cover while an air-raid was in progress? Most certainly not. They must come on deck to see the ' fun ', the mess-deck wag wearing a battered bowler hat and holding an opened umbrella.

One remembers the fogs and the gales – the tearing, snorting easterly winds of winter and early spring, and the short jabble kicked up outside in the shallow, yellowish-grey water. It broke over our low decks in sheets of icy spray as we drove through it at twenty knots past the Cork lightship, and out to sea by way of the Sledway and Shipwash, or the Rough Buoy and the Sunk lightship. Once in the open water it usually became worse – a confused, breaking sea which made life supremely wet and cold and uncomfortable. Wind and sea seemed generally to veer to the westward to give us a dead muzzler for the return journey.

Some of our expeditions were exciting, some deadly monotonous. But always there was the chance of something happening, particularly when we escorted those convoys of straggling merchantmen to and fro between England and Holland. A few steamed at fourteen knots, some at no more than seven. They tailed out in a lengthy procession stretching over miles of sea frequented by hostile submarines. It was a worrying job to give them adequate protection.

At night, we went to action stations immediately on clearing the harbour, since Zeebrugge, with its flotillas of German destroyers, was no more than seventy miles away as the gull flies. And the U-boats were ubiquitous.

Life at Harwich was peculiar in war time, full of

strange incongruities. One might be depth-charging an U-boat, chasing destroyers, or assisting in a bombardment of the Belgian coast at dawn, and at three in the afternoon be playing tennis on the hard courts at Dovercourt.

Leave was as liberal as it possibly could be in the circumstances. During the summer we were allowed ashore in the afternoons between one-thirty and seven, so that those of us who were married and had our wives living in Dovercourt could see something of them.

The Sports Club was a favourite rendezvous in summer – crowded with naval and military officers and their wives, naval wives whose husbands were away at sea, and the few real civilians that remained in the place. It was a representative gathering of both Services. Khaki tunics, and blue, gold-laced monkey jackets worn over white flannels, mingled with the light summer dresses of the women. Here was a red-tabbed staff officer of the local garrison, there the commanding officer of a submarine who had returned that morning from his ten-day patrol among the minefields of the Bight. There was a subaltern with the M.C. and a couple of wound stripes recuperating before returning to France – naval officers from every sort of ship in the harbour, and varying in rank from four-striped captains, to acting sub-lieutenants and midshipmen of the R.N.V.R. But for the fact that we all wore uniform, war seemed very far away.

However, we lived, so to speak, on the proverbial split yarn, and the signal ' Q.O.' – ' Raise steam for full speed and report when ready ' – was of fairly common occurrence during our afternoons ashore, and soon lost its novelty.

When it did come it meant that the enemy was probably at sea, so there was no dalliance. And while the harbour became enveloped in rolling clouds of black oil-fuel smoke, officers and men, if ashore, were immediately recalled to their ships by prearranged siren signals and by telephone. The Sports Club instantly became a turmoil. The tea-room emptied and games of tennis broke up. People hurriedly telephoned for taxis, if any were available, or asked others to give them a lift. Some, mounting their bicycles, pedalled off at full speed. Others ran home to change before undertaking the two-mile sprint down the dusty road to Parkeston Quay, where a concourse of motor-boats, whalers and dinghies awaited them.

One arrived on board. Then a hurried shift into seagoing clothes, and a signal fluttering at the Commodore's masthead : ' Slip. Proceed out of harbour.'

Half an hour later five or six cruisers and a score of destroyers would be forming up outside.

Twenty knots. Twenty-two knots.

Dovercourt and its amenities became a thing of the past as the land faded away astern and the first whiff of spray came sweeping over the bows.

What the wives thought about it as they saw their husbands' ships circling the buoys off the harbour mouth and disappearing over the skyline on some unknown errand, it is impossible to say. They knew that on occasions some of the Harwich Force had never returned, and that ships had come back with killed and wounded. Some of them had even helped to console newly-made widows in the first agony of their sudden bereavements, and at any moment their own turn might come. But the women never flinched. They were very brave, very patient and loyal in those long days and nights of anxious waiting.

Their lives ashore were unnatural. Housekeeping was difficult, and Harwich became a ' prohibited area', which meant that the naval wives, even though they may have had houses in Dovercourt before the war, had to possess special permits from the Competent Military Authority to enter the ' Harwich Special Military Area ' for the purpose of ' residence ' in the ' said area '. My wife's red permit book, number 114,192 of October 17, 1916, contains her photograph, with particulars of her height, build, colour of hair and eyes, and ' distinctive marks '. The details were entered by someone called P. S. Borrer, evidently a police officer.

At one time there was some idea of a German landing in Essex and Suffolk, and troops were sent to the

MINE EXPLOSION.

coast to repel a possible attack, and to dig trenches and erect barbed-wire entanglements along the coast. All residents received orders what to do if the place had to be evacuated. Livestock, wines and liquors had to be destroyed, and the civilian inhabitants, taking a few days' food with them, were to move inland – on foot, if I remember rightly.

We decided that our two dogs, the Irish terrier and a most obstreperous Sealyham, did not come under the heading of ' livestock ', in that they were not edible. They should march with my wife, carrying their own rations in home-made haversacks strapped round their middles – dog biscuits in one compartment, bones in the other.

Where we seamen should have been while the exodus was in progress heaven only knew ! It was lucky for our peace of mind that no enemy landing was ever attempted.

In our frequent excursions to sea we always saw the minesweepers at work outside the harbour, particularly round the buoys and lightships, and in the War Channel between the Sunk and the Shipwash. They were on the job in all weathers, and since them essage – ' The port of Harwich is closed on account of mines ' – was not infrequent, we realised that they had an unenviable task and a dangerous one. They had our sympathy and our gratitude at the time, particularly as the so-called ' closing ' of the port made no difference whatever to our comings and goings.

But how dangerous that minesweeping round about Harwich really was I, personally, had no conception until after the war.

3

The minesweeping force stationed at Harwich on the outbreak of hostilities consisted of seven trawlers. They were under the command of Commander H. S. Lecky, A.M., R.N.,[1] and Commander H. F. Cayley, R.N. (Retd.).[2] Commander Cayley was afterwards

[1] Now Captain H. S. Lecky, C.B., A.M., R.N. (Retd.).
[2] Now Captain H. F. Cayley, D.S.O., R.N. (Retd.).

Port Minesweeping Officer, retaining the appointment until 1917 when he was relieved by Commander T. J. S. Lyne.[1]

Each day for the first seven months of the war they swept two channels for the use of Commodore Tyrwhitt's light cruisers and destroyers, and the submarines, which were constantly moving in and out of harbour on their frequent excursions to, and return from, the Heligoland Bight.

No mines were found, but the trawlers had much practice in sweeping, and the continual annoyance of parted sweep-wires because of the shallow water in which they worked. The only excitements which came their way were a few abortive submarine hunts, some of which were obviously based on false information.

In those early days of the war people saw spies everywhere, and submarines where they never could have existed. There was the clergyman who reported having seen a periscope – a thing no thicker than a stout broomstick – at a distance of fifteen miles ; and the lady who sighted a submarine steaming at full speed up the river Exe – in which there was a depth of no more than fifteen feet at high water.

Her story was investigated. Asked to describe a periscope, she said it was ' a thing like a snake '. What she *had* seen was a length of coir hawser which had floated down river to become entangled in one of the fairway buoys. Rippling downstream in the strong current, it gave the buoy the appearance of moving through the water. Ergo, it was the conning-tower of an U-boat on her way up-river for some fell purpose known only to her commander !

And so it was at Harwich, where the trawlers,

[1] Now Rear-Admiral Sir Thomas J. S. Lyne, K.C.V.O., C.B., D.S.O. (Retd.).
Rear-Admiral Lyne was promoted from Gunner to Lieutenant in 1901 for the notable feat of *sailing* a broken-down torpedo-boat into Saldanha Bay during the Boer War. Promoted to Commander in 1912 and a captain on December 31, 1918, he afterwards commanded the *Impregnable*, the ship he had entered as a bluejacket boy over forty years before. Retired as a captain under the regulations for age, his case is the first for many years where a boy entering as a bluejacket has become a Flag Officer.

accompanied by some destroyers, were sent to the entrance of the Blackwater to sweep for a submarine which was supposed to be lying hidden on the bottom. There was not sufficient depth for the smallest U-boat to have submerged herself. All the sweeping did was to cause considerable damage to the local oyster beds !

In March, 1915, no mines having been discovered, the Harwich sweepers were used for experimental work with indicator nets laid out at sea for the purpose of locating the elusive U-boats. The idea was simple. A submerged submarine would steam blindly into a net, wrap it round herself, and then move off towing buoys or calcium flares along the surface to disclose her presence. Then patrol vessels would chase the buoys and fire explosive charges over the submarine. On one occasion, at least, this device was successful, though not, I believe, off Harwich.

However, the Harwich trawlers continued this work until June, 1915, when the first clutch of submarine mines was discovered near the Sunk lightship by the loss of four merchantmen and a couple of destroyers of the Nore defence flotilla. At once the trawlers were re-fitted with their sweeps, and reverted to their legitimate business.

Like the trawlers elsewhere, the little ships at Harwich were manned by their ordinary fishermen crews. In the first few months of the war, we are told, their discipline left something to be desired, and some persuasion was necessary before they could be made to realise that they were now part and parcel of a fighting Service. At first the monotony and apparent uselessness of their work rather got on their nerves and induced a want of imagination, and while very anxious to please, the men seemed to lack initiative.

But things very soon improved when discipline was tightened up and the fishermen realised they might be detached from their own calling for many months, even years. Self-respect increased. They began to absorb naval ideas and traditions, and the lack of imagination proved rather a blessing in disguise. When mines started to appear, first in isolated bunches, then in regular consignments, it permitted them to live and sleep and eat with fearlessness and self-confidence in conditions of extraordinary hazard and danger.

The change effected in the trawlermen by a few months of war, says one report, was amazing. Many of the skippers could hardly read or write. Nevertheless, they cheerfully accepted risk and responsibility, obeyed orders to the letter, and could take their ships anywhere.

As their one-time senior officer at Harwich wrote : ' Right well they did their job. If the term " gentleman " applies to one who is chivalrous, conforms to a code of honour, and who plays for his side and not merely for himself, then I claim that 90 per cent. of those who served in the Minesweeping Service during the war fully earned the title of " Gentlemen of the Sea ".'

The first batch of mines was actually swept up by the Harwich craft on August 5, 1915, while they were searching the channel from the South Shiphead buoy to the Sunk lightship. Thereafter, mines were laid in the Harwich area regularly once a week, while sometimes two distinct groups would be put down the same night. The first loss to the minesweepers occurred on August 16 when the trawler *Japan* was blown up at the south end of the Shipwash shoal.

During the period May to December, 1915, fifty-five vessels including merchantmen, patrol craft and sweepers were lost either by torpedo or through enemy mines between the Kentish Knock and Aldeburgh Ridge. The area was rapidly becoming a maritime graveyard. One remembers the chart dotted with the newly-drawn red symbols denoting wrecks. More and more mines were laid, and a number of patrol trawlers were withdrawn from their normal work and transformed into sweepers.

The two minesweeping gunboats *Spanker* and *Seagull* had been attached to the base in July, 1915 ; but at the end of the year the Admiralty had to be asked for more fast, light-draught sweepers, which resulted in the arrival of the *Atalanta* and *St. Seiriol* in the following January. The first was a triple-screw turbine steamer of 486 tons gross owned by the Glasgow and South Western Railway, and the *St. Seiriol* a new twin-screw turbine vessel of about 900 tons belonging to the Liverpool and North Wales Steamship Company. The *Atalanta* is still afloat and on service. Both ships did consistent good work in the Harwich area until the *St. Seiriol* was mined and sunk on April 25, 1918.

The first really serious loss was the mining of H.M.S. *Arethusa*, the cruiser bearing Commodore Tyrwhitt's broad pendant, on February 12, 1916, on her way back to Harwich. She struck a mine in the Sledway close to the South Cutler, the channel not having been swept that day because of the unusually bad weather. Abandoned in a sinking condition, she drove upon the Cutler shoal and eventually broke her back. This was the first group of mines laid inside the Shipwash shoal, the submarine responsible having probably used the Rough Buoy, which at that time still carried a light, to verify her position.

Motor launches using a light form of the ' A ' sweep, the two hired turbine steamers already mentioned, together with more trawlers, were gradually sent to Harwich, which made it possible for the swept channel used by the cruisers, destroyers and submarines to be extended further to the eastward. By some curious anomaly, however, the regular War Channel passing north and south through the area and used by a huge mass of merchant shipping, was still swept by vessels based upon Lowestoft. It was an unsatisfactory and uneconomical arrangement which resulted in many merchantmen being lost in the Channel because the Lowestoft sweepers were working unnecessarily far from their base.

It was not until March, 1917, that Harwich became responsible for its own section of the War Channel with a minesweeping force that by the beginning of this same year had been augmented to 4 hired paddlers, the 2 hired turbine steamers, and 29 trawlers. With this number of vessels it was just possible to cope with the continuous minelaying in the area that went on in 1917.

The greater number of mines were laid in the War Channel, and drifters provided with wireless were stationed at the north and south ends of the Harwich patrol to stop all traffic the moment the fairway was discovered to be foul.   The responsibility of the officer in charge of the War Channel was considerable, while an error in making a rapid decision when alternative courses of action were open to him might often have led to disaster.

It sometimes happened that when the low tides made it unsuitable for sweeping, the choice had to be made between holding up all traffic, or risking the sweepers and convoying the merchantmen through the danger zone.   And a minefield might occasionally be discovered while sweeping was actually in progress, with the traffic closely following the sweepers.   This meant that a crowd of merchant ships of every nation-ality had to be made to anchor until the area had been cleared, no easy matter where shipmasters, particularly the neutrals, were sometimes inclined to resent the giving of orders peremptorily issued by erstwhile fish-ing craft flying the White Ensign of the Royal Navy.

Two mines short of 1,100 were swept up off Harwich during hostilities.   In the opinion of those who are qualified to judge, the performance of the sweepers in this area during 1917 was one of the outstanding features of the minesweepers' campaign.   Six hundred and twenty-nine moored enemy mines were disposed of during this critical year of the unrestricted sub-marine war – 500 of them between March and October, both inclusive.   This record is only surpassed by Dover, where, in the larger area off the English and French coasts, 755 mines were sunk in the same year – 580 of them during the eight months mentioned.

Many fine deeds were performed off Harwich.

In June, 1916, or thereabouts, the hired turbine steamer *St. Seiriol* was sweeping off the Sunk lightship in a spot where a Norwegian steamer had been mined. The minesweeping kite came unexpectedly to the surface, and orders were given for it to be hove in. The winch was going very hard, and the kite came out of the water with a mine hanging alongside it and its mooring-rope entangled. It came up to within six inches of the head of the arched gallows before the winch could be stopped.

The R.N.R. petty officer in charge, a man named Lee, luckily retained his presence of mind. He cleared everybody off the after deck except himself and the winchman. Very gingerly, the mine was lowered clear of the ship's stern, when Lee went over the side with an axe and hacked at its mooring. In the words of Admiral Lyne, ' he had practically to sit on the mine, and then to work it off with his feet, apparently oblivious of what would happen if it suddenly shifted its position and one of the horns crumpled against the kite '. The deadly thing was eventually cleared and exploded close under the *St. Seiriol's* stern. Petty Officer Lee was awarded a well-deserved Distinguished Service Medal.

The *St. Seiriol* had many other adventures. In October, 1917, there was a period of strong easterly winds when the War Channel could not be swept for several days. ' Arrived off Sunk light-vessel with paddle-sweeper *Eagle III*,' the *St. Seiriol's* commanding officer writes. ' Heavy N.E. sea with moderate gale. Decided to try and sweep War Channel. Sweep passed successfully. Proceeded on our way, both ships making very heavy weather. After some time *Eagle III* signalled that one of her paddle-boxes was being washed away. I replied that we would sweep till we had cleared the channel or broke down, whichever happened first. Channel was swept and three mines accounted for. Traffic was resumed. *St. Seiriol* and *Eagle III* returned to harbour badly battered.'

Two months later the *St. Seiriol*, while sweeping, sighted S.S. *French Rose* of Liverpool heading to the southward with a mine about two cables (400 yards) ahead of her. It was about two hours before low water, blowing hard from the north-east with a very heavy sea. Slipping his sweep, the *St. Seiriol's* cap-

tain headed across the *French Rose's* bow between her
and the mine, thus forcing her to stop. ' I ordered
her to anchor,' he writes, ' as she was in a minefield
the extent of which was unknown.'

Patrol craft and sweepers were sent north and south
to stop all traffic, but a few minutes later the *French
Rose* was mined. ' I placed *St. Seiriol* alongside sinking vessel and all hands were saved. By this time
three mines were showing on the surface, and I could
see no way clear. I gave the unusual order ' Stand
by to blow up '; but by wonderful good luck we de-
ferred the evil day and got safely back into harbour.
Sixteen mines were afterwards swept up in a very
small area in the spot where the *French Rose* was sunk.'

Two months later, again, while sweeping the channel
between the Sunk and Shipwash, the lookout man reported a mine on the *St. Seiriol's* starboard bow. ' A
little later,' writes her commanding officer, ' when
standing on the port side of the bridge, I saw a mine
rubbing against the ship's side directly under me. I
shouted to the helmsman to put his wheel hard over
to swing us clear, and shut my eyes while waiting for
the worst. Nothing happened. It went clear, so the
pair of us turned 16 points and swept it up.'

The *St. Seiriol's* end came on April 25, 1918, while
she was sweeping a minefield off the Shipwash with
the *Atalanta*. She struck a mine under the bridge
and broke in two, the fore part sinking almost immediately, and the stern portion being taken in tow
until it grounded on the Shipwash shoal. One officer
and 15 men were killed, and 5 men were wounded.

Mines were not the only enemy with which the
sweepers had to contend. They endured bombs from
German Zeppelins and aeroplanes. On one occasion
a Zeppelin dropped seven bombs among a division of
trawlers and failed to secure a single hit.

The loss both in sweepers and lives was considerable,
and many were the occasions when trawlers and drifters
courageously went to the rescue of ships that had been
mined or torpedoed, and saved the lives of passengers
and crews. No fewer than 1,065 men, women and chil-

dren were so rescued up till December 31, 1917. One hears of trawlermen putting out in their cumbersome boats in the heaviest weather to save life, and of a boat from one trawler that rescued some airmen from the dangerous Longsand shoal when the seas were breaking over it.

The continuous minelaying involved a terrible risk to small craft. Large steamers with watertight compartments stood a fair chance of survival on being mined, and so did their men. Not so the trawlers and the little drifters of 100 tons and less, many of which were built of wood. Thus the curt official message reporting the loss of the 89 ton, wooden drifter *Forward III* off the Shipwash on March 31, 1917 : ' *Forward III* mined. No survivors.'

The little vessel struck a mine amidships by the keel, to vanish in a mighty upheaval of smoke and spray. When it in turn disappeared there was nothing to be seen on the water beyond a few broken pieces of wood. Not a man of her crew of nine was ever seen again. A large section of her wooden keel came whizzing down from the air to pierce the deck of the drifter *White Lilac*, where it remained, standing upright, like a monument to the gallant souls who had gone.

There was the trawler *Kelvin*, mined off Harwich on July 7, 1917, whose commanding officer, Lieutenant Thomas, R.N.R., might well have been saved if, when in the water, he had not insisted on giving up the piece of wreckage that was supporting him to one of his crew who could not swim. Thomas, an elderly man, had given loyal and devoted service at Harwich, and in 1913, as master of the sailing ship *Criccieth Castle*, had been wrecked off Cape Horn while homeward bound from Australia. During a heavy gale the ship sprang a leak and sank, and Captain Thomas, with his wife, his boy of four, and eight of the crew, got away in one of the boats with very little biscuit and water, which was rigorously rationed.

The wind blew furiously. The sea ran mountains high, and it was bitterly cold. The boat was constantly filled with water, so that they had to bale for

their lives.   Thomas was washed overboard while trying to improvise a rag of sail, but managed to get
back with the help of an oar.   The biscuit became
sodden with spray, and the drinking water brackish.
There seemed no hope of salvation.   One by one the
crew died, until only three remained, together with the
captain, his wife and their little son.

After a week's terrible ordeal a ship was sighted on
the horizon, but in that tumbling, wind-flecked waste
she passed them by unnoticed.   The next day they
reached a rocky islet, where Thomas, the only one who
could crawl, managed to get ashore and procured a few
handfuls of snow for drinking.   There was no food of
any sort, not even shell-fish.

By this time the child was suffering from frostbite
and his tongue was swollen in his mouth.   The rest of
the crew were quite incapacitated.   After a few hours
on the island, starvation seemed their inevitable fate,
but as the weather had moderated they put to sea
again in the hope of sighting another vessel or reaching a more hospitable shore.   After a voyage of twelve
days they eventually reached the Falkland Islands,
where after weeks of nursing, Thomas, his wife, the
child, and one member of the crew regained their normal health.   The other two men of the crew died.

It was after an adventure like that that Thomas
volunteered on the outbreak of war, became a temporary Lieutenant of the R.N.R., and lost his life in a
minesweeper.

Reverting again to the Harwich minesweepers, there
was the trawler *Burnley*, commanded by Lieutenant
Heap, R.N.R., who on November 25, 1916, heard an
explosion out at sea off Orfordness, sent his other ships
into harbour, and himself went out to investigate.   The
Burnley struck a mine and was lost with all hands.

One hair-raising incident succeeded another.   On
July 20, 1917, the hired paddler *Queen of the North*
was mined while sweeping off Orfordness with the loss
of 7 officers and 22 men.   Her commanding officer
and other survivors continued in the Minesweeping Service, several being in the paddler *Mercury* when that

vessel was mined. Sweeping off the Sunk lightship, she brought up three mines in her sweep. They exploded and blew off her stern. The bow portion was towed safely into harbour and a new stern fitted, and the *Mercury* resumed her duty sweeping. On her very first trip she was again blown up close to the scene of her former accident, on this occasion losing her bows with two of her crew.

There was the trawler *Lord Roberts*, commanded by a Lieutenant R.N.R. who was 'a sailor to his fingertips and also a prominent Bond Street merchant'. This little ship led a charmed life for nearly two years, and was responsible for saving many lives in heroic circumstances. Like so many of her sisters, however, she was mined and sunk off the Shipwash on October 26, 1916, with the loss of one officer and eight men. Her commanding officer, who had had a narrow escape and was badly shaken, was given an administrative job in harbour. 'He stuck it for about seven days, and then insisted on going to sea again to continue the good work.'

'*Cape Colony*. Hired Drifter, 82 tons, 8-1-17. Sunk by mine off Harwich,' runs the laconic announcement in the list of 'Navy Losses'.

This little ship had anchored for the night near the Shipwash light-vessel, and was weighing at dawn next morning when the mate, looking over the bows, saw a mine and its mooring foul of the cable within a few feet of the stem. With great presence of mind he jumped to the steam capstan and stopped heaving in. Unable to reverse the engine, however, he warned everyone, ran aft, and jumped overboard, followed by the rest of the crew. Almost before the last man had swum clear the mine struck the stem and the forepart of the *Cape Colony* was blown into matchwood. The rest of her sank instantly. All her crew were picked up by other vessels close by.

Sweeping had to continue, whatever the weather, and gales, fogs and snow often made the work more dangerous than ever. On one occasion a division of trawlers had swept up eleven enemy mines, but before they could be sunk by rifle fire a blinding snow-storm reduced the visibility to zero. The R.N.R. officer in charge of the group exercised his good sense by taking his vessels out of the dangerous area, wait-ing until the weather had cleared and then returning to sink the mines.

Salvage. One day in November, 1915, the trawler *Resono*, commanded by a Lieutenant R.N.R. – 'one of God's own seamen,' as Admiral Lyne describes him – saw a steamer called the *Ulrikon* blown up by a mine off the Galloper lightship. He rescued all the crew before the ship sank. No sooner had he done this, than he noticed another vessel, a Greek vessel called the *Athomas*, strike a mine and start to sink. Going alongside her, the *Resono* rescued all on board.

But the Greek ship did not sink. She drifted to-wards a British minefield, so the *Resono's* captain, seeing a chance of saving her, decided to take her in tow. The Greek chief officer and some of the crew were ' desired ' to get into their boat, to go back to their ship, and to get a line on board. They refused.

Finally, the *Resono's* own men were persuaded to go, their Captain having informed them that if they didn't make a move in two minutes by his watch he'd steam them over the minefield under his lee and blow them all to hell !

They went – and in spite of the foul weather the *Athomas* was eventually towed into the Thames es-tuary and handed over to tugs, while the *Resono* went back to her station in the War Channel. The stirring record of this fine trawler ended on December 26, 1915, when she was blown up off the Sunk lightship with heavy loss of life. Her captain was among the sur-vivors, and continued his good work until the end of the war.

Another fine piece of salvage work was carried out in the gathering darkness of a winter's day during a strong south-westerly gale with a heavy sea running, when the ' mark boat ' drifter *Lloyd George* was steam-ing down the War Channel between the Shipwash and Sunk light-vessels. She sighted the large steamer *Ber-*

wen which had been mined and was not under control. Going to her rescue, the skipper of the *Lloyd George* discovered that she had been abandoned by her crew, and was rapidly drifting to leeward towards a minefield, several mines in which were visible in the dusk in the troughs of the waves.

Realising the necessity for immediate action, the skipper with great skill and at no little risk, put his tiny ship alongside the 10,000 ton bulk of the *Berwen*, and managed to transfer three men out of his total crew of ten. By heaven only knows what efforts, these stalwarts managed to pass a hawser from ship to ship, whereupon the drifter steamed ahead with her huge charge in tow.

The *Lloyd George* was not fitted for towing, and had insufficient engine power to deal with the great mass astern of her. Little progress was made in the teeth of the increasing gale, but she held gamely on throughout the dark night and managed somehow to claw the *Berwen* off the minefield which threatened both vessels. Meanwhile, help had been asked for by wireless, and when the morning came the damaged ship was handed over to tugs. She eventually reached the Thames, with only a few hundred tons damaged out of the 7,000 tons of sugar which was her cargo.

The skipper and crew of the *Lloyd George*, it should be added, were refused the usual award for salvage on the grounds that the sugar was Government property !

One particularly fine piece of salvage work was performed by the trawler *Etoile Polaire*, commanded by Lieutenant A. Lansley, D.S.C., R.N.R. Early one morning in 1915 she was escorting a vessel employed in repairing a telephone cable near the Sunk lightship, when Lansley saw the S.S. *Volscian* mined in the neighbourhood. The crew deserted their ship in their boat, which was at once picked up by the trawler. Noticing that although the *Volscian* was down by the head she was not sinking very fast, Lansley decided to take her in tow and try salving her. The steamer's crew would not return to their ship, so Lansley put a few of his own men on board and managed to get the lines across.　There was a strong tide, and the *Volscian* was in a mined area.　Nevertheless, the *Etoile Polaire* took her in tow, tugged her through several dangerous areas, and brought her into shoal water near the Rough buoy off Harwich, where she was handed over to tugs. Being in shallow water, the steamer was practically salved before the tugs arrived.　The sum of £75 was awarded to Lansley and his men for saving a ship and cargo worth at least £10,000 !

The *Etoile Polaire* belonged to Dover, and with another officer in command was mined off the South Goodwin lightship on the night of December 3, 1915. It was blowing hard from the south-west with a considerable sea.　The tide carried the boat with the survivors towards the breakers on the Goodwin Sands. Then, luckily, it turned, and drifted them down-channel.　Sighting the riding-light of the South Goodwin lightship, the crew pulled for all they were worth and eventually reached the light-vessel after a very narrow escape of their lives.

Apart from those vessels already mentioned, and a large number of merchantmen, I can count at least fifty auxiliary vessels of the Royal Navy that were lost off Harwich during the war, and mostly through striking mines.　Among them were the trawlers *Javelin, Agamemnon II, Briton, Worsley, Japan, Dane, Nadine, Malta, William Morrison, Ameer, Commandant, Hirose, Narval, Lord Airedale, Tervani, New Comet, Holdene, Sisters Melville, Agile, Vitality, Strymon, John E. Lewis, Adrian, Numitor, Achilles II,* and the drifter *Hastfen.*

A mere recital of names is monotonous, but the point is that these vessels were almost entirely officered and manned by men of the Merchant Navy and the Fishing Fleets serving temporarily under the White Ensign.　As says one senior officer of my acquaintance – ' We should have lost the war without them.'

And Harwich, let it be remembered, was only supplying its quota to the 246 hired trawlers and 130 hired drifters that were lost throughout the war in practically every area where there was fighting at sea.

CHAPTER XIV

DOVER AND THE BELGIAN COAST

I

SIX trawlers fitted out as minesweepers arrived at Dover soon after the outbreak of war to work under the orders of Lieutenant-Commander W. G. Rigg, R.N., a retired officer who had rejoined the Navy from an appointment with the Royal National Life-boat Institution.

Having undergone some preliminary training, these little ships were employed on daily sweeping between the South Goodwin light-vessel and Folkestone. They discovered no mines. Unlike Lowestoft, the Humber and the Tyne, the Dover area was not troubled by surface minelayers within a few weeks of the opening of hostilities. It remained immune until the U.C. submarines from Zeebrugge started their operations in the middle of 1915. Thereafter, however, it received more than its fair share of attention.[1]

But during the first few months of war, the trawlers had various interludes in the dreary monotony of sweeping for non-existent mines in fierce tides and in every sort of weather. In September, 1914, for instance, four of the crews were employed in the novel task of embarking London omnibuses into transports alongside the Admiralty pier at Dover. Taken straight off the streets of the metropolis and driven to Dover by their ordinary drivers, these vehicles arrived in France in all the glory of their vermilion paint with

---

[1] The number of German mines destroyed by British sweepers in the Dover area between July, 1915, and the end of the war was 1,507 – 132 in the last half of 1915 ; 313 in 1916 ; 755 in 1917 ; and approximately 307 in 1918. During the same period French sweepers on the other side of the Straits destroyed 427 enemy mines.

the theatre advertisements still displayed on their bill-boards.

In December, and again in January, 1915, the traw-lers were sent to Dunkirk to sweep ahead of Rear-Ad-miral Hood's heterogeneous squadron then employed in bombarding the enemy positions on the Belgian coast. Though not actually hit, they had their fair share of excitement when they came under heavy shell-fire.

Meanwhile the U-boats were using the Dover Straits in increasing numbers for their war upon shipping in the English Channel and the western approaches. The losses were increasing, and the first lines of drift nets laid across the Straits did little to stop the free passage of the undersea raiders. As for the British protective minefields, they were treated with con-tempt. The mines failed to explode.

During the early months of 1915 Admiral Hood pressed the Admiralty for more patrol craft. Ordin-ary herring drifters began to arrive at Dover in January, and by June, 1915, three yachts and 132 drifters were engaged upon anti-submarine work under the command of Captain F. G. Bird, R.N. (Retd.), whom Admiral Sir Reginald Bacon describes as 'an ideal officer for the work' and 'always cheery'. His little fleet was manned by upwards of 1,500 officers and men of the Merchant Navy and Fishing Fleet, with less than a dozen naval officers and ratings in some of the more responsible administrative positions.

These drifters laid nets of thin galvanised steel wire with a mesh of between ten and twelve feet. They were supplied in lengths of 100 yards in depths vary-ing from 30 to 120 feet, and each vessel carried ten nets, making a 'fleet' of 1,000 yards. They were floated from the surface by various means, and were designed to wrap themselves round an U-boat travel-ling submerged, which would indicate her presence by towing a buoy or calcium flare along the surface. Electrically-fired net-mines were also used at a later date in conjunction with the indicator nets.

The work of the Dover drifter fleet, however, is

H.M.S. *ZULU*, T.B.D.

MINED, DOVER STRAITS, OCTOBER, 1916.

VIEW SHOWING DAMAGE TO AFTER-PART OF SHIP.

(This Fore-part was joined to After-part of *Nubian*, and the resulting ship re-christened H.M.S. *Zubian*.)

hardly germane to the story of the minesweepers, though to those interested in the former I would recommend the chapter on the subject in Admiral Sir Reginald Bacon's *The Dover Patrol*. He speaks of them in glowing terms – ' Twenty-five miles of nets hidden below water, heavy moorings and buoys rising and falling with the sea, and a mill-stream of tide racing past ; the hour or so of slacker water to effect repairs ; the cold, the cheerless disappointment of damage worked by tide and gale combined ; miles of nets to be renewed. . . . They worked as thoroughly, steadily and pluckily as if fighting was their trade. . . . They had fought the sea all their lives, and they fought the enemy with equal confidence. . . .'[1]

As part and parcel of the Dover forces, however, Admiral Hood had also asked for 66 trawlers for patrol work, which arrived in the area by the middle of 1915.

They were organised in units of six under the command of a Lieutenant R.N.R., with a sub-Lieutenant R.N.R. as sub-divisional leader. Later, as the skippers became more experienced, they were promoted to ' group skippers ' and put in command of a half-unit of trawlers ; finally to ' chief skippers ', where they were placed in charge of a complete division of six.

On Admiral Bacon's taking over the command of the Dover Patrol in April, 1915, Captain W. Vansittart Howard, R.N.,[2] an officer who had been on the retired list for nine years, and had been in charge of patrols in the Dover area in the armed yacht *Diane* since October, was appointed C.T.P. (Captain, Trawler Patrol), with Lieutenant-Commander Rigg, the Port Minesweeping Officer, as his assistant.

Captain Howard's early experiences of the war are interesting as showing that the Admiralty had previously arranged for the appointment of retired officers, and because they are typical of many others on the retired list who came back to the Navy and served throughout the period of hostilities.

[1] *The Dover Patrol*, vol. ii, pp. 440–1. [2] Now D.S.O.

'On August 1', he writes, 'I received my war telegram "Mobilise", and at once proceeded to take up my
appointment as Deputy Naval Transport Officer at
Belfast.   When all the troops in Northern Ireland had
gone, my work there ceased, and I came to London
and reported myself to the Admiralty on September
14.   Owing to my seniority, the Transport Service
held out no hope of an immediate appointment, so I
enlisted the services of a friend and went to see the
Fourth Sea Lord.   I offered myself in any capacity
whatever, and was asked, "Will you command a
yacht?"   I replied, "Yes, sir. Certainly", and was
told to be prepared to take up an appointment in two
or three days.   I left the Admiralty feeling very
youthful and intensely delighted at the prospect of
hoisting my pendant as a captain R.N. in war. . . .
We commissioned the *Diane* at Portsmouth on September 21, and arrived at Dover on October 1.'

Captain Howard's trawlers had the duty of minesweeping, as well as the protection of the traffic-routes
and merchantmen in the Dover area against the increasing activities of the German submarines.   It is
unnecessary here to go into details of the organisation.
Briefly, however, the great volume of trade passing
through the Straits was confined to certain restricted
traffic lanes protected by armed trawlers at intervals
of three to five miles, backed up here and there by the
older destroyers of the '30 knotter' type.

Some 24 or 26 trawlers were normally stationed to
the southward of the traffic lane between the South
Goodwin and Beachy Head.   They remained on patrol
for four days and four nights, and horrible as the
weather often was, never once left their stations to
take shelter.

The next four days were spent 'resting' in harbour,
and to the uninitiated the routine would not seem very
onerous in time of war.   Let it be said at once, therefore, that the rest was only nominal.   At least seventy-
five per cent. of the vessels supposed to be in harbour
would actually be at sea for three days out of every
four escorting ships containing specially important

cargoes, cross-Channel steamers, cable-ships, Trinity House steamers and the like.

In the first winter of the war a boom had been laid between Folkestone and Cape Grisnez for the purpose of stopping submarines. It consisted of heavy wire hawsers stretched between buoys and floated by huge baulks of timber each weighing four tons. In the gales and strong tides, portions of this obstruction were constantly breaking adrift, which meant that the ' resting ' trawlers had again to be sent out to tow them clear of shipping.

Later, when minelaying was almost a daily occurrence, there was more work still. The trawlers off duty were frequently sent post-haste to rescue mined vessels ; as well as to sweep newly-located minefields, and over the routes to be used by specially important personages and cargoes crossing over to France. They had also to sweep round lightships, buoys and barrages before the craft attending on them were permitted to approach. There was also the laborious job of bottom-sweeping, which meant towing a length of chain cable between two trawlers. Every fathom of the sea-bed had to be scoured in this way after a minefield had been swept in the ordinary manner, in order that any mines remaining on their sinkers should be brought to the surface and destroyed. This work was carried out in all weathers, and on every possible occasion.

So the trawlers nominal four days ' rest ' usually dwindled to one or two. As Sir Reginald Bacon writes[1] :

' One unit for twenty-four hours was called a duty unit, and was ready to go to sea at five minutes' notice, no leave being given to anybody on board. The next resting unit was coaling . . . the third . . . had to provision and draw stores. The fourth resting unit was called the stand-off unit, and . . . the whole of the crew that could be spared came on shore for instruction in gunnery and signals ! '

The Admiral adds that the trawler crews had practically no rest, but they undoubtedly ate well, slept well, and, having plenty of work, were always fit.

[1] *The Dover Patrol*, vol. i, pp. 121, 122.

From what I heard at Dover during the war, however, and since, I have no doubt that the trawlers, like the destroyers, were *overworked*, which was perhaps inevitable. That the officers and men were able to stand the conditions of service was nothing short of wonderful. They growled among themselves but never really complained.

And there was some justification for growling. To those of us who know it, the Dover Straits is a place of swirling tides, fierce gales, heavy seas and not infrequent fogs. At sea a trawler is never still, and in anything approaching a lop her motion will upset anything but the strongest stomach. Add to this a constant state of wetness; the snow and bitter cold of winter; the presence of enemy submarines and multitudinous minefields; the extinguishing of shore lights and removal of many off-shore buoys; the danger of the shoals and sandbanks and various floating obstructions; and the ever-present possibility of a raid by the enemy from a base no more than two hours away at a destroyer's full speed, and one begins to realise the strength, fortitude and endurance of the Mercantile Marine officers and fishermen who manned these ubiquitous auxiliaries during over four years of war.

And whereas in an ordinary small man-o'-war there were three or four officers to keep the watches, the trawlers not commanded by Lieutenants R.N.R. or chief skippers had only two watchkeepers – the skipper and the second hand. The latter, though an excellent seaman, might not be much of a navigator, which meant that the skipper had always to be on the look-out when near the land, when sweeping or looking for submarines – indeed in anything but the most normal conditions. Conditions as I knew them at Dover were generally abnormal.

Even in harbour at Dover they had no rest as we more ordinary mortals know it. The area enclosed by the breakwater may be a haven of refuge, but it is one of the most uncomfortable in the world. In the south and south-westerly gales, even the large destroyers sometimes rolled twenty-five degrees each way while lying at their buoys, so that, with the constant movement, and the rattle and clatter, sleep was largely a matter of luck and meals a purgatory. (I defy anyone to be fully normal in a deeply-rolling ship in harbour.)

At times, too, Dover was congested with a miscellaneous collection of twenty-four different sorts of fighting ships – everything from monitors and cruisers to submarines and coastal motor-boats. The trawlers, poor Cinderellas, had to be anchored near the detached mole, or wherever else room could be found for them. Sometimes they even had to be banished to the Downs, or to Ramsgate, Margate, Folkestone or the coast of France – depending on the congestion of Dover harbour, and the state of the wind and weather.

At Dover, when we were lying at a buoy and rolling, what is vulgarly termed, ' our guts out ', we sometimes watched the trawlers oscillating even more dizzily with most of their crews on deck trying to prevent violent contact with some other little ship at anchor.

No. Several years before the war, when I first visited Dover in a small destroyer, I came to the conclusion that it was the last haven of refuge that the Almighty had ever made. In 1916, 1917 and 1918, when I was there again in a destroyer of over 1,000 tons, I became doubly certain that it was the most God-forsaken harbour I had ever struck in anything approaching bad weather.

We rolled, and rolled – and rolled. There was little swinging room as we lay at our buoys, the stern of one ship being practically up to the bows of the next. Picking up a buoy at night in that crowded harbour was a perfect nightmare, with the probability of going hard and fast aground if a sudden gust of wind swung one's bows off at a critical moment and caused one to miss it. There was no room to manœuvre.

As for the trawlers lying at anchor near the breakwater – they waltzed through half the compass, plunging, surging sickeningly from side to side with their mastheads cutting the wildest capers against the background of grey sky. Heaven knows how those on board them lived, ate, slept or did anything!

We assumed they must be inhabited by a breed of supermen – fierce, unshaven, loud-voiced Robot creatures with no stomachs, men who were not heirs to the pains and ills of ordinary civilisation, men of steel and whalebone and indiarubber.

They were.

Of that I am fully convinced now that I know more of what they endured.

2

The first minefield was laid off Dover by an U.C. boat from Zeebrugge on June 18, 1915. Thereafter, mines appeared with startling regularity off the buoys and lightships likely to be used by the cross-Channel traffic, off the entrances to harbours, and across the routes used by the coastwise shipping.

Captain Vansittart Howard was appointed ' Traffic Manager ' in the Straits from the South Goodwin lightship to Beachy Head, and across the Channel to the French coast. At the South Goodwin lightship, the Senior Naval Officer at Ramsgate, Captain G. N. Tomlin, M.V.O., R.N., took charge of the traffic and was responsible for its safety through the Downs.

Figures convey little to the imagination, but here are a few statistics for the Dover area during the period August 5, 1914, to November 11, 1918.

	Total Movements
Merchant vessels passed north through Downs	62,400 } 125,100
Merchant vessels passed south through Downs	62,700
Merchant vessels passed south through Downs and afterwards to French ports	36,200
Hospital ships and ambulance transports despatched from Dover . . .	3,875 } × 2 = 22,574
Troop transports, store carriers, etc., despatched from Dover . . .	2,094
Various vessels from Folkstone . .	5,318
Total movements through the Dover area	147,674 vessels

In addition, 10,000 laden barges of a gross tonnage of 1,250,000 tons carried 650,000 tons of amunition safely to France, while the approximate number of troops ferried to and fro was over 16,000,000.

During this period :

One hospital ship was mined.
One empty transport was bombed and sunk.
Forty-seven merchant vessels were sunk by mines.
Thirteen merchant vessels were sunk by torpedo.
One merchant vessel was sunk by enemy bombs.
One merchant vessel was sunk by air torpedo.
One merchant vessel was sunk by gunfire.

This record is one of which the vessels of the Dover Patrol have every reason to be proud.

The moment submarine minelaying started, however, it was very soon realised that the number of minesweepers was insufficient. All patrol trawlers were therefore fitted with minesweeps, and the traffic lanes were divided up into sections – up and down the Channel route from the South Goodwin lightship to Beachy Head ; Folkestone to Boulogne ; Dover to Calais ; Dover to Dunkirk.

During their four days out the trawlers were busy sweeping all day, and patrolling all night. In addition, regular spiral sweeps had to be undertaken round the light-vessels and lighted buoys near the traffic routes, while trawlers had to be stationed more or less permanently at Boulogne and Dunkirk to keep the approaches clear of mines. In order to make the daily sweep, which approximated to 600 miles a day, ten or twelve of the ' resting ' trawlers had to assist during daylight, while another pair had to leave Dover each morning to make certain that the entrance to Calais was carefully swept the following dawn.

On July 14, 1915, the first six hired paddlers arrived at Dover. They had been taken up and fitted out by Lieutenant-Commander W. G. Rigg, who also had his hands full in training newly-joined officers and men in minesweeping. These ships were the *Jupiter II, Marmion II, Duchess of Montrose, Ravenswood, Albyn* (ex

Albion), and *Balmoral,* all of which were familiar to excursionists on the south coast or in the Bristol Channel. During 1916 and 1917 they were to be reinforced by six more with names equally familiar.

The paddlers, useful because of their shallow draught, and because they could sweep at ten or eleven knots and thus cut the moorings of any mines encountered instead of dragging them in the mine-sweep as did the slower trawlers, were very soon hard at work. Drawing no more than $9\frac{1}{2}$ feet at the most, they were at least 75 per cent. safer than trawlers with their draught of $14\frac{1}{2}$ or 15 feet. It is true, however, that they were so lightly built that their paddles were liable to break up in bad weather, which made them useless for sweeping when it blew hard.

But the weather did not often deter them. Commanded by officers with temporary commissions in the R.N.R., officered by the R.N.V.R., and manned by volunteers from every walk of life and every profession a large proportion of whom had never been to sea before, they did yeoman service, both off Dover and the Belgian coast during the subsequent bombardments of Zeebrugge and Ostend. They had many adventures.

On July 29, 1915, the *Albyn* – Lieutenant A. Daniels, R.N.R. – and the *Jupiter II* – Lieutenant G. P. Spooner, R.N.R. – came across their first minefield near the South Goodwin. Two mines came up to the surface, and the crew, who were unfamiliar with them, gathered on deck to watch the fun while they were sunk by rifle fire. Some of the officers, together with an ex-soldier and a trimmer, opened fire. The trimmer's third shot hit a horn, and the mine exploded. The devastating shock precipitated half the interested ship's company down the hatchway.

On the following August 22, the paddlers swept at night ahead of the monitors proceeding up the Belgian coast for a bombardment of Zeebrugge. After daylight the *Albyn* sighted an enemy seaplane, which made straight for her. Daniels, who was watching the machine through his glasses and could see the pilot quite plainly, started to zig-zag at full speed. When he thought the seaplane was in a position to drop a bomb, he put his engines to full speed astern. The ship had barely lost her way, when a cluster of three bombs fell close ahead. Wheeling round, the German pilot made another attempt ; but the commanding officer watched him carefully as before and repeated his manœuvre at the critical moment. Four bombs were dropped this time, the nearest missing by twenty yards. The seaplane retired disgusted.

The first loss among the paddlers occurred on October 6, when the *Brighton Queen*, sweeping at night off Nieuport, struck a mine and sank almost immediately. All but seven of the crew were saved. The loss of this ship brought home to everyone the great danger, if not the impossibility, of minesweeping at night.

For months at a stretch, from April, 1916, until the end of the war, the paddlers, half a dozen or more at a time, were stationed at Dunkirk. They were used for sweeping off the Belgian coast along the barrage of mines and mine-nets laid to cover the coast between Nieuport and the entrance to the Scheldt for the purpose of stopping the enemy submarines from Zeebrugge from entering the English Channel. The route was regularly patrolled by monitors and destroyers, and was actually marked by buoys, some of which were illuminated. It lay at an average distance of twelve miles from the coast. One remembers that on clear days it was possible to count the windows in the hotels and other large buildings on the waterfront at Ostend. The coast, moreover, mounted 112 guns of 4-inch calibre and upwards, including thirty-three 11-inch, 12-inch and 15-inch, some of which had a range of 40,000 yards. Apart from submarines, fast, well-armed German destroyers were usually stationed at Zeebrugge or Ostend.

I have been able to look through the terse minesweeping diaries of Commander A. E. Buckland, D.S.O., D.S.C., R.N., who, as a lieutenant, spent nearly thirty months in charge of a division of paddle-sweepers in this area. From time to time he served in no less than eight ships, first the hired paddlers, and then the Admiralty-built paddle minesweepers. His record is one of practically unremitting work. For instance, between April 21 and May 31, 1916, his flotilla was thirty-one days at sea, steamed 1,357 miles with its sweeps out, and swept up eleven German and eighty-six English mines.

The sweeping was drearily monotonous as a rule, with moments of intense excitement and danger. The flotilla incurred the inevitable losses, some of which will be described later ; but for the most part it meant being at sea day after day in practically every sort of weather, with occasional shell falling around from the enemy coastal batteries, and frequent bombing from aircraft.

Here are extracts from a few typical days in Commander Buckland's diary :

'H.M.S. "Nepaulin". Monday, May 1, 1916.

' All paddlers sailed 7 a.m. Proceeded to No. 3 buoy escorted by *Attentive* and destroyers. Then swept up English minefield at north-east end of Dyck Bank. Weighed buoys and marked the next line by two dan buoys. Work completed at 12.45 and sweepers returned to Dunkirk at 2 p.m. Mines destroyed, 18.

' The *Kylemore* had two men killed and one slightly injured by mine exploding when hit by rifle bullet. The pieces instead of going upwards swept the decks.

' Sailed again at 6.30 p.m. and proceeded to No. 3 buoy. Swept up to No. 5. Sweep parted there. Attempted to pass it again, but weather too bad so abandoned operation and returned to Dunkirk, anchoring at 1.30 a.m.'

On August 14 of the same year, the *Eglinton*, *Goodwood* and *Sandown*, with Lieutenant Buckland in the first-named, went out sweeping at 5 a.m. ' Swept patrol line to No. 7 buoy,' he writes. ' Swept back round S.W. Hinder and Cliffe d'Islande Bank. On way back observed small airship not under control, with a large bend in her. *Eglinton* followed her across banks until told to leave her by *Mastiff*.[1] – *Mastiff*

[1] An ' M ' class destroyer.

then proceeded to anchor in her path. Airship flew on top of him, and, as was only to be expected, caught fire. One man killed and 8 injured. Both occupants of airship uninjured. Paddlers anchored in Dunkirk Roads at 9 p.m.'

' *Sunday, September* 2, 1917.

'. . . Very large air raid from 9.30 to 11.30 p.m. *Albyn* hit by bomb. After part of ship absolutely gutted. Lieutenant King and second engineer killed. *Lingfield* had over 100 holes put in her, and two trimmers killed. Had a hard job to put out fire in *Albyn*. Great help from Drummond[1] and chief engineer of *Plumpton*.'

Air raids on Dunkirk, which was within twelve miles of the enemy lines, were very common. During one period of two months that the sweepers were based there, there were fifty such raids and several long-range bombardments. Considering the weights of metal and explosive dropped on this devoted town the casualty list was surprisingly small. In all, 7,514 bombs and projectiles fell in Dunkirk during the war, 233 people being killed and 336 wounded. The civilian population remained in the place, and the work of unloading the steamers which brought all the food for the British Army in France continued.

A monotonous, uncomfortable task punctuated by moments of hideous excitement – that was certainly the lot of the minesweepers operating off the coast of Flanders. Referring to Commander Buckland's diary, I find that in December, 1917, for instance, his flotilla spent twenty-three days actually sweeping. On six days furious gales from the north, west and south-west prevented any work from being done, while on two other days there was thick fog.

Commander Alexander D. Thomson,[2] D.S.C., R.N.R.

[1] Lieutenant G. A. Drummond, D.S.C., R.N.R., commanding the *Eglinton*.

[2] Now in the employment of the Asiatic Petroleum Company (N.C.), Ltd., Shanghai. Writing on September 28, 1932, from Chungking, he was then in command of the S.S. *Shu Kwang*.

(Retd.), who in 1917 was commanding the hired paddler *Duchess of Montrose* as a lieutenant, also has something to say of the work.

'Nearly every day,' he writes 'we would sweep ahead of the monitors from Y buoy to the entrance to the Scheldt. I often had visions of finishing the war in a German prison camp. On many occasions our little fleet would consist of three paddlers and the old *Marshal Soult*, or some other monitor equally fast and furious (about five knots), and our own escort of destroyers often out of sight on some job or another. Twelve miles away on our starboard beam was Zeebrugge with all its ultra-modern destroyers. Why the Germans never tried to cut us off was a mystery. It would have been simple. At times, of course, we went along in grand style with our Dover fleet augmented by you fellows from Harwich, and I suppose that kept the enemy guessing.'

And so the work continued.

Here are a few of the more exciting incidents.

On January 1, 1917, a large cargo vessel, the *Sussex*, struck a mine near the West Dyck shoal on her way into Dunkirk. The paddle minesweepers at once went to help her, to find that the steamer had damaged herself in the mine-nets laid by the drifters for the destruction of enemy submarines.

Thomson's ship, the *Duchess of Montrose*, and the *Nepaulin*, crossed the mine-nets in safety; but the *Goodwood*, Lieutenant J. Trenance, D.S.C., R.N.R., one of the Admiralty-built paddlers drawing rather more water, struck a mine. The *Redcar*, Lieutenant A. Daniels, D.S.C., R.N.R., at once went to the *Goodwood's* rescue and succeeded in towing her to Dunkirk in a sinking condition, where she was handed over to salvage tugs and put into dry-dock. The *Redcar* then returned to help the *Duchess of Montrose* and *Nepaulin* with the *Sussex*. The three small paddlers succeeded in towing their huge charge clear of the minefield, and she was eventually salved.

Mines were constantly laid by German submarines in the western approaches to Dunkirk, and a fortnight after the last incident the *Redcar* and *Chelmsford* were returning after completing their daily sweep when they saw a large cargo-vessel, the S.S. *Port Nicholson*, strike a mine about five miles west of the Gravelines buoy. They took her in tow, with the intention of beaching her on a three-fathom shoal near by. The *Chelmsford* parted both her hawsers; but she and the *Redcar* succeeded in towing the damaged ship within half a mile of the bank, when the *Port Nicholson* suddenly turned turtle and sank. It was sheer bad luck, particularly as the two paddlers had gone to her rescue in the middle of a dangerous minefield in which four German mines had been seen awash.

Hairbreadth escapes were of frequent occurrence, and rarely came to the notice of the authorities. On February 15, 1917, for instance, when the *Eglinton* – Lieutenant G. A. Drummond, D.S.C., R.N.R. – was heaving in her sweep-wire, a mine came up foul of it. It actually hit the *Eglinton's* stern before those on board were aware of its presence, but luckily fell back into the water without exploding. Some time later, the *Redcar* had precisely the same narrow escape of destruction.

It is difficult to convey any adequate impression of the daily, almost hourly, risks incurred by the sweepers. Yet the gallant men in them accepted the danger as a matter of course, and carried on. Sweeping was accounted ' dull ' when there were no mines to be found. The ex-pleasure steamers, in particular, were very lightly built, and practically fell to pieces when struck by a mine. There was rarely any hope of saving them. They had to be abandoned just as fast as the survivors could leave them. The unostentatious heroism of those who continued to work in these ships after once having been blown up, or having seen their friends blown up, can hardly be exaggerated. They had none of the excitement of battle against a visible foe – nothing of the supreme satisfaction of being able to hit back. The work was entirely one-sided – ' Heads you win. Tails I lose.'

I feel certain that none of us in the fighting ships

really understood what the minesweepers were doing during the war, or the risks they underwent. And Britain does not realise now, when both the Merchant Navy and the Fishing Fleets, from which two sources the Minesweeping Service was principally manned, have been smitten by the prevailing depression, with the result that thousands of its men have been cast workless ashore to swell the ranks of the unemployed.

On March 18, 1917, the *Duchess of Montrose* struck a mine off the Gravelines buoy and sank in less than a minute, with a loss of twelve lives. I have an account of her going from Commander A. D. Thomson, whom I have mentioned before.

' I remember leaving Dunkirk that morning with the harbour covered with a thin film of ice – a fine day for a dip. We began to sweep at about 9 a.m., and had swept up five mines, when the prohibited hours for sweeping interfered with our work. (Prohibited hours, I should explain, were one hour before to one hour after low water slack.) On resuming the job the sweep had been passed about an hour when the *Duchess* hit a mine amidships. I was using the rangefinder at the time, and as a result was knocked silly and didn't quite know what happened until I found myself in the icy cold water with various survivors. The bow and stern of the *Duchess* were pointing heavenwards, and the middle of the ship was under water.'

Commander Thomson wrote that account in 1932, fifteen years after the incident. It is possible he has forgotten details, for the contemporary description of one of his shipmates states that as soon as he recovered consciousness on the bridge he ran down the ladder to the after part of the vessel to find a stunned and semi-conscious crew. Rallying them, he ordered them to throw overboard everything that would float, and, as they still seemed too dazed to understand, told them to save their lives by jumping overboard.

' I remember seeing the engineer officer and steward with their heads stuck out of ports on the after bulk-head of the wardroom,' Thomson continues. ' The ports were too small for their escape, and they couldn't get out, poor chaps, because the entrance to the ward-room was under water.'

'We were picked up after about ten minutes in the icy cold water,' he goes on, and while the men were swimming about and holding on to any wreckage they could find, Sub-Lieutenant R. T. Ingram, R.N.R., by his cheery encouragement, coolness and self-possession, managed to keep up their spirits. In all, thirty-one officers and men were rescued. 'I was all in,' Thomson adds. 'I could do nothing for myself through numbness and shock, and had to be undressed by the steward. . . . I had a lovely pair of black eyes through looking through the eye-pieces of the range-finder when the mine went up. They lasted for some time, and people didn't always know where I'd got them – thought I'd been drunk and disorderly, perhaps. Anyhow, I was sent off on three weeks' sick-leave in someone else's clothes, and then, by special request, I returned to another ship at Dover.'

On Friday, April 20, 1917, the *Nepaulin*, another hired paddler commanded by Lieutenant R. J. Car-ruthers, R.N.V.R., struck a mine off No. 3 buoy in Dunkirk Roads, and sank in a very short time with a loss of 22 lives.

At dawn on June 24, three paddlers, the *Kempton* (Lieutenant A. E. Thomson, D.S.C.,[1] R.N.), *Redcar* (Lieutenant A. Daniels, D.S.C., R.N.R.), and *Gatwick* (Lieutenant W. H. Evans, R.N.R.), sailed from Dun-kirk to sweep the approaches to Calais. It was a calm day with good visibility. No mines were found, and two hours before low water slack Lieutenant Thomson took his three ships inshore to anchor during the 'pro-hibited period' for sweeping. While still at anchor he was informed by a patrol drifter that enemy moored mines had been sighted. As soon as the tide was run-ning, the three paddlers weighed and proceeded to clear the area.

'We were sweeping three abreast,' he writes. 'The area was dotted with wrecks – quite safe for navigation, but the devil as far as sweep-wires were concerned.

[1] See p. 53.

As soon as we were coupled up mines began bobbing up to the surface. Then the *Gatwick's* sweep parted, so I ordered her to sink the three mines that had appeared, while the *Redcar* and ourselves continued to sweep.

'No sooner had the signal been sent, than the *Redcar* struck a moored mine fair and square under her mess-deck. The fore-part of the ship was blown away as far as the bridge, and the water was covered with debris and wounded men supporting themselves as best they could.' The gun's crew, and four other men in the bows, were killed instantaneously.

The Admiralty-built paddlers were more stoutly constructed than the ex-pleasure steamers, and having ordered his crew to stand by the boats, Lieutenant Daniels, the *Redcar's* commanding officer, went below with the chief engineer to examine the foremost bulk-head of the forward boiler-room. They found the bottom part of it blown away, and the water pouring into the hull. It seemed unlikely that what remained of the ship would stay afloat. Her wounded end was nearly under water, and her stern lifting. Returning on deck, however, Daniels ordered his crew to abandon ship in the boats, while he and his chief engineer remained on board to make fast a hawser in case the *Redcar's* stern portion could be taken in tow and salved.

'We immediately closed the wreck,' Thomson continues, 'and sent away all our boats to pick up survivors. Incidentally, she was well down by the bows, and appeared to be anchored on a shoal by the mass of wreckage forward. Most of the survivors came on board my ship, and as there was considerable delay in getting them inboard, and I was anxious to get out of the area and to transfer the wounded to a drifter for passage to Dunkirk, I left the bridge to try to hasten things.

'On my way forward again I found the chief engineer working over a casualty on the starboard sponson. The poor man had lost one foot, and the other was hanging by about an inch of flesh, while his abdomen was cut clean open with the intestines hanging

H.M.S. *NUBIAN*, T.B.D.

WRECKED, DOVER STRAITS, OCTOBER, 1916.

After-part of vessel salved.   (This After-part was joined to the forward portion of *Zulu* and result known as H.M.S. *Zubian*.)

out. We amputated the foot with my sheath-knife, put on tourniquets, replaced his inside, and tied him as best we could. As I began to walk forward towards the bridge a mine hit us in the engine-room just beneath where we were standing. All the engine-room staff were killed. The chief engineer was telescoped (we picked up his body next day), and the casualty from the *Redcar* was blown into the water. Rescued by an Able Seaman called Morrison, the poor fellow lived for forty-eight hours and then died of shock.

One of the *Redcar's* boats had not been made fast to the *Kempton* when the men were disembarking, and drifted some twenty-five yards away when the latter blew up. Two of the *Redcar's* men, a petty officer and a signalman, realised at once there would not be enough room in the remaining boats for the survivors of the two ships. They immediately jumped overboard, swam to the boat, and paddled it alongside the *Kempton*, where it was at once filled with men. This action was the means of saving many lives.

' When the explosion came,' Thomson writes, ' I was thrown about twenty feet, and landed in a sitting position on the quarter-deck. I heard no sound, but felt exactly as if I had suddenly been placed in a London fog. Both masts had come down, and the ship's back was broken. The officer of the watch was blown from the upper bridge to the lower, and his trousers were split from clew to earring. I gave the order to abandon ship, and in company with the officer of the watch, Lieutenant Eric Richardson, R.N.V.R., went below to inspect the after stokehold bulkhead, and then down forward to examine the after mess-deck bulkhead. Both seemed to be holding out, but the ship was steadily settling amidships, with the bow and stern rising out of water.

' As we were drifting towards the barrage, I decided to let go the anchor, so Richardson and myself went forward to the forecastle and cleared away the port anchor. Just as I was knocking off the slip, I remember Richardson remarking, " What happens if we

19

drop the killick on another bloody mine ? '' Luckily we didn't.

' By this time everyone was out of the ship except four A.B.'s – (I heard afterwards that the first person over the side was my Chow dog '' Bruin '') – and as she had taken a heavy list to port, Richardson and I went to my cabin to save what we could. On the way I remembered I still had a destroyer's allowance of confidential books on board – relics of the days when the *Kempton* had been sweeping the approaches to the Firth of Forth – so knotted the neck of a cricket shirt and used it as a sack. By the time we had got them all it was time to leave, so grabbing a tin of cigarettes and the remains of a bottle of whisky, we made a hasty exit for the boat. We were on our way over to the *Gatwick* when the old *Kempton* turned over and sank, her forefoot remaining above the water for some time. I felt very sad. She was the best built of all the paddle minesweepers, and during her year of service had never let me down.'

Ignoring strict chronological sequence, for presently I shall have more to say of the work of the trawlers and other minesweepers round about Dover and in the Straits during 1916, 1917 and 1918, it is here desirable to continue the story of the sweeping off Dunkirk and the Belgian coast to its logical conclusion, that is, until the German evacuation of Flanders.

In Appendix 6, section 4, I have mentioned the ten ' tunnel minesweepers ' of the ' Dance ' class, originally built for service as tugs in Mesopotamia. They started to join the Dover Patrol in December, 1917, and the first mention I can find of one of them in Commander Buckland's diary is on December 13 of that year. On this date the *Cotillion*, commanded by Lieutenant A. Daniels, D.S.C., R.N.R., who, it will be remembered, had been blown up in the *Redcar* in the previous June, was sweeping off Dunkirk with the paddler *Ravenswood*.

The *Hornpipe*, *Quadrille*, *Coverley* and *Minuet* also arrived before the end of the year, and the *Mazurka*, *Gavotte*, *Pirouette*, *Tarantella* and *Sarabande* in the early months of 1918. Most of these ships were commanded by Lieutenants R.N.V.R., with Lieutenant Daniels (afterwards succeeded in turn by Lieutenant M. Archibald, R.N.R., and Lieutenant E. Broad, R.N.R.) in command of the flotilla. With their light draught, the ' Dance ' class were very useful for sweeping off Dunkirk, though, as has been said elsewhere, they were useless in anything approaching bad weather.

On October 1, 1918, the German Marine Corps ' was ordered to evacuate the Flanders base. Twenty-four torpedo-boats and twenty submarines made their return to German ports ; but U.B.10, U.B.40, U.B.59 and U.C.4, together with eight torpedo-boats, were blown up during October 1–2. On the 17th, Ostend was evacuated. The enemy left Zeebrugge and Bruges on the 19th and the Flanders coast was clear on the 20th.' [1]

At that period Commander Buckland was Port Minesweeping Officer at Dover, and on October 18 he went to Ostend in a motor-launch with Captain Hamilton Benn, M.P., R.N.V.R.,[2] who was in command of the motor-launch flotilla. ' The people were very pleased to see us,' Buckland writes, ' cheering and shaking us by the hand. . . . About one hour before high water began sweeping with tunnel minesweepers, but their light sweep-wires parted as soon as they encountered mines. Mines are obviously very heavily moored. Enemy batteries also opened very heavy fire on us, so had to abandon sweep. . . .'

Thereafter, however, until the time of the Armistice, the paddlers and tunnel minesweepers, assisted by motor-launches and seaplanes, were locating minefields and clearing channels to Ostend and Zeebrugge, and chain-sweeping the bottom. The work was sufficiently exciting. Many mines were discovered and exploded, some even inside Zeebrugge mole.

Quite early in the proceedings, on October 19, the *Plumpton* was mined off Ostend. ' The bridge and port side of the after end of mess-deck and stokehold

[1] *The German Submarine War*, p. 324.
[2] Now Captain Sir Hamilton Benn, Bart., C.B., D.S.O.

were completely blown away,' Commander Buckland wrote. 'I went on board the *Quadrille* and took *Plumpton* in tow by the stern, and eventually beached her about ¾ mile east of Ostend piers. *Plumpton's* C.O., Lieutenant G. A. Drummond, D.S.C., R.N.R., Sub-Lieutenant Collet, and seven ratings were killed.'

'Friday, November 8,' runs the last entry in the diary. 'Chain-sweeps off Ostend and Zeebrugge continued. Nothing to report. All routine sweeps carried out. Nothing to report.'

In the nineteen days, October 18 to November 6, inclusive, Commander Buckland mentions 93 mines as having been destroyed off the Flanders coast. Some 21 of these were found inside the mole at Zeebrugge.

A mere recital of these figures conveys little impression of the real danger of the work. Nor does the bald statement that a mine exploded ' quite close to *Gavotte* and smashed her condenser ' !

What were trivial incidents of the day's work to those who spent most of the war minesweeping sound hair-raising enough to us. Sufficient risk and excitement to last the ordinary man a lifetime were sometimes concentrated into a few hectic hours or minutes.

3

Every one of the sixty odd trawlers stationed at Dover was used as a minesweeper, as well as a patrol and escort vessel. A dozen were even fitted out as minelayers.

The many adventures of trawlers in the Dover area would fill several books. For every story or incident which came to the notice of the authorities and thus found its way into official despatches and reports, possibly into the newspapers by way of the *London Gazette*, scores of others passed into oblivion. The men who commanded those little ships were not the type to put pen to paper more often than they could help, certainly not for the advertisement of their own deeds.

On a dark night of low visibility, with a moderate gale blowing from the south-west and a correspondingly heavy sea, the trawler *Elysian*, on her way back to Dover from the French coast, miscalculated her position, mistook the lights and had the misfortune to run ashore. When daylight came, she found herself on the north-eastern part of the Goodwin Sands. As the tide rose, heavy seas started to break over both sides of the little ship. The Deal lifeboat came out in answer to the signals of distress, and as the *Elysian* was driving higher and higher up the sands and being severely battered in the process, the commanding officer was persuaded she would become a total loss. Accordingly, he decided to abandon her, and all the men were brought safely to shore in the lifeboat.

But the *Elysian* did not break up, and the next night Lieutenant W. G. Morgan, D.S.C., R.N.R., stationed on patrol near the South Goodwin in the trawler *Lord George*, sighted a ship without lights. The squalls were very violent, it was blowing a full gale, and the visibility was poor. Closing the vessel, Morgan challenged repeatedly, and received no reply. He was about to open fire, when the weather cleared a little and he saw that the strange ship was a trawler. Then he recognised the *Elysian*, which had floated off the Goodwins due to a change in the wind. Remaining close by until daylight, Morgan approached the deserted vessel, got a few of his men across in his boat, passed a tow-rope, and brought his prize safely into Dover.

Lieutenant Albert J. Coles, D.S.C., R.N.R., commanding the trawler *City of Dundee*, was the means of saving some of the crew of the *Hull Trader*, when that ship foundered in heavy weather two miles south of Dover harbour after having been mined. His own ship was sunk off Folkestone on September 14, 1915, after collision with a merchant ship. Coles was on the upper bridge at the time, and the *City of Dundee*, nearly cut in two, began to sink at once. Before he could get clear, he became entangled in the signal halyards and was carried under water with the wreck. Managing to fight his way clear, however, he came to the surface and swam to a raft, to which he helped three men who might otherwise have been drowned. They were an hour and a half in the water before being picked up.

The trawler *Othello II* struck a mine off Leathercoat on October 31, 1915. Broken in two, she sank almost immediately. The wheelhouse was so badly shaken by the explosion that neither the doors nor the window would open. Inside, were the skipper, second-hand, helmsman and a deck-boy. The three men managed to push the lad out through a half-open window, and he was the only man saved of the whole ship's company.

The boy was sent to another trawler, the *Weigelia*, which was sunk by a mine off Dover in the following February. On this occasion only one man was lost, and again the deck-boy escaped with his life.

After the *Othello II* incident, orders were given to remove all the sliding doors of the trawlers' wheelhouses, and to substitute light canvas doors which could easily be pushed or kicked out in a sudden emergency. They were the means of saving many lives.

Trawlers were conspicuous in saving life when the hospital-ship *Anglia*, carrying wounded from France to Folkestone, was mined and sunk in the Channel on November 17, 1915, with a loss of about 80 of her hospital staff and wounded.

This same minefield was responsible for the loss of three other vessels, one of which was the trawler *Falmouth III*, Lieutenant H. Beadle, D.S.C., R.N.R., which actually sank on top of the wreck of the *Anglia* and remained there for several days until dislodged by a gale.

Two young R.N.R. officers were learning their minesweeping duties under Lieutenant Beadle's instruction. One of them, Sub-Lieutenant W. A. McIntosh, was drowned. The other, Lieutenant W. E. Eglinton, suffered so severely from shock that he was unfit for service at sea for about three months. However, as soon as the doctors allowed it, he volunteered for sea service and came back to minesweepers in the Dover area, where he assisted in clearing many minefields.

Some people will remember the loss of the 12,000 ton P. & O. liner *Maloja* which foundered with a loss of 122 lives after striking a mine off Dover on February 27, 1916. Once more the ubiquitous trawlers were conspicuous in the work of rescue, among them being the *H. E. Stroud*, commanded by Lieutenant R. J. McClorry, R.N.R.

This gallant officer was killed eight months later, on October 26, when enemy destroyers from Zeebrugge, made one of their ' tip and run ' raids on the patrol protecting the anti-submarine nets between the South Goodwin Sands and the French coast. Fired upon at close range, a shell exploded on the brass boss of the wheel in the *H. E. Stroud's* wheelhouse, killing the commanding officer, the helmsman, and the man on the lookout. The steering gear was also wrecked, but the second hand improvised relieving tackles and brought the damaged ship safely into Dover.

In March, 1916, the trawler *Flicker* was patrolling off the minefield which had sunk the *Maloja* to warn passing shipping. On the morning of the 4th she was reported as not being on her station. No sign of her, or of any wreckage, was ever discovered, only the body of one of her deck-hands floating in a lifebelt. It was presumed she was blown up in the minefield. Her skipper, J. West, says the official report, ' was one of the steadiest and most valuable of men '.

On the 28th of the same month another trawler, the *Saxon Prince*, went a-missing. She had been on patrol for four days off the South Goodwin, and was due to return to Dover. It was blowing a furious gale and there was a raging sea off the eastern entrance to the harbour, and the *Saxon Prince* did not arrive at the expected time. Search was at once made for her, but without result. Neither bodies nor wreckage were recovered. She was assumed to have been overwhelmed and sunk with all hands. ' Disappeared in storm off Dover ', is the laconic announcement of her passing in the official list of Navy losses.

On March 15, 1916, the steamship *Shenandoah* was

mined off Folkestone. Lieutenant A. H. Barnes, R.N.R., of the trawler *Macfarlane*, at once went to her at full speed and advised the master to try beaching his ship. The master complied, and all went well until some of the bulkheads collapsed and the ship suddenly sank by the stern, leaving the bow portion afloat. The *Macfarlane* sent her own boat to the rescue, and picked up the occupants of two others from the *Shenandoah*. Then she found another boat bottom up with three men holding on to the keel, and others clinging to wreckage in the water. The rescued men reported they could hear someone knocking inside the boat, so Barnes ordered the trawler *Returno* to go alongside and right her with a tackle. This was done, when the wireless operator and a fireman of the *Shenandoah*, who had been some twenty minutes confined in the capsized boat, were rescued in an exhausted condition.

Whenever a trawler was mined, the enginemen and trimmers had little chance of survival. Steam-pipes usually burst ; boilers often exploded with a rush of scalding steam ; hatches were closed, and ladders shaken away from their fastenings. It was a miracle if any of the men below escaped with their lives.

On March 27, 1916, the trawler *Tourmaline* was damaged by a mine explosion, and her main injection valve fractured. The pumps were started at once, but the water gained rapidly. Some men would have deserted the engine-room. Not so Chief Engineman W. Harris, R.N.R., who remained below encouraging his men in spite of the rising flood. His aim was to get the ship into Dover, where she could be beached and eventually salved. This the gallant fellow succeeded in doing, though the water had risen to his shoulders when the *Tourmaline* made the harbour. Harris was given a well-deserved Distinguished Service Medal, while one of his men was ' mentioned in despatches '.

This incident was only typical of many others where the engineers' squad behaved with the greatest bravery and devotion to duty. For instance, on April 14, 1916, the trawler *Electra II* was badly damaged in collision. The water rose rapidly in the machinery space, but Chief Engineman Thomas Stark stuck to his post up to his waist in water, kept his ship afloat, and enabled her to be taken into harbour. On arrival, the *Electra II's* deck was actually awash, and the level of the water was within six inches of the fire-bars in the furnace and still gaining rapidly. Stark also received the D.S.M.

The *Dagon*, stationed on patrol near the Royal Sovereign light-vessel, was the only trawler torpedoed in the Dover area during the war. The incident occurred on December 8, 1916. The explosion was particularly violent and the ship sank almost at once, none of the officers and crew below being saved.

On the evening of February 8, 1917, the armed trawler *Highlander*, commanded by Lieutenant R. S. Bainbridge, R.N.R., was steaming down-channel between Dungeness and Beachy Head. It was a very dark night, blowing hard with a heavy, tumbling sea, when, at 7.45 p.m., Bainbridge heard a heavy explosion on his starboard bow. Steaming in that direction he soon saw the destroyer *Ghurka*, which had been mined and was in a sinking condition. Making an S.O.S. signal by wireless giving the position, he at once set about the work of rescue.

Only a small portion of the *Ghurka's* bows still remained above water. Practically all the officers and crew had been drowned. But getting alongside the wreck the *Highlander* tried to hoist out her boat with the derrick. Unfortunately, she was rolling so deeply that the painter carried away, the boat fell into the water, and was carried rapidly away to leeward by the wind and heavy sea. Bainbridge decided not to waste time in trying to salve her, but to save the men in the water. He managed to rescue five, three more, benumbed with cold, being drowned when practically alongside. The whole surface of the water was covered with a thick scum of oil fuel from the *Ghurka*. The clothes, faces, hands and arms of the survivors were so covered with it that they appeared like negroes.

Commander F. H. L. Lewin, R.N.,[1] the flotilla gunnery officer, happened to be on board the *Ghurka* as a passenger. He was uninjured by the explosion and was a very strong swimmer. He had already saved a man entangled in the sinking fore-part of the wreck at the risk of his life. And though close to the *Highlander*, he now refused to leave the water or to accept help until the four ratings with him had been rescued. For his gallant conduct on this occasion he received the Royal Humane Society's silver medal, and afterwards the Stanhope gold medal for the bravest deed of the year.

On February 26, in the same year, the trawler *St. Germain*, commanded by Lieutenant Lansley, whose name has already been mentioned in connection with the salvage of the *Volscian*,[2] struck a mine near Folkestone, the foremast being thrown over the side by the explosion. The trawler *Strathgairn* – Skipper Waters, D.S.C., R.N.R. – at once went to the rescue. Lansley, thinking the *St. Germain* was about to sink, ordered Waters alongside, and set about transferring his confidential documents, ammunition, depth charges and small moveable gear. Then, going below, he examined the damage to his ship. She had struck the mine with her bows, and he found that a great volume of water was pouring in through a large crack in the foremost bulkhead.

With three men – William Forsyth, the second hand ; Charles M. Foot, an engineman ; and Albert Edwards, a leading seaman R.N.R. – Lansley determined to make every effort to save his ship. Having stopped up the crack in the bulkhead as best they could with mats, canvas and bedding, a tow-rope was passed to the *Strathgairn*, and Waters was told to tow the *St. Germain* stern first towards the shore. The fires of the damaged ship had been extinguished by the inflow of water, but sufficient steam remained in the boiler for the pump to be kept going. The weather became bad on the way in towards the shore. However, Lansley managed to keep the water from rising, and was able to beach his vessel at Folkestone. For their share in

[1] Now Captain F. H. L. Lewin, R.N. (Retd.).   [2] See p. 269.

preserving the *St. Germain*, Forsyth, Foot and Edwards each received the D.S.M.

Skipper A. Geddes, R.N.R., a man about 54 years of age, was domiciled in New Zealand when the war began. He held a master's certificate, and at once came home to volunteer in any capacity as a seaman. Too old to be taken as a Lieutenant R.N.R., he was accepted as skipper of a minesweeper. 'He was a bold and fearless sweeper,' wrote the Captain of the Trawler Patrol, Captain Vansittart Howard. 'He had done such good work that I recommended him for promotion to Chief Skipper.' But his promotion came after his death. Geddes was lost with several of his crew when his trawler, the *Fraser*, was blown up and sunk off Boulogne on June 17, 1917.

When H.M.S. *Ariadne* – an old cruiser converted into a minelayer – was torpedoed off the Royal Sovereign lightship on July 26, 1917, the trawlers in the vicinity again performed excellent service in saving life. The same thing happened when the monitor *Terror*, which had been torpedoed off the Belgian coast on October 19, 1917, was proceeding to Portsmouth after temporary repairs at Dover. On the 23rd, before arriving off the Royal Sovereign lightship, she met a fresh gale with a very heavy sea. She began to leak so badly with the labouring, that at midnight, off Beachy Head, she was forced to make signals of distress.

The trawler *Elysian* happened to be in the neighbourhood, with Skipper Daniel McCarthy on watch. He at once called Chief Skipper Herbert G. North, his commanding officer. In spite of the wind and sea they took the trawler alongside the monitor's quarter and rescued her entire crew, the *Elysian* being much damaged in the process. At daylight next morning, however, the weather had moderated, and the *Terror* was still afloat. The officers and crew were accordingly put back on board, and the monitor was eventually taken in tow by tugs and arrived safely at Portsmouth. Chief Skipper North received a well-earned D.S.C. for taking his ship alongside in 'conditions of sea and

weather which required the greatest skill and pluck ',
while Christopher Darnell, the engineman of the *Elysian*, was ' mentioned ' for keeping his engines and
pumps running when the ship was making a foot of
water an hour through the damage sustained during
the work of rescue.

But many acts of bravery and exceptional seamanship perforce went unrewarded. For every incident
I have mentioned there were dozens of others which
never came to the notice of the authorities. Where
some hundreds of officers and some thousands of men
were employed in the Minesweeping Service, the great
majority went unrecognised. The wearing of half-an-
inch of blue and white ribbon did not make a man any
more gallant than his fellows.

4

The barrages of mine-nets laid across the Dover
Straits from the South Goodwin to the French coast
between 1915 and 1917 did little to stop the German
submarines from Zeebrugge from entering the Channel.
Nor did the obstruction of wire hawsers, buoys and
huge baulks of timber stretched between Folkestone
and Cape Grisnez in 1915. In the strong gales, heavy
seas and abnormally swift currents, portions of the
barrage were always breaking adrift, the buoys themselves dragging their anchors and parting their cables.

The Belgian coast barrage, which was really a zareba
of mines and nets stretched between Dunkirk and the
entrance to the Scheldt, has already been mentioned.
Laid in April, 1916, and renewed the following spring,
it acted as a deterrent to the U-boats so long as it
could be regularly patrolled. The moment the patrol
was withdrawn, however, as it had to be during the
winter, the enemy's submarine activity increased and
minelaying recommenced. From the beginning of
1917, until the end of November no less than 253
passages were made through the Straits by submarines – an average of 23 each month.[1]

[1] *The German Submarine War*, p. 222.

Something better had to be done, and in 1917 Sir Reginald Bacon, the Vice-Admiral Commanding the Dover Patrol, proposed laying a regular wall of mines between Folkestone and Grisnez. If carried out in its entirety the project would take between 28,000 and 30,000 mines placed in parallel lines at depths of 100, 80, 70, 60, and 40 feet to catch diving submarines.

The Admiral 'was strongly opposed to having the line marked by a patrol in the first instance, and also anxious to let submarines be destroyed without the enemy having the slightest inkling of how they were lost'.[1] If patrols afterwards became necessary because submarines came through the minefield on the surface, they should, he considered, be to the westward of the barrage, which would be illuminated at night by searchlights ashore at Folkestone and Grisnez, and by searchlights from three or four armed light-vessels moored across the Channel in the vicinity of the mine-field. If the submarines dived, they would encounter the mines. If they remained on the surface, they would be shown up to the patrols in the rays of the searchlights and could be attacked. As a deterrent to submarines on the surface, or to surface craft, the Admiral suggested a double line of shallow mines right across the Straits with 'gates' off Folkestone and Grisnez.

He deprecated the use of the flares which were after-wards introduced to illuminate the mine barrage, and recognised the danger of the patrols of destroyers, trawlers, drifters and other craft being attacked with probable heavy loss if enemy destroyers, at their own selected moment, made 'tip and run' raids at night from Zeebrugge or Ostend, as they undoubtedly would.

These raids, carried out at high speed at night, were always difficult to counter. It was impossible to cover the whole area with the number of destroyers available at Dover, and there was never any guarantee, or even a probability, that the attackers would be brought to action. The odds were all on them. They could emerge when they chose, steam full pelt for the British

[1] *The Dover Patrol*, vol. ii, p. 401.

patrol line, sink any ships they saw, and then go full speed back to their harbours.

The destroyers at Dover, on the other hand, were on the job day and night. Indeed, they were over-worked. For seventeen days and nights, as a general routine, they had steam actually on their engines, with only brief spells in harbour for fuelling, provision-ing and storing. At the end of seventeen days they were laid up for three days for boiler cleaning, while once every four months or so they went to a dock-yard for a refit lasting about twenty days. 'None of the captains ever broke down,' the Admiral wrote, 'although, as their three days stand-off for boiler-cleaning approached, they also reached their limits of endurance, and I could see by their pinched faces that they were badly in need of rest.'[1]

Little wonder. The strain of constant watchfulness in small vessels at sea in all weathers in time of war must be experienced to be properly understood. Nevertheless, the Admiral had no alternative but to work his small craft almost to breaking-point. Dover, like other areas, really had insufficient vessels to pro-tect the huge volume of traffic passing through it, and at the same time to guard the Straits. The wonder of it is the ships were able to do what they did. And what applied to destroyers, applied with equal force to other small vessels like minesweepers, trawlers, drifters and motor craft.

However, to revert to the new Folkestone-Grisnez barrage, the new-pattern H.2 mines – modelled, let it be said, on those used by the enemy since the begin-ning of the war – began to be available in quantity in November, 1917. The first section was actually laid on November 21. Within four weeks the first sub-marine was destroyed – U.B.56, sunk in the minefield on December 19. At 11.42 p.m. there was a heavy ex-plosion. One German seaman was seen in the water, but he died soon after coming to the surface.

Cargo by cargo the deep minefield was added to and built up, finally to be completed by October, 1918.

[1] *The Dover Patrol*, vol. ii, p. 331.

Some submarines got through undamaged, but many others were lost, and in February, 1918, the High Sea Fleet submarines from the Heligoland Bight were forbidden to use the Dover Straits. By September the Straits were effectually closed, and no further U-boats tried to pass. The smaller ones from the Flanders ports thus found themselves confined to the North Sea.

During 1918, the Dover barrage was the grave of the following thirteen U-boats, most of them being forced to dive into the minefield and being blown up after sighting British patrol craft.

U.	109.	Gunfire of drifter *Beryl III* and mines.	January	26
U.B.	35.	Depth charges of T.B.D. *Leven* . .	January	26
U.B.	38.	Mined in Barrage	February	12
U.B.	58.	Mined in Barrage	March	10
U.B.	33.	Mined in Barrage	April	11
U.B.	55.	Mined in Barrage	April	22
U.C.	79.	Mined in Barrage	April	22
U.B.	31.	Depth charges of drifters . . .	May	2
U.C.	78.	Depth charges of drifters . . .	May	2
U.C.	64.	Mined in Barrage	June	20
U.C.	77.	Depth charges of trawlers . . .	July	10
U.B.	109.	Mined in Barrage	August	29
U.B.	103.	Depth charges of drifters . . .	September	16

The principal credit for this result must go to Admiral Sir Reginald Bacon. He originated and worked out the details of the Folkestone-Grisnez Barrage, but, to his bitter mortification, was relieved in command of the Dover Patrol by Vice-Admiral Sir Roger Keyes on January 1, 1918, and did not see the fruits of his nearly three years of arduous experience and labour.

5

Sir Reginald Bacon's plan was not carried out in its entirety.

Flares of 1,000,000 candle-power arrived in quantity, and twelve trawlers were fitted out to burn them continuously at night on the mine barrage.

' Six flare trawlers were placed each side of the minefield,' Captain Vansittart Howard writes. ' The gaps between them were filled by " P " boats, monitors, and as many drifters and minesweepers as could be found. These used their searchlights, thus making a continuous line of light each side of the minefield between Folkestone and Grisnez. – When the barrage searchlight vessels were placed in position and their apparatus was fairly tested, the flare-burning trawlers were gradually released. However, there were never less than six, three each side of the minefield, until the Armistice was signed. – Searchlights at Folkestone were used on either side of the minefield, and until the powerful searchlights were installed at Cape Grisnez, three flare-burning trawlers were placed in position to prevent enemy submarines passing close to the French coast. – Patrolling destroyers had the duty of protecting the flare-burning trawlers, as well as the drifters steaming to and fro on their beats between them.'

The ' Brock ' flares gave an intensely brilliant light. In clear weather they lit up Dover harbour, seven miles away, as though it were bright moonlight. Their glare was even visible in Canterbury and all over the surrounding country. But they were not very popular with those who had to use them. ' With all the lights showing, and our searchlights going,' one commanding officer writes, ' keen vision was impossible.' – ' When the flares were burning,' says another, the trawlers ' could not possibly see any enemy which was about to attack them, and they made a splendid target for any enemy destroyer which could slip through our destroyer patrols on a dark night '.

On the night of February 14–15, 1918, an enemy submarine was reported in the minefield by the drifters, and heavy firing began. The ' P ' boats, monitors and destroyers on patrol concluded that the firing was at the submarine. They were unaware that a flotilla of German destroyers had steamed through the patrol and were attacking the paddle minesweepers, trawlers and drifters who were burning lights to assist in illuminating the minefield.

The trawler *James Pond*, commanded by Chief Skipper A. E. Berry, D.S.C., R.N.R., was burning

H.M. TUNNEL MINESWEEPER *COTILLION*
(ORIGINALLY T. 92. TWIN-SCREW TUNNEL TUG FOR TIGRIS).
The ship is here seen battened in for a sea voyage.

her flares near the French coast when she saw three destroyers approaching from the eastward at high speed. Flashing past at very close range, they each fired salvoes. It was impossible to miss. A shell exploded in the *James Pond's* wireless cabinet, killing one operator and severely wounding the other. Another struck the wheelhouse, wounded Berry, and lit the remaining flares, which were stowed well forward close to the forecastle.

The raiders disappeared into the darkness, to leave the trawler damaged and blazing. The wounded wireless operator was dragged out of the burning débris in the wireless cabinet, while Berry ordered his men to fire quarters in the hope of putting out the flames. Unfortunately, the canvas hose was burnt through.

A French destroyer came alongside with an offer of help. Berry replied that as his ship was still afloat he needed no help, and hoped he would be able to extinguish or reduce the blaze by throwing the flares overboard. Gallant attempts were made to do this, but soon after the destroyer had steamed away all the remaining flares became ignited.

The fire was at no great distance from the magazine and was rapidly gaining. The heat was unbearable, and forced to discontinue his efforts Berry hoisted out his boat and abandoned ship with the rest of his crew and the wounded telegraphist. They started to pull towards the French coast, the *James Pond* blowing up with a tremendous report soon after they had left her. The wounded telegraphist unfortunately died on the way ashore.

Berry might quite well have embarked in the French destroyer with all his men when the chance came, but preferred to remain in his blazing ship on the off-chance of saving her. For his bravery he was awarded a bar to the Distinguished Service Cross he had already earned in the Dardanelles. His second-in-command, Skipper Henry Bennett, received the D.S.C., and two men, Alfred Boynton and **Alexander Sandison**, the D.S.M.

But the enemy destroyers had not finished. After

20

passing the *James Pond* they turned sharply to the
north-north-west along the line of drifters, firing salvoes into them as they steamed by. These little ships
did not hesitate to return the fire with the tiny guns
they possessed; but 3- and 6-pounders were nothing
of a match for the 4·1's of the enemy. The *Christina
Craig, Clover Bank, Cosmos, Jeannie Murray, Silver
Queen, Veracity* and *W. Elliott*, all between 60 and 96
tons, were sunk one after the other. Still more were
damaged.

Then came the turn of the paddle minesweeper *Newbury*, commanded by Lieutenant Alexander D. Thomson, D.S.C., R.N.R., whose name has previously been
mentioned in this book. This ship lay near the Folkestone ' gate ' with her searchlight burning. Four
enemy destroyers steamed up from astern, two on
either quarter, firing close-range broadsides. The
Newbury was instantly a shambles, and the officer of
the watch was killed.

' They simply wrecked the whole outfit,' Thomson
himself writes. ' The bridge, foremost 12-pounder,
searchlight and after 6-pounder were shot away with
their entire crews. To make matters worse, our depth-
charges exploded, wrecked the after part of the ship
besides setting her on fire, and killed three officers and
a steward who were below. The siren started blowing
and couldn't be shut off. Altogether we were in a
proper mess.'

The time was about 1 a.m., and the ship was gradually settling down in the water. Thomson immediately
passed an S.O.S. signal to Folkestone pier, which transmitted it to Dover, and then set about shoring up bulkheads and effecting what temporary repairs he could.
Thanks to his efforts, and the stout build of the ship,
he was able to keep her afloat. All the spare fireworks
had been used, so a bonfire was built on the forecastle
head as a further signal of distress, and fed with broken
woodwork and oily waste. When clear of the minefield Thomson anchored. As he remarks, ' It was certainly *some* night.'

Meanwhile, ships had been sent to the *Newbury's*

rescue. But the night was dark and misty, and it was not until about 6 a.m. that she was eventually found by her sister vessel the *Lingfield*, which took her in tow stern-first – as the bows had been severely damaged – and eventually brought her to Dover with the help of tugs. By that time the top of the *Newbury's* stern was level with the water.

For saving his ship on this occasion Thomson added a bar to the D.S.C. he had already earned ; Engineer-Lieutenant A. A. Kirkham was awarded the D.S.C., and two men, Horace Neller and George Miller Barnes received the D.S.M.

Apart from ships, the British casualties on this occasion were 22 killed, 54 missing and 13 wounded. But the loss, grievous though it was, was more than counter-balanced by the gallantry and heroism of the men, particularly those manning the trawlers and drifters. On the very next night these little ships were again in full strength on their patrol, burning their flares, and carrying on with their work as though nothing unusual had happened.

They continued to do so until the Armistice. The monument to their bravery is unseen and largely forgotten – the rusty hulls of U-boats silted up in sand, hidden beneath the swirling tides of that twenty miles of turbulent water which lies between Folkestone and Grisnez.

You, who pass across or through the Dover Straits on business or pleasure – remember the men who strove and fought and died there, so that Britain might live.

CHAPTER XV

MINE CLEARANCE

I

THE important matter of eventual mine clearance had been considered before the end of the war, when it was decided that one of the Allied and Associated Powers should be chosen to collect and co-ordinate all the results of the work as it went on, and to publish periodical reports of progress for the benefit of the shipping of all nations. In this way it was hoped to obviate the duplication of information, and to establish one uniform system to cover the navigable waters of the globe.

Not unnaturally, Great Britain was asked to undertake this work, and agreed to do so.

When the Armistice came, the Admiralty appointed an 'International Mine Clearance Committee',[1] to which all maritime countries except the late enemies were invited to attach a 'Mine Clearance Intelligence Officer'. Twenty-six countries did so, and the ex-enemy countries were invited to join as soon as the peace treaties were ratified.

The officers appointed by the Powers were in direct communication with their Governments, and with the I.M.C.C. They kept the latter informed of all mine clearances effected by their respective nations; and in return received the collected information of the work of all the countries. This was largely embodied in

[1] The Committee consisted of Captain B. H. Smith, C.B.E., R.N., representing the Mercantile Movements Division at the Admiralty; Commander H. M. J. Rundle, O.B.E., R.N., representing the Minesweeping Division; Commander D. B. Le Mottée, representing the Hydrographic Department, with Lieutenant-Commander G. Cunningham Glen, D.S.O., as secretary. The Committee worked under the general supervision of Rear-Admiral J. A. Fergusson, C.B., the Assistant Chief of the Naval Staff.

pamphlets styled 'Mine Notices to Mariners', which were reproduced in different languages.

These mine warnings, which became very well known to merchant-vessels during the post-war period, were printed in green. They were issued free by the same

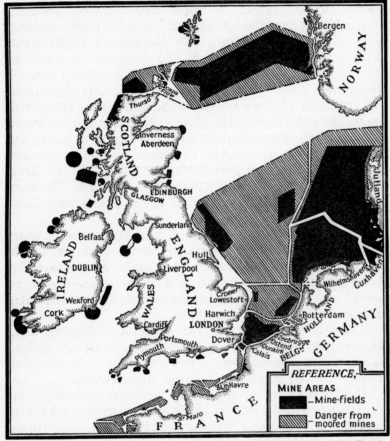

(Reprinted with the permission of *The Times*.)

MINED AREAS AT THE TIME OF THE ARMISTICE – NOVEMBER 11, 1918

channels as the ordinary 'Notices to Mariners'. The chart which appears in this chapter is to all intents and purposes a reproduction of one prepared by the I.M.C.C. and published on February 10, 1919. It shows more clearly than can be expressed in words the definitely dangerous minefields round about the British Islands, in the North Sea, and English Channel, and the areas which *might* be dangerous through moored mines having dragged their moorings.

Appendix IA, and its attached chart, shows that 235,983 mines were laid all over the world during the period of hostilities. Of these, 190,454 were planted in the North Sea, the ' Northern Barrage ' easily coming first with 71,126 mines ; the Heligoland Bight next with 42,899 British and 10,886 German, a total of 53,785 ; and the eastern part of the English Channel third with 40,286 British mines. The chart contained in Appendix IA does *not* show the mines that remained to be cleared away at the time of the Armistice ; while the size of the symbols does not show the area or density of minefields. It merely indicates the approximate positions of mines laid during the war in the area covered. When the war ceased most of the German and many of the British mines round the British Isles had already been swept up.

Nevertheless, on November 11, 1918, there were only a few comparatively narrow lanes of water which could be guaranteed to be clear, while, as has already been shown, it was no small task to keep these channels swept so that the coastwise traffic might proceed with a reasonable degree of safety.

The labour of mine clearance was a prodigious one. It involved a close search of over 40,000 square miles, while a large proportion of the area had to be covered twice, and in some cases three times, over.

It had been necessary to lay a considerable number of British mines very shallow – sometimes under ten feet below low water ordinary spring tides, sometimes only eighteen inches below L.W.O.S. Clearing these particular fields was hazardous, and involved the strictest attention to tides and weather conditions.

The Supreme War Council allotted various areas for mine clearance to the different Powers. The Americans became responsible for their portion of the Northern Barrage ; the French for an area between the Belgian and French coasts ; and the Germans the large

area in the Heligoland Bight to the eastward of 4°E.
But a large percentage of the areas was allotted to
Great Britain, and to expedite and facilitate the work
a special ' Mine Clearance Service ' was established in
February, 1919.

Among other matters, this Service overcame the
difficulties in regard to *personnel* by the enlistment on
a common basis of all classes of seamen, except active
service ratings of the Royal Navy who could not be
spared from the Fleet. There were special rates of
pay and conditions of leave, while officers and men
were permitted to wear on their left sleeves the Mine
Clearance Badge approved by His Majesty for all those
engaged in minesweeping.

In June, 1919, the Service consisted of about 700
officers and 14,500 men. The names of the Mine
Clearance Officers in 22 different areas at home and
abroad, and in command of the 55 different flotillas or
groups of vessels engaged in the work, will be found in
Appendix 4. Reductions in the *personnel* took place as
ships were gradually paid off on completing their work,
and the task was finished by November 30, 1919, at
which time the British minesweepers had cleared up over
23,000 Allied and 70 German mines since the Armistice.
A very fine performance was the sweeping up of the
mines in the Northern Barrage by the ships and men
of the American Navy, which will be described later.

The British Mine Clearance Service had the advantage of war experience in minesweeping unrivalled
among the world's navies. Its general direction at
the Admiralty was also in the most capable hands of
Captain Lionel G. Preston, C.B. – many times mentioned in this book – who had been associated with
minesweepers since before the war.

People in Britain in 1919 who were conversant with
what had gone on at sea during the past five years
felt gratified that, mainly through British and American efforts, the seas had been so quickly cleared up
and merchantmen were once more immune from the
deadly mine menace which had beset them during the
four years and three months that the war had lasted.

But the clearance was taken largely as a matter of course. It was never properly understood what an enormous debt of gratitude was owed by the nation in general, and the sea-traders of the world in particular, to the *personnel* of the Mine Clearance Services who prolonged their war service in order that the seas might be made safe for peace-time traffic.

The spirit shown by both officers and men in their dangerous, monotonous and thankless duty was particularly fine. One hears of men who were in the habit of cheering whenever they steamed over shallow mines which were plainly visible and gave little clearance for their ships. One particular crew was twice mined in the *Penarth* and the *Cupar*, but still continued to work.

While the task was in progress three sweepers were lost at home, and two in the Mediterranean. On the other hand, only six merchantmen were mined from the time of the Armistice up till the end of 1919. Three of these disobeyed orders by navigating unswept waters, three others struck mines which had dragged their moorings.

For some time after the war, however, the danger of floating mines still existed ; while mines which had been sunk without exploding could not be considered safe if brought up in a trawl. Earlier in this book I mentioned the case of the trawler *Uvalaria* which was blown up in December, 1919, and the skipper and mate of the *Gurth* who were severely injured through tampering with the detonator of a mine fished up in 1926.

When the mine clearance started, it was at first intended to ' bottom sweep ' all areas in which mines had been sunk in any numbers. This, however, proved to be too expensive and laborious, added to which bottom sweeping was by no means a certain antidote.

Time alone rendered perfectly innocuous those thousands of explosive steel canisters punctured by rifle bullets, which, with the wrecks of many fine ships, littered the waters all round the British Isles, gradually to become silted up and unrecognisable in the ooze and eddying sand of the sea bottom.

2

Few personal records are available of the dangerous and monotonous work of the post-war mine clearance flotillas. Nevertheless, I have been able to collect a little that may be of interest.

In the first winter after the war the *Totnes* flotilla of sweepers under Lieutenant-Commander (now Captain) M. W. S. Boucher, D.S.O., R.N., was employed clearing up the mines off Zeebrugge. It was bitterly cold, with the thermometer a few degrees above freezing, so that the men's fingers were apt to stick to any metal they touched. The flotilla was sweeping an area strewn all over with wrecks and other obstructions so that the sweep sometimes parted as many as nine times a day. Yet, with their numbed, bleeding fingers, the men would regularly make the two short-splices necessary to repair a heavy sweep-wire in the average time of four and a half minutes.

There were occasional touches of comedy. For instance – it was sometimes necessary for men to go inside the paddle-boxes, and on one occasion, on completing one section of his sweeping, the senior officer in the *Totnes* made the usual signal to heave up the kites close in and shorten sweep-wires preparatory to turning the flotilla. This done, the ships flapped along little more than 100 yards apart. The *Haldon* happened to be next to the *Totnes*, when from the side of the *Haldon's* paddle-box a frightened face appeared.

' Oi ! ' it shouted.

Reluctant to return the greeting in similar fashion, Boucher at first took no notice. The man repeated his hail.

With his third ' Oi ! ' he added the information. ' 'Ere ! Tell the bloke up topsides to stop the blinkin' engines ! I can't git out o' 'ere ! '

How the man had got into his wet and rather uncomfortable position, and why he could not get out, was never discovered. The *Totnes*, however, signalled to the *Haldon* – ' There is a man hailing me from your port paddle-box. What is the matter with him ? '

It was explained that the man was a newly-joined
Mercantile Marine trimmer who, just before sailing,
had gone into the paddle-box for a purpose best known
to himself. As soon as the paddle revolved his retreat
was cut off. He felt like a spider trying to get out
through an electric fan. It was lucky the flotilla had
not set out on a long voyage.

Some types of mines were susceptible to countermining – in other words, the concussion of one might
explode another and so on right down a line if they had
been laid closer together than they should have been.
While sweeping was in progress, mines usually detonated
far enough astern of the sweepers to be harmless. If
countermining occurred, however, a second or third
mine might explode *under* a sweeper with disastrous
results.

' A classic example of this occurred when a flotilla
had been sent to skim a British deep minefield which
had been laid against submarines,' Captain Boucher
writes. ' The object was to skim the deep field to
sweep up any mines that had taken up their depth
shallow, and might be dangerous to surface ships.
The minefield was large, and roughly covered the area
between Rathlin Island and Skye.

' Sweeping began, and presently a mine went off in
the sweep. Within a few seconds, the sea became
chaos – spouting plumes of spray and smoke. Each
line of mines went off in a succession of terrific detonations until none was left. The entire minefield,
deep and shallow, was thus involuntarily and automatically cleared in three minutes ! By sheer good
fortune no sweepers were sunk, though they all returned to harbour leaking at every seam from the
frightful concussions they had sustained during a most
terrifying experience.'

Captain Boucher describes a similar incident when,
with five ships abreast, he was about to sweep up two
lines of mines. The *Leamington*, in which he was
then serving, was the starboard wing vessel, and her
neighbour would not, or could not, keep station,
but lagged astern. More than one signal had been

sent to her, and the senior officer was fast losing his patience.

Presently a mine went off in the port wing sweep. A second later, two more exploded simultaneously – nearer to the ship this time and obviously not touched by the sweeps. Countermining had started. Things were becoming exciting. Everyone looked on in apprehension, wondering where the next explosion would be.

The thundering upheavals had now passed the ships on the port wing and were coming down the line. A moment later a heavy concussion was felt in the bottoms of all the sweepers, and a huge dome of white water rose close at the stern of the next ship to the *Leamington.* 'We hung on, waiting for the next crash, with feelings that may be imagined. But our luck was in that day. The countermining stopped. What is more, our neighbour was never again astern of station. The mine had done what signals couldn't achieve. She had had a severe nudge from behind, greatly to the amusement of the flotilla.'

Sweeping always had its excitements.

3

Immediately after the Armistice, the Seventh Fast Flotilla from Grimsby, still commanded by Commander Basil R. Brooke, D.S.O., in the *Penarth,* with the *Cattistock, Sligo, Cupar, Clonmel, Badminton, Burslem* and *Sherborne,* began sweeping up the large German minefield off the Dutch coast.

A small cruiser was sent to Imuiden to act as their parent ship, and the new base was a welcome change to everyone concerned. Passing through the locks and mooring up alongside a jetty in a quiet canal was bliss indeed after rolling about in a more or less open anchorage off Grimsby. Incidentally, they found that the neutral Dutch had suffered much through the war. Food was very scarce, and one of the pilots said he had completely forgotten the taste of meat. No provisions of any kind were brought on board the ships for sale, though someone succeeded in buying a skinny rabbit ashore for 5s. 6d.

The clearing of the minefield took several weeks, and only one untoward incident occurred. This was when a ship, detailed to sink mines by gunfire, had punctured the case of one which slowly sank to the bottom. Failing to take the tide into account, the commanding officer allowed his vessel to drift over the spot where the mine had sunk. It struck the bottom, and, most unexpectedly, exploded. A plate was driven in in the engine-room, which promptly filled with water. But the bulkheads held, and the ship was towed to Imuiden, there to be patched up and taken on to Sheerness, where she was soon repaired and did more useful work in mine clearance. There were no casualties.

Early in 1919 most of the minesweepers were concentrated at Grimsby for a massed attack on the British east coast minefield which stretched from Flamborough Head to the Tyne and contained 11,783 mines. It was probably the biggest task they undertook.

Lieutenant Blackmore, still in the *Cupar*, describes the work in some detail : 'Mines were swept up in large numbers, and all sorts of methods were tried to effect their speedy destruction on the surface. We realised that if they were merely sunk without being exploded they would become a source of danger, particularly to trawlers. The *Cupar* used a special net of my design, but on many occasions during the work we were only too thankful that British mines were made in accordance with the Hague Convention, whereby they were safe when on the surface and adrift from their moorings. When manœuvring among floaters it was quite impossible to prevent some of them rolling along the side, which did not add to the joy of the crew. My scheme simply consisted of a large net, floated and kept open by otter boards like the mouth of a trawl. At the cod-end was an E.C. mine electrically connected, and when about twenty mines had been collected we veered the contraption to a safe distance astern, fired the E.C. mine, and destroyed the whole bunch by detonation. In some cases we saw whole mines blown a great distance, and at all times we had to take cover before touching off the explosion. The bang, when it came, was usually a mighty one. I believe the idea was later improved by the net, with several E.C. mines attached to it, being towed by a drifter at each end.'

Early in February, when a large reorganisation took place on the formation of the 'Mine Clearance Service', Commander Basil Brooke became Mine Clearance Officer for the North-Eastern Area with his headquarters at Grimsby, while Lieutenant Blackmore came ashore as one of his assistants. It was a coincidence that within a few days both their old ships, the *Penarth* and *Cupar*, were blown up and sunk with considerable loss of life.

Lieutenant P. A. C. Sturrock, D.S.C., R.N., a very fine and most popular officer who had been Captain Preston's navigator in the *Skipjack*, *Hollyhock* and *Lupin*, had taken over the command of the Seventh Flotilla from Commander Brooke. He was engaged in laying buoys to mark the eastern limit of the large minefield, when, on approaching the northern end, the *Penarth* struck a mine and sank.

She seems to have had no other vessel in close company, and the last seen of her commanding officer was in the after part of the ship apparently making no effort to save himself after doing all he could for his ship and his crew. As says one account : ' He died, as we had always found him, a perfect gentleman.'

The cold-blooded gallantry of Lieutenant David Wainwright, R.N.,[1] came out in evidence at the subsequent Court Martial on the survivors for the loss of the vessel. This officer, who had been a prisoner of war in Germany and had been made commandant of his camp because of his exceptional personality, displayed the greatest bravery in searching the stokehold of the sinking *Penarth* for injured men before making his escape in a Carley float with several others. The ship was about thirty miles off the Tyne when she disappeared, and because of a heavy snowstorm and the very bad weather which followed it, the float was

[1] Now Lieutenant-Commander David Wainwright, A.M., R.N. (Retd.).

adrift for over twenty-four hours before being sighted and picked up by one of the ships sent out in search. Meanwhile, four men had died of exposure, and Wainwright and the survivors were utterly exhausted. It was due to the officer's encouragement and cheerfulness during those horrible hours of suspense and uncertainty, without food or water, in the bitter cold, and a breaking sea which constantly washed them off the float, that any men remained alive to be rescued. Wainwright's bravery earned him that rare distinction, the Albert Medal.

At the Court Martial it also came out that the line of mines on which the *Penarth* had been blown up had not been laid precisely in the position plotted on the chart. There was an error of $1\frac{1}{2}$ miles, which was fully confirmed when they were eventually swept up.

The *Cupar* met a similar fate soon after her sister ship. Although taken in tow by a consort and actually moving towards the Tyne, she foundered on the way after a loss of several lives caused by the explosion.

4

In December, 1918, Commander (now Captain) Colin S. Inglis, D.S.O., R.N., was appointed in command of a flotilla of sixteen drifters to be used for mine clearance off the Belgian Coast. His right-hand man was Lieutenant W. W. Storey, D.S.C., R.N.R., who had had great experience in minesweeping during the war round about Dover and Dunkirk.

With few exceptions the *personnel* was confined to non-active service ratings. Among others, Inglis had his excellent Chief Petty Officer McGraw, torpedo coxswain, who also acted as Master-at-Arms, and a handful of engine-room ratings with previous experience of drifters. There were also two temporary acting gunners (T.), who were really pensioner chief torpedo instructors ; four pensioner torpedo-gunner's mates ; a leading signalman (officially unfit for sea service !) ; and a very aged Royal Marine pensioner as the commander's personal attendant.

The rest were almost entirely fishermen – mostly from Stornoway, Lerwick and Aberdeen, with a few from Hull and Lowestoft. Most of the skippers found their own crews, though a small number of undesirables had to be weeded out and replaced by men ' picked up from all over the shop '.

Inglis's own skipper in the *Imbat* was a worthy named Mr. Wright of Hull, or ' Uhl ', as he called it. He was a unique character who navigated almost entirely by his sense of smell, and was almost incapable of reading a chart. Nevertheless he always knew his position within a mile or so, and invariably assumed an old bowler hat whenever he took the wheel to take his ship in or out of harbour. He wore a kapok life-saving waistcoat with £100 in Treasury notes sewn up inside it, and, in spite of having already been blown up once or twice, entertained the most lively contempt for the German mines.

A drifter's normal complement consisted of the skipper, mate, four deck-hands, a cook, signalman, telegraphist (if fitted with wireless), two enginemen and one trimmer. Here is a list of the ships of Captain Inglis's Flotilla.

Imbat (Senior Officer, Commander Colin S.
    Inglis, R.N.) . . . . . . Skipper Wright
Shadow . . . . . . ,, Satterfield
Black Night . . . . . ,, Berriman
Sheet Lightning . . . . . ,, Besford
Hailstorm . . . . . . ,, Williams
Pack Ice . . . . . . ,, Pells
    (afterwards relieved by Lieut. Morgan, R.N.R.)
Runnel . . . . . . Skipper Gates
Scour . . . . . Mr. Brightman. Gunner (T.)
Swirl . . . . . . Skipper Harrison
Heat Wave (2nd in Command, Lieut. W. W.
    Storey, D.S.C., R.N.R.) . . . . ,, Sparrow
Anticyclone . . . . Mr. Clegg. Gunner (T.)
Storm Centre . . . . Skipper Catchpole
Firmament . . . . . ,, Bird
    (afterwards relieved by Lt. Puckering, R.N.R.)
Sunlight . . . . . . Skipper Perret
Red Sky . . . . . . ,, Porter
Scend . . . . . . ,, Cooke

All sorts of vexatious delays occurred before operations could be started. The drifters only became available in ones and twos at uncertain intervals ; though Storey was able to go to Ostend with two ships at the end of February, 1919, to organise the base.

Inglis followed him there in April, and, as he writes, ' we came under the orders of the Vice-Admiral, Dover Patrol, and got all our stores and provisions, etc., from Dover. Our base was Ostend, and we worked out of Zeebrugge. As well as my flotilla, we had there the ordinary sweepers and their attendant motor-launches, together with a number of salvage vessels working on the blockships sunk at Zeebrugge and Ostend. A large contingent of Royal Marine Engineers lived ashore at the latter place, and the S.O. Belgian Coast was eventually transferred from Dunkirk to Ostend. Subsequent to Captain F. Larken[1] leaving, E. R. G. R. Evans[2] was appointed S.O. after a short interregnum during which I officiated. All the various sweeping operations were in full swing by May, 1919, and only finished when the railway strike occurred at the end of September.'

Besides its other work, Inglis's little fleet did some 3,000 square miles of bottom-sweeping ; carried out systematic patrols for sinking floating mines after every little blow ; provided a ' duty drifter ' for the Senior Naval Officer ; did many odd jobs, and, last but not least, undertook one or two fishing trips a week with its own private trawl gear to keep all the sweepers in fresh fish. During the whole period the only casualty occurred when a seaman had a finger badly broken when a kite-wire jammed in one of the ships.

A dangerous task was the destruction of all mines washed ashore, of which there were many. For this a special party was told off, the men in which did very fine work.

' Keeping discipline in a flotilla of nondescripts was

---

[1] Now Admiral Sir Frank Larken, K.C.B., C.M.G. (Retd.).
[2] Now (November, 1934) Vice-Admiral Sir E. R. G. R. Evans, K.C.B., D.S.O.

OFFICERS, H.M.S. *CUPAR*, FEBRUARY, 1919.

Back Row : ———, Lieut. Wm. S. Tate, R.N.V.R., Temp. Eng.-Lieut. Geoffrey Taylor, R.N.

Front Row : Lieut. Frank L. Wyatt, R.N.R., Lieut. G. E. Blackmore, R.N., Lieut. Francis A. Orr, R.N.R.

rather a problem,' Inglis goes on to write. ' I can
never speak highly enough of the way Chief Petty Officer
McGraw, as Master-at-Arms and general factotum,
handled the men. Their general behaviour all through
six months would not have disgraced a Sunday-school
treat. – My aged marine attendant was a gem while he
lasted. Officially his age was 57, and he had 39 years'
service to his credit. I attended the wedding of his
granddaughter in January, '19. She was 22, so goodness only knows the old villain's real age. He admitted 10 years' Army service, mostly in India, before
joining the Marines as a recruit at the nominal age of
18 ! '

' When the " Mine Clearance Force " was constituted marines weren't allowed for, and the problem
arose as to how the old boy should be shown in the
complement. We therefore made him an Ordinary
Seaman 1st class, but as volunteers for the mine-
clearing weren't given any fresh kit, we told him to
put up a sergeant's stripes as being roughly the equiva-
lent of a chief petty officer. That tore it. He got so
hopelessly tight at the wet canteen that he got pneu-
monia and very nearly passed out. He was invalided
home, and I'm afraid I shall never see his like again.
He was the nearest approach to the immortal Private
Paget I've ever met, and was never defeated by anything.'

Captain Inglis goes on to say that he warned all his
men that there was no room for ' passengers or bad
hats '. They were told that everyone would be allowed
one run for his money – unless it was something altogether too desperate, but that a second offence
would entail immediate dismissal. There were plenty
of others waiting to take their places. The result was
that the men rose to the occasion and behaved like
lambs.

One of the best workers in the flotilla was an old
engineman of the R.N.R., trawler section, a grandfather, and a pillar of the kirk at home in Scotland.
His engine-room was a picture in paint and polished
metal, and the engines and boiler always in apple-pie

order.   He never went ashore except for a gentle amble on the jetty and back again, so when he asked for a long week-end to visit some friends in Brussels, it was immediately granted. He was due back on board his ship on a Monday night, as she was going to sea at daylight on the Tuesday. The ship sailed without him.

The old gentleman broke his leave for six whole days after having had 'the time of his life'. He returned penniless, and looking about 100.

' He duly came before me, and I told him exactly what I thought of him. I asked him what excuse he had to offer, and he blandly replied in his broad Scots dialect – "Weel, sorr, ye promised us a' 'ane 'rin for 'oor money ; but woe betide us if we came 'afore ye a second time. I've had me 'ane 'rin, an' a damn 'guid 'ane it was too. I'll no be wantin' anither, thankin' ye kindly ! "   What *could* I do but let him go and forget it ? ' says Captain Inglis.

The flotilla finished its service by doing odd jobs and carrying yeast during the railway strike of September, 1919. 'The men who stayed with me right through', observes their senior officer, 'were as fine a lot as I could have wished for.'

Immediately after paying off, Inglis was appointed to the *Heythrop* – one of the twin-screw minesweepers – as senior officer of a flotilla of four for service in the Baltic. They were sent to relieve the paddlers who ' had started knocking their flappers off as soon as the sea froze over '. The other ships were the *Cattistock* (Lieutenant J. D. Campbell, D.S.C.) ; *Holderness* (Lieutenant D. Wainwright) ; and *Oakley* (Lieutenant A. E. Thomson, D.S.C.). The names of the last two officers have appeared earlier in this book.

They made three attempts to cross the North Sea at the end of October, 1919, but on each occasion were recalled because of bad weather, the twin-screw minesweepers having rather an evil reputation as seaboats. Finally they were sent out by way of the Kiel Canal, being piloted through by a man who had been chief officer in one of the biggest German liners which had been surrendered to the Allies. The pilot almost wept with gratitude when Inglis gave him a 1-lb. tin of canteen margarine to take home to his wife and children.

Arriving in the eastern Baltic during the first week in November, the flotilla was unable to do any sweeping on account of the ice. All the same, they tried dropping the sweep-wires through the floes ; but found it quite useless, as everything carried away.

The monotony of life at Reval and Bjorko Sound was sometimes varied by odd trips as ' mine bumpers ' ahead of the British cruiser squadron. This rather tickled the sweepers, as the cruisers drew at least 10 feet more water than they did, and the British destroyers drawing 14½ feet or so were dashing ' all over the place without worrying in the least '. The weather was bitterly cold, and it was not easy to prevent everything from freezing up with a temperature down to about 25° below zero.

The flotilla was finally ordered home at the end of December, and was detailed to tow four motor-launches (M.L.'s) from Reval. Only one reached Copenhagen. One was stove in by the ice at Reval, and eventually broke her back as the Estonian authorities tried to lift her with a crane. Another broke adrift in the middle of a large minefield, and, after being salved with great difficulty, went sailing off again to be wrecked on some reefs west of Bornholm. The third, which was only held together by ice, broke in half, leaving the bow portion and capstan still attached to the tow-rope, while the stern portion sank. The fourth duly arrived at Copenhagen, where, on New Year's morning, 1920, Inglis figured at a Court of Enquiry assembled to enquire into the circumstances attending the loss of three of His Majesty's motor-launches. He was absolved from all blame in the matter.

' We returned home again via the Kiel Canal, and on January 15, 1920, paid off at Pompey. So ended my experience of mine clearance.'

5

I have already mentioned the Northern Barrage between the Orkneys and the Norwegian coast where 56,033 American and 15,093 British mines had been laid by the end of the war. Incidentally, their share of the barrage cost the Americans approximately $80,000,000 to lay. As says Mr. Josephus Daniels, the then American Secretary of the Navy – ' Admiral Sims estimates that the war cost the Allies $100,000,000 a day. Thus, if the Northern Barrage shortened the war by one day, it more than repaid its cost ' !

This is certainly one way of regarding the colossal expenditure, and we know also that the subsequent clearing of the American portion of the Northern Barrage cost the United States Government between $60,000 and $70,000 a day. But neglecting the purely *deterrent effect* of the Northern Barrage upon enemy submarines, we know that six U-boats are supposed to have been destroyed there, and that, therefore, an expenditure of about 11,686 mines was incurred for each submarine sent to the bottom. I am unaware what proportion of these submarines were sunk by the American or British mines, and what was the cost of the British share of the Northern Barrage. However, if their portion cost the Americans $80,000,000, then it cost at least $13,333,333 for every U-boat demolished – or about £2,777,777 at par !

These figures are illuminating. According to the official Navy Estimates, a modern British submarine of a large type costs roughly £340,000 to complete, which means that about *eight times* this sum was spent by the Americans alone in destroying each U-boat in the Northern Barrage.

The United States Mine Clearance Force was assembled at Kirkwall, in the Orkneys, under the command of Rear-Admiral Joseph Strauss who flew his flag in the *Black Hawk*. He had under his command 6 repair ships and auxiliaries ; 3 British oilers ; 34 minesweepers ; 24 ' sub-chasers ' ; 2 tugs ; 2 tenders ;

and 20 British trawlers manned by United States naval *personnel*.[1]

The American mine, known as the Mark VI, was of peculiar design, and had novel firing gear. It consisted of an electrical device inside the spherical mine case, and a thin wire antenna of any desired length, supported by a small buoy or float within eight or ten feet of the surface.

The mine itself had a destructive radius against submarines of about 100 feet. However, it was not necessary for a vessel actually to strike a mine to explode it. If a steel ship of any sort – indeed, any steel object, or even a minesweep – touched the antenna, the mine to which it was attached exploded. The main idea was economy, fewer mines being required to cover a certain area with the mines laid at different depths below the surface.

The American minefields being dangerous to *any* steel ship like an ordinary trawler or minesweeper, much ingenuity was displayed, and many experiments had to be carried out before the actual sweeping could start. Briefly, the ordinary sweepers had to be rendered more or less immune by providing them with an electrical protective device to prevent the mines from firing within a certain distance.

It was also necessary to determine the actual condition of the mines in the Barrage. Due to defects in their design, many had exploded soon after being laid ; others had broken adrift, to be discovered on the coast of Norway. As steel vessels could not be used for this purpose, the protective device not having been perfected, two *wooden* fishing smacks from Lowestoft were taken over by the Americans, and refitted at Inverness. These two vessels were the *Red Rose* and the *Red Fern*, manned by American naval ratings, and commanded respectively by Lieutenant Noel Davis, U.S.N., and Lieutenant Olaf Maatson, U.S. Naval Reserve Force.

In tow of the *Patapsco* and *Patuxent* they sailed for

[1] For names of ships employed, see list at end of Appendix 4, ' Post-War Mine Clearance '.

the Barrage on December 22, 1918, reaching it the next day. The two steamers stood off at a safe distance, while the smacks set sail, passed their sweep-wires from ship to ship, and shaped course to cross the first minefield.

' A few minutes before noon, as the vessels crossed the first line of invisible mines,' says the official American account,[1] ' a giant column of discoloured water sprang high into the air close astern of the *Red Rose*. The first mine in the North Sea Barrage had been swept. Separated as it was from that vessel by only a short length of manila rope, which insulated the sweep-wire from her stern, the tremendous shock of the explosion all but crushed in the wooden hull of the vessel ; water spurted in between the timbers in countless places ; the pump was started at once, but was barely sufficient to keep her dry.'

' It was a pretty sight,' the account continues, ' to see these little craft sailing back and forth across the minefield, wearing and tacking in unison, and keeping station on each other by furling topsails or streaming sea anchors.'

In all, the lines of mines were crossed four times, and six were exploded, which proved that they were still there ready to explode, and that every possible precaution must be taken when they came to be cleared by the ordinary sweepers.

Caught in a furious gale that same evening, the *Red Rose* and *Red Fern* lost touch with the *Patapsco* and *Patuxent* and were driven southward. After a severe buffeting they managed to reach Peterhead and St. Andrew's Bay respectively, having been given up for lost. Nevertheless, the experience gained in the minefield was of the greatest value.

The actual mine clearance started on April 29, after the heaviest snowstorm of the year, when the sweepers and a division of sub-chasers set out for the Barrage. It continued for five months, and was carried on in

---

[1] Navy Department. Office of Naval Records and Library, Historical Section. Publication No. 4, *The Northern Barrage* (Taking up the Mines), p. 12.

circumstances of great difficulty and danger. The weather was often vile, with a very heavy sea, but the gravest risks of all came from mines being dragged up in the sweeps, and from the explosion of one mine setting off another in close proximity to a sweeper.

On May 12, when the *Patuxent* was hauling in the end of her sweep-wire which had been severed by an explosion, a mine came up foul of her kite. The commanding officer sent his men to the bows of the ship, and himself went aft with his chief boatswain's mate. The gallant pair managed to clear the mine at the risk of their own lives, but it detonated within ten feet of the stern of the ship. Several men were blown overboard by the shock, or washed overboard by the falling column of water. But no lives were lost. Only the captain's thumb was cut off by a flying sliver of steel.

Two days later the same thing happened when the mine-sweeper *Bobolink* also brought up a mine foul of her kite. The captain, Lieutenant Frank Bruce, put most of his crew in a place of comparative safety, and went aft with four others to clear the mine. Before anything could be done it exploded – killing Bruce instantaneously, blowing the boatswain and three other men overboard, and severely damaging the ship. All four men were rescued from the water, with the boatswain unconscious from shock. The *Bobolink* had to be towed into Scapa Flow for repairs.

One day in July the sweeper *Pelican* was severely damaged by six mines detonating underneath and around her, probably due to countermining. The great mass of water thrown up by the explosions wrecked and flooded the fore-part of the ship.

Captain R. C. Bulmer, U.S.N., who was in charge of the operations, at once took his ship, the *Auk*, alongside the sinking *Pelican*. Connecting his hose to the compartments in the damaged vessel's bows, he started his pumps. The *Eider* came alongside the other side and did the same. Then the *Teal* took the three ships in tow, and started to steam slowly back towards harbour. The *Pelican's* bows were just showing above water, but for several hours the pumping kept her from foundering.

Then it started to blow hard from the westward, kicking up a heavy head sea. Tugging at their hawsers, the *Auk* and *Eider* started to plunge and roll, with the inanimate *Pelican* between them. The pumping hoses broke, and the water started to rise in the wreck, threatening every moment to buckle and to crush in the foremost bulkhead, which would have meant the ship sinking like a stone. It was decided that only a few volunteers should remain on board. Twelve were asked for, and the whole ship's company held up their hands. The twelve strongest were chosen, and the others, much against their will, ordered to seek safety in the *Auk* and *Eider*.

They were fifty miles from the shore. Darkness had come. All through the night, with their ships plunging and straining, the crews of the *Auk* and *Eider* struggled to keep their hoses intact and the pumps going. Men stood ready with axes to cut the securing wires in case the *Pelican* went to the bottom. But thanks to the gallant efforts of all concerned she was kept afloat, and soon after dawn reached the sheltered waters of the Bay of Tresness, in Sanday.

There were many narrow escapes, but the most serious calamity occurred when one of the trawlers, the *Richard Bulkeley*, brought up a mine in her wooden minesweeping kite. It was seen close to her stern near the surface, and orders were given for the kite-wire to be veered in the hope that it would clear itself. Unfortunately, the mine exploded, shattering the whole stern of the ship and causing her to sink in seven minutes.

Commander Frank R. King, U.S.N., was her gallant captain. When the explosion came, his first thoughts were for his crew. Whipping off his own lifebelt, he buckled it round a man who was half-dazed, and helped him to get clear of the ship before she sank. And when the *Richard Bulkeley* took her last plunge, Commander King, oblivious to his own safety, was still searching for any of the crew who might be left on board. He went down with her, a heroic figure who had sacrificed his life for others. A few months later a fitting tribute was paid to his memory by naming one of the new American destroyers the *King*.

Two officers and nine men of the American naval forces were killed during the clearing of the mines from the Northern Barrage, and twenty-three ships were damaged. 'Regrettable as was this loss of life,' writes Mr. Daniels, 'it was small in comparison with that of our comrades in the British minesweeping service.'

The entire minefield, spread over about 6,000 square miles of one of the most unsheltered and stormiest seas in the world, was swept up by September 30, 1919, a remarkably fine achievement by the officers and men of the United States Navy. According to the American official account of the operation, 21,295 mines were disposed of while the work was in progress. Of the 56,033 mines originally laid, 3,814 are stated to have exploded prematurely soon after laying. The remaining 31,924 had apparently been sunk or carried away from their moorings.

A magnificent spirit was shown by the American *personnel*. Like their comrades in the British service, a large portion of the crews of the minesweepers came from the Naval Reserve.

6

The sweeping up of the mines in and about the entrance to the Dardanelles immediately after the Armistice with Turkey was a matter of some difficulty. Mudros was used as the storing and fuelling base, and Kephalo, which was closer to the minefields, as the working base. The parent ship was supplied with several kite balloons, manned and handled by the Royal Air Force, to assist in locating mines.

A paddler, or a light-draught sweeper, went out on to the mined area towing a kite balloon at a height of about 350 feet. There were usually two observers in the car of the balloon, one to keep a look out for the

small, dark blobs in the clear blue water which repre-
sented mines, and the other to speak through the telephone directly into the headphones worn by the officer
on the bridge of the sweeper below.

Marking the positions of the mines at the entrance
to the Dardanelles was not altogether easy.   No official
chart of the German or Turkish minefields, which over-
lapped a considerable portion of the British, was ever
forthcoming.   There was also a swift current of between four and five knots, while some of the mines
were in very shallow water.   However, the ship detailed to mark the field approached it until the ob-
server aloft in the balloon reported a mine.   The vessel
was then conned from the balloon until her bows were
within five or six feet of the mine, when she would stop,
and let go a small moored buoy known as a ' pellet ',
roughly the size of a football.

In this way every third or fourth mine would be
marked, until the whole line – possibly three miles in
length – had been delineated.   Returning along the
line the sweeper then dropped larger dan buoys with
flags at intervals of 150 or 200 yards.

While clearing up the mines with the ordinary ' A '
sweep, one vessel kept just inside the line of dan buoys,
and the other about 300 yards on her beam.   The
pellets were swept up with the mines, while two mark-
boats followed close astern sinking the mines by rifle
fire the moment their moorings were cut and they
bobbed up to the surface.

The process was not so easy as it sounds.   The
strong current flowing across the line made steering
an accurate course at slow speed very difficult.   As
many as thirty or forty mines might be on the surface
at one time, which meant that the risk of sinking, and
possibly exploding, them at short range had to be
accepted.   If they had once been lost sight of they
might have drifted away on the tide and have become
a menace to shipping.

The whole of the mines moored in deep water off
and in the Dardanelles were cleared in this manner,
says one account to which I have had access, though

it will be remembered that in the Dardanelles operations of 1915 aircraft had been comparatively useless
for locating deep-laid mines inside the Straits where
the water was more or less opaque compared with
that outside.

Mines laid in shallow water near the shore were
almost impossible to sweep in the ordinary way because the sweep-wires continually fouled the bottom
and carried away. However, some officers located
them with the kite-balloon, and then lassoed each
mine in turn, which proved quite safe and practicable.

' I put three of my best A.B.'s right forward,' writes
Mr. A. Merton Brown, who was commanding a minesweeper in this area. ' Each had hold of a large wire
loop arranged as a bight or lasso. Directed by the
balloon above, I approached within three or four feet
of the mine, when the so-called ' cowboys ' did their
job. Having caught the mine, I then went slowly
astern and dragged it with its sinker into slightly
shallower water. The towing wire was then loosened,
the mine came to the surface, and we sank it by rifle
fire.' Although it was slow work at first, the men soon
became very efficient.

The clearance work at the Dardanelles was completed in July, 1919. Over 3,000 mines were removed
with a loss of four out of the sixteen sweepers, and a
casualty list not exceeding 50 lives. Though the loss
of life was regrettable, the result was satisfactory, as
many of the mines were laid very shallow and the
work was more dangerous than usual because the rise
and fall of the tide was no more than six inches. (In
home waters, sweeping was carried out only for a
certain period on either side of high water, when the
rise of the tide gave a definite safety margin if the
mines were not showing on the surface at low water.)

' When two or more mines got into our sweeps at
the same time,' Mr. Brown writes, ' they would sometimes foul each other and explode. This parted the
sweep-wire. Before it could be hauled in, the sweepers
often drifted on to the next line of mines, which of
course was unmarked, with fatal results. In one case,

when the wire was being hauled in, two mines came up foul of the kite, struck the stern of the ship, and exploded with very sad results. On another occasion my marking boat was actually sinking a mine, when she drifted over it. She had disappeared completely before the smoke and spray of the explosion had drifted away, though many more of her men were saved than we might have expected. Rescue work was always risky as we had to dash in at full speed across the lines with the mines only three feet under the surface. We were lucky to have no casualties.'

Just before the regular sweeping operations began, great loss of life was caused by steamers carrying refugees blundering across the minefields before they had been swept and marked. The sweepers had to steam in and warn these ships not to proceed except under escort, but in some cases they struck mines before warning could be given.

They were generally old, unseaworthy ships carrying as many as 1,000 people, mostly old men, women and children. They sank very fast, and rescue work was difficult again because of the number of people in the water, and the damage likely to be done by propellers while the rescuers manœuvred among them. Though most of them wore lifebelts, numbers succumbed to shock and through becoming panic-stricken and dragging each other under.

By the end of August, 1919, practically all the kite balloons had been destroyed by lightning. They were always pulled down as low as possible at night ; but a particularly close flash would strike them and they would drop in a mass of flames just astern of the vessel to which they were moored. Blind sweeping had to be resorted to, and the removal of a small Bulgarian minefield off Dedeagach, north of the entrance to the Dardanelles, was a work of particular danger. However, it was accomplished without loss.

There was more difficulty in September, 1919, when British sweepers were sent to the Bosphorus. Owing to the internal trouble in Russia, no plans were obtainable of the Russian minefields laid in the Black

Sea off the Bosphorus, and off the Bulgarian ports of Burgas and Varna. Moreover, the Russian mines were reputed to be especially potent. They had no horns, whiskers or other protuberances – merely an interior device like a saucer containing a chemical liquid which upset and caused them to detonate at the least definite shock or concussion.

But like the mines in every other part of the world, they were swept up – somehow.

7

The mine menace no longer exists. Ships can pass on the sea and along the coastwise traffic routes without the constant fear of sudden, under-water explosions which may send them reeling to the bottom.

Some of those 726 little vessels which formed our ubiquitous minesweeping flotillas at the time of the Armistice have gone the way of all good ships – to be cut and broken up into scrap-metal with oxy-acetylene and hammers and chisels in the dusty, forgotten corners of the shipbreakers' yards. Others, the trawlers and drifters, are still plying their business on the fishing grounds. Some of the hired paddle-steamers still carry excursionists during the balmy days of summer, when the sea is sufficiently peaceful for the uninitiated.

As for the gallant fellows who manned this heterogeneous fleet while they served under the White Ensign during those four strenuous years of war – some have gone the way of all flesh, others have long since scattered to the four quarters of the globe.

But to those who have had the patience to read to the end I would say : ' Remember the Minesweepers. They also helped to make history. Remember, too, that they were manned for the greater part by officers and men of our Merchant Navy and Fishing Fleets, officers and men of the R.N.V.R., and numbers of civilian volunteers who had never been to sea before the outbreak of hostilities – all of whom flocked to enrol themselves for this hazardous service when the call came.'

APPENDIX I

LOSSES THROUGH MINES

H.M. Ships

Battleships, 5 ; Cruisers, 3 ; Torpedo-gunboats, 2 ; Monitors, 1 ; Sloops, 5 ; Destroyers, 20 ; Torpedo-boats, 3 ; Submarines, 4 ; Patrol boats, 1 ; Armed Merchant Cruisers, 1 ; Armed Boarding Steamer, 1. *Total* 46.

Auxiliaries on Admiralty Service

Store Carriers, 3 ; Minesweepers (apart from sloops, hired trawlers, drifters, etc.), 12 ; Fleet Messengers, 2 ; Colliers, 22 ; Oilers, 2 ; Special Service Ships, 2 ; Yachts, 4 ; Whalers, 1 ; Admiralty Trawlers, 4 ; Hired Trawlers, 140 ; Hired Drifters, 32 ; Motor-launches, 1. *Total* 225.

Minesweepers

Sunk or seriously damaged in the following areas : Lowestoft, 48 ; Dover, 33 ; Harwich, 24 ; The Nore, 15 ; Grimsby, 15 ; Portsmouth, 13 ; Granton, 9 ; Queenstown, 7 ; The Tyne, 6 ; Bristol Channel, 6 ; Belfast, 6 ; Fleet Sweepers, 5 ; Plymouth, 3 ; Kirkwall, 3 ; Cromarty, 3 ; Falmouth, 2 ; The Clyde, 2 ; Peterhead, 2 ; Portland, 1 ; Lerwick, 1 ; Stornoway, 1 ; Foreign waters, 9. *Total* 214.

The figures give a fair indication of the intensity of the German submarine minelaying in the northern and southern approaches to the Thames, used by the enormous volume of traffic passing in and out of the port of London.

Merchant Vessels [1]

Sunk : 259 of 673,417 tons	. . .	1,493 lives lost
Damaged : 84 of 432,446 tons	. .	64 lives lost

Fishing Craft [1]

Sunk : 63 of 8,545 tons	. . .	332 lives lost

[1] For these figures I am indebted to that invaluable book *The German Submarine War*, by R. H. Gibson and Maurice Prendergast. They represent only a small proportion of the 7,829,900 tons of British mercantile shipping sunk, and the 7,807,900 tons damaged, during the war by enemy action. Lloyd's Register of Shipping gives a total of 5,861 British merchant ships of over 100 registered tons as having been sunk by the enemy during hostilities.

335

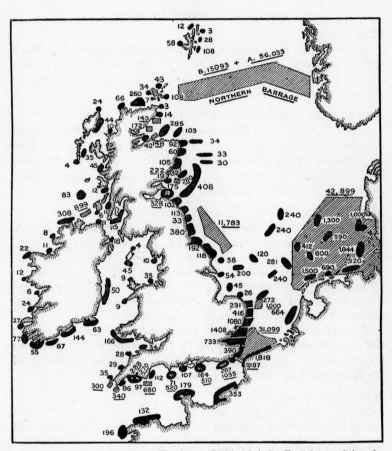

(Based on a British Admiralty Chart, by permission of
H.M. Stationery Office and the Hydrographer of the Navy.)

DIAGRAMMATIC CHART SHOWING BRITISH, AMERICAN AND GERMAN MINES
LAID IN THE NORTH SEA, ENGLISH CHANNEL AND ROUND BRITISH ISLES.
AUGUST, 1914–NOVEMBER, 1918

German mines are shown in black ; British and American, shaded. Figures
show numbers of mines laid in each area during the war, those underlined
being British and American. Positions are only approximate, and the size
of the symbols bears no relation to the extent or density of the minefields.

336